THUCYDIDES: MAN'S PLACE IN HISTORY

THUCYDIDES

Man's Place in History

H.-P. Stahl

The Classical Press of Wales

First German edition published in 1966.
This edition first published in 2003 by
The Classical Press of Wales
15 Rosehill Terrace, Swansea SA1 6JN
Tel: +44 (0)1792 458397
Fax: +44 (0)1792 464067

Distributor in the United States of America:
The David Brown Book Co.
PO Box 511, Oakville, CT 06779
Tel: +1 (860) 945–9329
Fax: +1 (860) 945–9468

ISBN 0-9543845-2-0
A catalogue record for this book is available from the British Library

Typeset by Ernest Buckley, Clunton, Shropshire
Printed and bound in the UK by Gomer Press, Llandysul, Ceredigion, Wales

––––––––––––––

The Classical Press of Wales, an independent venture, was founded in 1993, initially to support the work of classicists and ancient historians in Wales and their collaborators from further afield. More recently it has published work initiated by scholars internationally. While retaining a special loyalty to Wales and the Celtic countries, the Press welcomes scholarly contributions from all parts of the world.

The symbol of the Press is the Red Kite. This bird, once widespread in Britain, was reduced by 1905 to some five individuals confined to a small area known as 'The Desert of Wales' – the upper Tywi valley. Geneticists report that the stock was saved from terminal inbreeding by the arrival of one stray female bird from Germany. After much careful protection, the Red Kite now thrives – in Wales and beyond.

CONTENTS

PREFACE

It is with mixed feelings that one returns to a book written long ago, and written in a language one has hardly used in more recent publications. Should the literature be updated? That, it quickly turns out, amounts to rewriting references without necessarily improving contents. Is the book's thesis perhaps outdated? To my surprise I found that this is not the case. (Which was not to deny that numerous revisions would help streamline the original.) The intellectual setting which places Thucydides outside the narrow national perspectives of many interpreters is still valid today—as is the thematic concentration on man's self-inflicted sufferings. And the new final chapter, on the Athenian Expedition in Sicily, confirms my earlier findings that planning and outcome are leading categories employed in the historian's investigation, and also that narrative detail can lead us to the critical core of Thucydides' work.

My heart-felt thanks go to all who have helped to bring about this English edition. Dr David Seward provided a lucid and smooth basic translation of the unrevised original. Ms Jana Adamitis, with her usual skill and scrutiny, performed the final copy-editing. In between, she and Mr Benjamin Haller alternated in keeping an eye on my revisions. Ms Karen Hoover drew the maps which go with Chapter 10.

Special thanks go to my publisher, fellow Vergilian scholar and friend, Dr Anton Powell. He not only suggested publication in English but, in his subtle and unobtrusive ways, nudged me on to actually going ahead with the undertaking.

The German edition was inscribed 'Hermann Kleinknecht zum Gedächtnis'. There are few today who have met the lively classicist. May this edition once more help to keep his memory alive.

Hans-Peter Stahl
Pittsburgh, PA, USA
29 April 2002

THE QUESTION
Book 6.53–61

In the summer of 415 BC the city of Athens is in an uproar. A series of arrests sweeps over the city. The surface reason for the arrests is a scandal that has arisen in the weeks preceding the Sicilian expedition: unidentified perpetrators have mutilated many of the Hermes figures displayed in the city. In addition, there are rumors concerning parodies of the Mysteries that are said to have taken place at night in the private homes of certain influential people (Thuc. 6.27).

This can certainly be interpreted as a bad omen for the Sicilian campaign, a reason not to treat the subject too lightly. An additional interpretation is current: the people sense revolt and conspiracy aimed at dissolving their sovereignty (27.3), and they are being encouraged in this suspicion by certain determined demagogues (28.2). Here we touch upon the deeper, emotional root of the general unrest.

Among the accused is one of the three generals chosen for the Sicilian undertaking. Because the leaders of the people fear his influence in the army (and indeed among the people themselves), they let him leave with the expedition (29.3). However, they do so with the intention of later recalling him and taking him to court at a time when he will be isolated.

The leaders use the interim to their advantage. While the fleet is operating in Sicilian waters, at home denunciations and arrests are multiplied (53.2). The people are co-operative. The merest utterance of suspicion justifies—sometimes irrespective of the low reputation of the informant and the public respectability of the suspect—intervention and an investigation, the first step of which is the arrest of the suspect.

What has led to this order-threatening mass hysteria?

> For the people knew by hearsay that the tyranny of Peisistratos and his sons had become oppressive towards the end and that, moreover, it had not been themselves [the Athenians] and Harmodios [i.e. the 'tyrannicide' and Athenian national hero] who had overthrown it, but rather the Spartans [i.e. their current enemies]—and therefore they lived in constant fear and became suspicious at every turn. (53.3)

At this point the historian interrupts his report of the chaotic situation in Athens to begin the famous excursus on the tyranny and its downfall. He introduces this passage with the explanatory[1] conjunction 'for', although, in view of the fact that the events he is about to describe occurred over a century earlier, the sense of the conjunction is not immediately clear.

The first sentence, which topples from their pedestals two national heroes, is already provocative, at least for Athenian sentiments.

> For the daring act (!) of Aristogeiton and Harmodios was undertaken as a result of a love affair (!), by a more detailed account of which I shall prove that neither the others nor the Athenians themselves (!) give an at all (!) accurate account of their own (!) tyrants and of the events. (54.1)

The—untranslatable—accumulation of negatives, the fact of a 'love affair' as the cause of a revolt against the tyranny, the choice of the word 'daring act' (τόλμημα in Thucydidean usage approaches the nuance of 'over-boldness'), the climactic 'nor the Athenians themselves' (who surely should know best), the (in Thucydides rare) 'I (ἐγώ) shall prove'—all this shows an emphasis which points (better: is intended to point) to a strong involvement on the part of the writer; that is, this is evidently a point of particular interest to our author.

What is the basis for this involvement? Is it merely, as has been suggested, the pride of one who 'knows better (more exactly)' than everyone else?

This would in any case be a possible, though in our view a naive, motive. Thucydides is after all the first author who programmatically announces his intention to achieve 'accuracy' in his account of events (1.22.2), and the complaint about the Athenians' failure to give an at all 'accurate' account is literally raised in the sentence quoted above. In addition, it is precisely this excursus which historians and philologists have again and again praised as a model of Thucydides' scientific precision.

The question is whether 'accuracy for its own sake' (or 'correction of existing misconceptions') is a sufficient category for understanding the passage, or whether the style of presentation suggests an opening for an additional point of view. To answer this question we must turn to the excursus itself.

It begins with a correction without which the story would be incomprehensible: it was not Hipparchos—as is commonly assumed—but Hippias who, as the eldest son, succeeded Peisistratos on the tyrant's throne. The younger brother Hipparchos sought without success to win the favors of a young man named Harmodios. In so doing, he hurt Harmodios' lover Aristogeiton, a citizen of the middle class.

Aristogeiton's immediate (!) reaction (out of jealousy and fear of Hipparchos' power) was to overthrow the tyranny—'so far as this was possible for a man of his standing' (54.3). That is, by emphasizing the disproportion between the power of the tyrant's brother and the scant means of a 'middle-class' citizen, Thucydides from the beginning stresses the absurd nature of the undertaking. At the same time he shows in a psychologically convincing way how the *private* motive of jealousy, because it cannot be satisfactorily dealt with in the private sphere, becomes a dangerous *political* factor. The fact that this transformation occurs in the absence of calm consideration (that is, without weighing the possible consequences), is emphasized in the characterization of Aristogeiton's reaction as spontaneous (εὐθύς, 54.3).

On the other hand, Hipparchos' reaction—it is characteristic of this author that he gives the reactions and motives of both sides at significant points in his presentation—is to aim in the *opposite* direction. After a second failure to win the young man's favor, he decides upon damaging him *privately*, that is, he seeks to avoid the open use of the political power so feared by Aristogeiton (54.4).

There is a certain balance of motives here. The 'tyrannicide', who acts out of jealousy, is no better than Hipparchos, whose vanity is wounded by the refusal of his advances.

Hipparchos' reaction is problematic. Why does the tyrant's brother seek satisfaction on the private level, when (in accordance with the Athenian concept of tyrannical behavior) he might well use force?

It is at this point that the second correction of contemporary misconceptions begins, and it takes the form (since it requires proof if it is to be convincing) of an excursus within the excursus: the notion that the tyrants 'ruled by force' and were unpopular is *false*.

On the contrary, this family of tyrants was guided in its undertakings by 'virtue and reason' (54.5: two words of very high praise which Thucydides bestows on very few people). The effects of this comportment were a blessing for the citizenry: low taxes, a rich building program for the beautification of the city, successful military campaigning abroad, and respect for religious practices. The tyrants did not even abrogate existing laws in their own interest: they only saw to it that a member of their family was always in one of the annual offices (54.5–6).

The answer, then, to the question posed above, is that Hipparchos would *in no way* have abused his official power because such an abuse would have interfered with and derogated from his family's governing principles (and therefore from their prestige). Aristogeiton's fear (and therefore his first, spontaneous reaction) arose from a false perception of the situation.

Taking the passage as a whole—and in this light the correction proves to be part of the narrative—we get the impression of a political community

3

which, before the intervention of the 'tyrannicides', was enjoying the blessings of domestic peace and order. At the same time, we get a picture which is in contrast to the Athens of 415.[2]

Thucydides is even able to support two of his assertions with archaeological evidence. An inscription on the altar of the Pythian Apollo bears witness both to the construction projects of the tyrant family and to its holding of Athenian magistracies (54.7).

The mention of the inscription leads to the identification of Hippias (eldest son of the tyrant Peisistratos) as the tyrant (i.e. it serves as evidence for the first correction of current opinion at the beginning of the excursus).

This is an important passage (55.1–3) insofar as Thucydides, conscious of his method as a convincing form of argumentation, applies a conclusion based on probability as a means of guaranteeing the truth—three times[3] in a row.

It should be noted here that the historian himself (on the basis of personal information) is anyway 'more accurately' informed than others (εἰδὼς...ἀκριβέστερον ἄλλων..., 55.1), i.e. he would not require these pieces of evidence for his own satisfaction. But for the sake of the general verifiability of his account, he is interested in evidence which is independent of his own person (γνοίη δ' ἄν τις καὶ αὐτῷ τούτῳ). In this way, the εἰκός, as applied to the past by the historian himself, becomes a means of leaving the realm of subjectivity.

Now the thesis that Hippias (not Hipparchos) was Peisistratos' successor is made probable by three considerations. First, there is the above-mentioned altar and the stele 'On the Injustice of the Tyrants': both inscriptions mention children of Hippias only, not of his brothers Hipparchos and Thessalos. This permits the conclusion that Hippias married first and was consequently the eldest. Second, on the same stele Hippias is mentioned directly after his father. This permits conclusions about his relative age and succession to his father's throne. Third, on the day of Hipparchos' murder Hippias could scarcely have reacted so quickly and effectively had he just at that moment taken power rather than having long since been accustomed to exercising it.

'But Hipparchos, known for his unhappy fate, also acquired the reputation among posterity of having been tyrant' (55.4). After refuting the misconception of his contemporaries, the historian—I would suggest this as an obvious interpretation of the sentence—adds a psychological explanation for how it came about: an assassination carried out against anyone but the tyrant himself is inexplicable to the patriotic consciousness (which has no room for private motives). As a consequence the murder-victim

4

becomes the tyrant and his brother the victim's successor: the gate to the myth of the two national-liberation heroes has been opened.

We return to the narrative of the excursus. The rebuffed Hipparchos impugns the honor of Harmodios' sister; the young man's resultant affliction spurs his lover on still further; now both are eager for action; the circle of conspirators is kept small for the sake of security: they hope for spontaneous assistance from their fellow citizens on the day of 'liberation' (we shall often see that 'hope', in Thucydides' view, is a weak element in any plan—56.1–3).

At the appointed time—the Panathenaea festival has been selected because one might carry weapons on that day without arousing suspicion—Harmodios and Aristogeiton see a fellow conspirator conversing familiarly with the tyrant ('but then Hippias was well accessible to all', adds the author, highlighting once again—just before the catastrophe—the peaceful domestic situation). The pair become frightened and imagine that they have been betrayed and are 'as good as arrested' (57.2).

Their reaction is consistent with an emotional response: if the political goal is now out of reach, they will at least—in a kind of substitution[4]—satisfy the original, private vendetta. Finding Hipparchos at the Leokoreion, they 'fall upon him immediately without reflection and in the height of passion—the one of jealousy, the other of wounded pride—they stab him to death' (57.3).

Let us observe the points of emphasis. Even at the most dramatic moment, the author cannot refrain from viewing the deed itself exclusively in the light of its irrational motives. The hoped-for popular uprising does not materialize. Moreover, the tyrant, responding rapidly, succeeds that same day in disarming the remainder of the conspirators (Harmodios had been killed immediately after the assassination and Aristogeiton captured shortly thereafter).

> In such fashion Harmodios and Aristogeiton arrived at the beginning of their plot because of lovers' grief—and at their unreasonable daring because of fear which arose at the moment of crisis. (59.1)

The beginning and end of the episode look to each other. A spontaneous, ill-considered reaction leads to the plan to overthrow the tyranny; spontaneous (εὐθύς at 57.3 repeats εὐθύς of 54.3), ill-considered action which abandons its plan leads to the deed. Both conception and execution take place under the sign of fear and erotic excitement (54.3–57.2–3). The 'daring act' (τόλμημα, 54.1) of the beginning is given an edge in the 'unreasonable daring' of the writer's concluding judgment (ἡ ἀλόγιστος τόλμα, 59.1; for the negative significance of this, cf. 3.82.4).

A foolish undertaking thus ends in pitiful failure. And yet this is only one side of the issue. The cross-over from the private to the public sphere, once accomplished (by the creation of a group of conspirators), cannot be undone: the attempted assassination and consequent exposure of the opposition must have an effect on the tyrant's behavior.

This is the other[5] side, and it brings about precisely the opposite of what the 'freedom fighters' had intended. From that time on, the tyranny becomes more oppressive for all the citizens because the tyrant is no longer sure of his personal security, which had been the guarantor of the aforementioned (54.5–6) liberal policies.

> But for the Athenians, the tyranny became harsher after this (μετὰ τοῦτο, 59.2; cf. μετὰ ταῦτα, 59.3), and Hippias, already more in fear, *killed many citizens* and at the same time looked abroad for some security for himself in the event of a sudden change in the situation. (59.2)

As has already been pointed out, this is the climax of the narrative: a foolish act arising from a private motive results in the destruction of the balance of an entire commonwealth. Now the reader also understands why Thucydides gave so full an account of the peaceful aspect of the tyranny. The narrative yields a gruesome result: murder (out of foolishness) begets multiple murders (out of fear).

Could the meaning of the whole excursus be contained in this result?

The author's points of emphasis—which highlight the tragic effects on the citizenry of what he considers a foolish assault—surely point beyond the opening perspective of merely setting straight for its own sake the record of contemporary misconceptions. For this reason scholars have attempted to give the excursus a broader significance by seeing it as parallel to the situation in Athens in 415 (when the similarly ill-advised and hasty recall of the general Alcibiades, according to this view, likewise leads to great misfortune for Athens).

However, this analogy does not seem entirely satisfactory because the presumed result of Alcibiades' recall (i.e. the failure of the Sicilian expedition) lies too far beyond the situation in which Thucydides has placed the excursus. Besides, an analogy could not account for the causal function of the excursus (γάρ, 54.1).

Finally, mere parallelism would devalue the unique and—to judge by Thucydides' presentation—paradigmatic value of the excursus to a simple, repetitive schema, and it would, at least at this point, be hasty to infer such a schema.

Before giving our own interpretation, let us first continue our examination of the historian's report. For the fact that the tyrant looks for

refuge abroad only *after* the attempted assassination (μετὰ ταῦτα, 59.3)
Thucydides is once more in a position to offer proof: Hippias married his
daughter Archedike to a son of the tyrant of Lampsacus (in comparison to
Athens an insignificant town: '...he, an Athenian, to a Lampsacan!', 59.3).
The implication is that an Athenian tyrant at the peak of his power would
never have condescended to this (we can leave aside the consideration that
the Lampsacan tyrant enjoyed great influence with the king of Persia).

As proof, the author cites the inscription on Archedike's tombstone at
Lampsacus. Further evidence for this foreign connection is the fact that the
tyrant did visit Lampsacus, among other places, after his fall from power
(59.4).

A summary mention—the climax of the narrative (59.1–2) is now behind
us—of Hippias' attempt two decades later to regain his rule in conjunction
with the Persian invasion brings the excursus to a close (59.4).

The next sentence (60.1) picks up the situation in 415 with a statement
nearly identical to that contained in the last sentence before the excursus
(53.3):

> Thinking of these things, and recalling what they knew of them by hearsay
> [that is, trapped in the un-corrected, false conception of the events narrated in
> the excursus], the Athenian people at that time [= 415] were harsh (χαλεπός:
> in 53.3 this word was used of the tyranny in its last stages, then translated as
> 'oppressive') and suspicious of those accused of profaning the Mysteries, and
> it seemed to them that it had all been done for the purpose of an oligarchic
> or tyrannical conspiracy.

The fact that the situation has not changed in any way since the
beginning of the excursus must raise the question: what is the reader
supposed to have learned from it that can add to his understanding of the
situation in the year 415?

In order to answer this question, let us summarize the points emphasized
by Thucydides in the excursus:

1. The Athenians live in ignorance of their own history (emphasized
stylistically; this case, we may now add, seemed to the historian so typical
that—in another context—he used it as one of two examples for the general
indifference of human beings towards the search for truth: 1.20.2–3).

2. (a) The famous 'tyrannicide' was a foolish case of private revenge;
moreover, (b) the victim had never been tyrant.

3. The rule of the Athenian tyrants was peaceful and beneficial to the
city (along with 2b, confirmed by epigraphic evidence; use of conclusions based on probability; insight into the origin of the legend about the
tyrannicide).

4. Hippias' rule became oppressive only when he (after the murder of his brother) began to fear for his own safety (confirmed by epigraphic evidence).

The notion current at Athens, on the other hand, is that the freedom fighters[6] Harmodios and Aristogeiton rebelled against the oppressive tyranny and murdered the tyrant. But the tyrant's brother took power immediately and the final liberation had to come from abroad.[7] It is upon this picture that the Athenian people's chronic fear of tyrannical ambitions is based.

And this gives us the key to the interpretation of the excursus: the national legend rests upon an *historical falsehood*; it states that the (supposed) tyrant was killed *because* his regime was oppressive rather than allowing the murder to be the cause of the regime's harshness. In other words, *cause and effect have traded places*. The act of murder (arising from private, purely emotional motives), which destroyed the domestic peace of the city, becomes in the myth a (morally justified) act of liberation for that same city. And that is not all.

It is precisely this *false myth* which becomes *in its turn*—a hundred years after the fact!—*a concrete political factor*, in that it excites the people's fear of tyranny to such a degree that *again* the domestic peace of the city is destroyed and the very order of Athenian society is threatened. The *demos* demonstrates behavior of the kind that its imagination ascribes to the tyrant himself (cf. our observation on the author's use of the word χαλεπός). We have thus discovered the causal function of the excursus:[8] while making a correction, Thucydides shows historical *misconception as a direct cause* of action which has jumped the rails of rational control.

The unavoidable question that arises is, what is the way out of such a situation?

To begin with, we should notice that Thucydides describes the climax of the chaotic situation only after the excursus:[9] the anger of the people (ὀργιζομένων, 60.2, reminiscent of the ὀργή of Harmodios and Aristogeiton, e.g. 57.3) increases daily in the degree of its savagery (ἐς τὸ ἀγριώτερον, 60.2), and more and more (respectable) people are taken to prison.

At last one of the prisoners comes forward—in return for amnesty (though he 'seemed the guiltiest of all'!)—to denounce the 'guilty parties' (in the mutilation of the herms), even though the reliability of his information remained questionable. 'For opinion is divided, but clear proof no one could provide (τὸ σαφές), neither then nor later, of who the culprits were' (60.2). The narrative becomes lively enough for the author to include a report in indirect discourse. '…the people gladly seized upon the, as they

8

believed, reliable information (once again τὸ σαφές, 60.4)…' The men accused by the informer are killed (those who have escaped are condemned *in absentia* and a reward is offered to anyone who will kill them), the others are set free.

'And under these circumstances it was *unclear whether those executed had been punished unjustly, but the rest of the city was clearly benefited in the present situation*' (60.5). The people behave in precisely the same way in the matter of the profanation of the Mysteries. Because they believed themselves in the case of the herms 'in possession of the clear truth (τὸ σαφές)' (61.1), they were in the case of the profanation of the Mysteries (of which Alcibiades, among others, had been accused) even quicker to assume an antidemocratic conspiracy. A Spartan army which happens (ἔτυχε, 61.2) to appear at the isthmus (and in reality is on its way to Boeotia) is seen as an acute external threat. It is immediately and loudly assumed that it is approaching at the behest of Alcibiades (61.2). Simultaneously, suspicions about Alcibiades' friends in Argos lead to the return of the Argive hostages (at the time in Athenian custody) to Argos *for execution*.[10] All of these factors result in the recall of Alcibiades (for whom the death sentence is planned in Athens, 61.4, 7).

We have sketched the events so far beyond the climax of the domestic situation in order to show how here, too, Thucydides takes into account unfortunate effects upon those who otherwise have no part in the events (the 300 Argive hostages). He adds this fact (irrelevant for the situation of Athens of that time, but significant of the people's wrath and its consequences) using τότε (we would translate emphatically, 'it was at that time also that the Athenians delivered…', 61.3).

Before concluding, there is still something to say about the supposed 'clarity' (τὸ σαφές).

We encounter the word three times in rapid succession (60.2, 4; 61.1). In the first instance the author explains that clarity about the truth of the accusations made by the informant proved at the time (as well as later) unattainable. In both of the other instances, he emphasizes that the Athenians only *believed* that they had clarity.

This word—just as the question of 'accuracy' (τὸ ἀκριβές) at the beginning of the excursus, taken together with the problem of human indifference vis-à-vis the truth—once again leads back to those sections of the first book, where Thucydides is discussing the goal and method of his work. In the concluding sentence of his program (1.22.4) Thucydides states that he wishes for readers who desire *clarity* (τὸ σαφές) concerning 'what happened and concerning what—in accordance with the human condition[11]—will again be such and similar'.

Through this triple reference to key concepts in the Thucydidean program, the entire section with which we have dealt up to this point acquires special significance.

In his own search for unambiguous clarity—in which he employs only the most reliable means available—the historian discovers that the actions of human nature (if we may apply a higher category of his program to the present problem) are guided by merely supposed clarity; the result is behavior which is no longer under rational control and so causes the death or suffering of those afflicted.

If we return to the beginning of the excursus (the historical ignorance of human beings and in this case especially of the Athenians) with this finding in mind, we can no longer understand the vigorous emphasis (54.1) as that of an enlightened know-it-all, but rather as at most an expression of regret—arising from insight into the *de facto* inevitability of what appears from rational hindsight to have been avoidable.

The events described at the end (61.1), surrounding the revenge for the profanation of the Mysteries, are secondary to our central theme insofar as Thucydides clearly says that the Athenians in this case were behaving in a manner analogous to their settling of the affair of the mutilation of the herms.[12]

The decisive statement is of course (we are once again taking up the question of a way out of such an emotionally charged situation) that the city was undeniably benefited by the informant's dubious declarations—in all of which the problem of justice must be left aside.[13]

In the context dealt with, this is the last of the Athenian domestic situations presented to the reader, and the manner in which this situation came about fits appropriately into the chain of events. Emotions excited by an historical falsehood are calmed by an only supposedly clear perception; in other words, *the devastating effects of a case of ignorance are here neutralized only by further ignorance.*

If our interpretation has come close to grasping the picture which in this case occurs to Thucydides from his insight into history, then another question arises. Is this picture the rule or an exception in the normal progress of human affairs? That is, what are the boundaries within which by its very actions human nature—to use one aspect of his characteristic category—defines itself in the author's view?

Notes

* Foreign quotations have as a rule been translated into English. Where required, the foreign quotation has been inserted into the text itself. All translations from

the Greek are the author's.

¹ γάρ may be used to introduce a digression; its causal function does not thereby automatically disappear: see below, n. 8.

² It must be mentioned that interpreters who have wished to see in Thucydides support for a particular type of constitution have, on the basis of this passage, seen fit to state an affinity for tyranny. In so doing they have overlooked the fact that the author is speaking not of tyranny in general, but of this particular family of tyrants (οὗτοι, 54.5), and that his praise is expressed for the peaceful domestic situation maintained by these tyrants—a point which one would like to observe when contemplating Thucydides' position on constitutional questions.

³ We can with good conscience speak of a conclusion based on probability in all three cases since the variation of expression ('probably', 'not improbably', 'it seems to me') arises only from stylistic considerations.

⁴ Cf. 1.20.2: βουλόμενοι δὲ πρὶν ξυλληφθῆναι δράσαντές τι καὶ κινδυνεῦσαι.

⁵ Thucydides contrasts private fate and public effect using μέν-δέ, 59.1–2.

⁶ As for the evidence outside the present text, cf. especially Scol. Campbell 893–896 = Athenaeus 15.695.10–13, which ascribes to the tyrannicides the success of their undertaking, and *IG* 1.77.

⁷ Cf. Herodotus 6.123.

⁸ A parallel excursus which reaches into the more distant past in order to *provide the cause of* a situation in the more recent past and is likewise introduced with γάρ can be found in the *Pentecontaetia* (1.89.1 ff.): the description of the rise of Athenian power (1.89 ff.) gives the cause of current Spartan fears (1.88). In this case as well—as in the Peisistratid excursus—the causal function is fulfilled by way of a correction (Thucydides mentions both themes: 1.97.2). Neither passage (1.89.1, 6.54.1) is discussed by Denniston (*The Greek Particles*, Oxford, 1959²).

⁹ It is clear from a comparison with Andocides 1 (e.g. 36, 48) that Thucydides' description (which, compared with his normal presentation, must count as rather lively) is actually quite reserved.

¹⁰ There is a certain horrible irony in this, for the Argive hostages (on suspicion of pro-Spartan leanings) had originally been brought to Athens by *Alcibiades himself* (5.84.1).

¹¹ For τὸ ἀνθρώπινον see below, p. 28 f.

¹² Of course this does not mean that we should overlook the extensive consequences of these condemnations (the betrayal of Alcibiades); only that Thucydides sees the decision to recall Alcibiades as having an accessory character in terms of its coming about.

¹³ It scarcely needs to be pointed out that the same viewpoint is present in this judgment as in the presumed 'Praise of Tyranny' (cf. above, n. 2), namely, 'preservation (or restoration) of domestic peace'.

2

RETROSPECTIVE
The State of Thucydidean Studies; Methodology

It would be a project rewarding in itself to consider the modern literature on Thucydides from the perspective of the history of scholarship. Preoccupation with the 'first *scientific* historian', as Thucydides has often been called, has time and again stimulated modern scholars to compare, or even identify, their own position with that of the 'founder' of the historical discipline. In the latter instance there is sometimes a tendency to use Thucydides as the star witness for one's own case: '…in his conception of what is required of a writer of history he is nearer to the twentieth century AD than he is to the fifth BC'.[1]

As surprising as such a judgment may be in its pointed formulation, it is not alone in its general tendency. The characteristics—variously marked in individual instances—which lend the ancient historian such a modern air are easy to enumerate: the (theoretically often conceded) unconditional love of truth; his awareness of problems of methodology; the high value he sets upon the individual fact (closely connected to his insistence on precision); his presumed readiness to recognize universal laws as operative in events; his consistently executed precision in chronology; and, not least, his insistence upon a strict, *immanent* causality (for which he is often contrasted with his 'religious' predecessor Herodotus, who thus serves as a foil for Thucydides).

At the same time these several aspects make it transparent to which concept of the historian's task Thucydides' work would seem most to approximate. The entrance of *positivist* methodology into the humanities could scarcely leave unnoticed the efforts of an author whose methodical effort seemed primarily to strive for ascertaining the historical facts.

The fact that the positivist concept of knowledge (with its well-known principle of objectivity as *scientific*[2] objectivity) has been applied also to Thucydides is not in itself very important for the aspects to be considered in the present work. However, to the extent that, under the influence of this method of inquiry, assumptions have been made also concerning the intention of the work and even the personal attitudes of its author, this line of interpretation deserves our full attention. Of additional importance is the fact that its influence, though seldom explicitly stated or (because of its complexity) even fully consciously applied, extends into the modern picture of Thucydides.

Near the turn of the nineteenth century Thucydides was already being discussed under the rubric 'The *Science* of History'.[3] Shortly thereafter, Cornford (1907) came forward with his book, *Thucydides Mythistoricus*, and claimed for the ancient historian a position diametrically opposed to the positivist one.[4] In his view Thucydides knows no causality at all,[5] has no developed sense of economic affairs,[6] and is deeply influenced by Aeschylus; Thucydides is supposed to have retained the tragedian's moral element, but abandoned his theology[7] and replaced it with 'supernatural powers'. In Cornford's view Thucydidean hope becomes the goddess Ἐλπίς, chance becomes the goddess Τύχη, Alcibiades becomes Ἀπάτη (and Ὕβρις). In short, Cornford was at pains to ascribe to Thucydides all the mythical powers the historian must have been proud to have overcome.

I mention this odd work in the present context only because it incited later positivist criticism. Cochrane's book (*Thucydides and the Science of History*)[8] may serve as an example here because it most clearly expresses the tendencies we are about to discuss.

First, Thucydides is once again allowed his awareness of causality, and an emphatically *immanent*[9] causality at that; Cochrane claims to see the influence of fifth-century atomist philosophy[10] and points out its aversion to traditional religious ideas. This is the cardinal point for the equation—unhistorical but in accord with Comte's famous schema—of Thucydides' attitude with the anti-metaphysical mind set[11] of his positivist interpreter.[12]

Significant for the further development of the scholarly view of Thucydides is that, by means of the reasoning just described, the Thucydidean concept of knowledge is shown to be *scientific*.

Already Littré,[13] writing in 1839, had pointed out the stylistic similarity between Thucydides and the Hippocratic Corpus. Cochrane expands this correspondence into the area of methodology—within limits an entirely justified view[14]—as well as to the goal of the work. The latter is possible for Cochrane only because he understands the process of reception as analogous to modern development. He writes that Thucydides' work represents 'an attempt to apply to the study of social life the methods which Hippocrates employed in the art of healing', and is an 'exact (!) parallel to the attempts of modern *scientific* historians to apply *evolutionary* canons of interpretation derived from *Darwinian* science'.[15]

I know of scarcely any passage in the modern secondary literature on Thucydides in which there is so frank an admission of nineteenth-century influence. The reference to Darwin's evolutionary theory shows what is basically at issue here: transference of the modern idea of progress (inclusive of all its complex associations) to Thucydides. It is a small step from here to conceive of the entire process which the historian describes—the course of the war—or even of the decline of a single political community—as parallel to the medical categories of a disease.[16] Thus it seems only consistent that Thucydides be equated with the 'healing' Hippocrates and, so to speak, become the physician at the bedside of ailing society:

> In the case of Thucydides…something akin to the *positive faith* of the modern scientist is needed to explain the note of calm *assurance* with which he commends his "Histories"…as a possession for ever. …it is perfectly evident that he has *no doubt* in the value and the *usefulness* of his own work.[17]

My intention is to go to the root of the utilitarian interpretation of this statement from Thucydides' program (1.22.4: that his work is a possession for ever). It has long been established that the interpretation aiming at usefulness, in the sense of practical applicability, rests upon faulty translation.[18]

However, that the aspect of utility has been supported by importation of a category alien to this work and by analogy to modern intellectual history, is a largely unconscious, but for that reason all the more weighty, presupposition.[19]

The consequences for interpretation are of several kinds. The most common is that Thucydides believed (in accordance with the physician's intention) he was able to help humanity by teaching a lesson with his work.[20] The interpretation sees as the foundation of this teaching the 'recognition'—which Thucydides is supposed to have adapted chiefly from contemporary medicine,[21] but also from the sophists and philosophers[22]—that human nature is a *constant*[23] whose actions (it would be more apposite to say: reactions) are generally predictable. With this prognostic skill, transferred from medicine to politics, Thucydides is supposed to have aimed at equipping his statesman-reader with the ability to predict and steer future developments[24] (possibly even to improve human nature, despite the dark qualities which Thucydides ascribes to it).[25]

Together with the work's prognostic intention arises the question of how to calculate probability, since the reactions of human nature can be predicted in approximate terms only, never with complete certainty.[26] Because the εἰκός concept is so significant for Thucydides' contemporaries—both in medicine and in the rhetoric of the sophists[27]—it is usually assumed that Thucydides himself (especially since he often lets his speakers argue on the basis of what is εἰκός) employs this method of arguing as a reliable instrument for gauging *future* events:

> …the various speakers in the *History* are constantly predicting the *probable* outcome of policies and the future course of events. Now to Thucydides the supreme requisite of a politician is his πρόγνωσις…and the *History* itself is, in essence, a *manual for future statesmen*, instructing them in the outcome of conditions destined to be repeated. Inevitably, therefore, he attributes to his speakers these same methods of deducing the typical results of given circumstances.[28]

One may call it 'a manual for future statesmen', 'Breviarium für den künftigen Politiker' ('breviary for the future politician'),[29] 'Techne für den Politikos',[30] 'rational zu handhabendes Werkzeug' for the 'politischen Menschen',[31] or even claim that Thucydides' work is intended to provide political insight 'whose rationality is to unlock a more *secure future*'.[32]

All such interpretations—even when they do not expressly begin from the positivist thesis—share the assumption that Thucydides, on principle, considered the forces at work in political events rationally comprehensible and therefore was able to pursue a more or less practical goal with his work.

However, an attempt to learn precisely what useful lessons the historian has to offer the statesman meets either with no answer at all or the response that the basic universal laws 'perhaps can hardly be defined precisely';[33] occasionally one encounters a more or less acceptable selection of quotes from the work itself, especially from the speeches.[34]

But let us—in the context of the problem posed by the recent image of Thucydides—assume that human nature is a predictable entity, one that can be pressed into service for statesmanly planning;[35] another important factor producing uncertainty for the supposed prognostic intention of the work comes into play. This is the role of chance, or more generally, the possibly blind course of events (which, of course, does not depend upon human nature alone). If Thucydides is to have written his work for politicians, for him as well as for his 'era of rationalism', τύχη must indeed have been 'a stumbling-block'.[36]

One way of allowing for this 'stumbling' is to place Thucydides among those contemporary philosophers who were optimistic on this point. Besides Thrasymachus (fr. 1) and Critias (fr. 21), Democritus' fr. 119 is a favorite citation:

> Human beings have formed an image of τύχη as an excuse for their own thoughtlessness; for only to a small extent does τύχη fight against reason: most things in life are set straight by shrewd intelligence.[37]

Quite apart from the fact that these passages likewise consider and attempt to render rationally comprehensible only *one* of the two desta-bilizing factors,[38] it seems worthwhile to pose the question whether Thucydides' attitude toward the course of events can really be sketched as follows:

> …the deeper the insight into things, the more clearly the rationally compre-hensible moments appear; Thucydides demands that these moments be observed not only by the hindsight of the historian, but also by the foresight of the statesman.[39]

In my opinion, such an interpretation is possible only if one either underestimates[40] the role of chance in a single chain of events or takes the position that each individual chance-influenced episode, looking at the war as a whole, contributes little or nothing to the total outcome.[41]

Both alternatives have in common the fact that they assign to the statesman the responsibility (and the opportunity) to include in his plans sufficient contingency (reserve) factors to allow for the unexpected:

> It is also true that Thucydides' tendency to understand τύχη as the remainder of what is calculable only confirms his basic practical motif: the remainder itself becomes an item in the equation.[42]

In this way both destabilizing factors seem to have been neutralized: human nature is seen as a 'constant'; chance is eliminated by allowing a sufficient 'margin for error in the equation'. What previously appeared to be a game of chance with two unknown quantities in play has been reduced to a system composed of manipulable factors.

And—one would like to ask—what has become of the tragic element (often cited, but not accommodated by such a system) in the work? We are told that it resides in the 'catastrophic course of events παρ᾽ ἐλπίδα'[43]— which evidently is to be avoided in the future.[44]

It might thus appear that nothing stands in the way of a 'successful probability computation' for the statesman. It is likely, however, that this appearance is deceptive. Let us leave aside the fact that the statesman is given no criterion for checking a pressing situation against the probable course it will take. One would still like to raise the question: does not this 'catastrophic course of events παρ᾽ ἐλπίδα' indicate a real problem for the author, precisely the one to which access is not gained through such optimistic interpretation; and further, does an area beyond the sphere of politics not open up behind this problem?

The complex of problems reviewed up to this point clearly places Thucy-dides in the framework of a *political* task. In my opinion it is quite right and makes sense to see Thucydides, from the point of view of the existing tradition of the historical discipline, as the inventor of political history.[45] For a philologist, however, the question must arise whether a writer (I use the word advisedly) would, at a time when prose was beginning to compete with poetry,—one scarcely need point out the deliberate individuality of Thucydidean prose—not have intended his work to be read with more far-reaching aspects in mind. Nor need I mention that, even when tragedy, the pre-eminent poetry of his time, wears a political costume, the political aspect of the work is not necessarily the ultimate one.[46]

It is remarkable that philologists—German philologists in particular— have contributed decisively to an analysis of Thucydides' work primarily along political (and thus usually practical) lines. The explanation for this will take us on a—perhaps surprising—detour.

Since the publication of Ullrich's *Beiträge zur Erklärung des Thukydides* in 1845/6, there has existed in the field of Classics the so-called 'Thucydidean Question'. In 1899 Ed. Meyer was already lamenting that it was 'not a good sign for the efficiency of the philological discipline'[47] that this problem had not yet been solved.

The problem as raised by Ullrich comes down to this: the work as we have it is not a unit but rather—I concentrate here only on the most important points—consists of two drafts or designs, written at different times, which the author did not have time to integrate consistently with one another. According to Ullrich, the first part consists of Books 1 to 4 (middle) and was written soon after the end of the Archidamian War (421); the later part consists of the remaining Books and reworkings of certain passages of the earlier part and was composed soon after the collapse of Athens (404).

The effects of the 'Thucydidean Question' become relevant to our point of view with Schwartz's (1919) work on Thucydides. This book has often been credited with lending fresh momentum to Ullrich's thesis, which by then had already undergone several attempts at modification: 'Schwartz for the first time raised this question decisively to the level of a problem of intellectual development'.[48]

But what at first sight might present itself as fruitful innovation proved fateful in the long run, particularly since Thucydidean studies have to this day not managed to free themselves from this book.

Schwartz understood the compositional layers in the work as 'stages in the development of Thucydides the historiographer who attempted to wrestle with the great historical *experiences of his time* by shaping them and at the same time himself'.[49] Schwartz's fatal step—Stenzel discreetly hints at this already in 1926[50]—was in understanding Thucydides' 'contemporary experiences' on the basis of his (i.e. Schwartz's) own time.

In itself, a current political interpretation is not a rarity (it might speak for the author's objective reserve in his work). In his book *Thucydides and the World War*,[51] Lord tries, on the basis of the Peloponnesian War, to make predictions about the further course of World War II.[52] In the introduction to his 1925 book Abbott openly admits that World War I provided some stimulus for his work.[53] The historian Gomme sees in a more recent quarter-century of European history the fulfillment of Thucydides' hope that his work would be a κτῆμα εἰς αἰεί.[54]

In Schwartz's work the contemporary interpretation turns up in scientific garb.[55] Terms such as 'Retraktation', 'Doppelfassungen', 'Herausgeber' and the labeling of certain features as 'Früh' and 'Spät' criteria (some of which already belonged to his predecessors' tool-kits) at first give the impression of strict objectivity and a method appropriate to the subject.[56] But it is precisely this method which disguises the content of Schwartz's argumentation.

For instance, when the reader unexpectedly discovers, instead of the question raised by Thucydides about the causes of the war, a discussion of Pericles' war-'guilt', and when Spartan fear of Athens' rising power (1.23.6, 88) is referred to as Sparta's 'jealousy',[57] we have a right to doubt the objectivity of such an interpretation.

The most momentous of Schwartz's 'doublets' occur in the great tetrad of speeches which Thucydides sets in Sparta before the outbreak of the war. Schwartz ascribes the speech of the Corinthians urging war and that of the Spartan king Archidamus warning against it to Thucydides' early stage. The speech of the Spartan ephor Sthenelaidas precipitating the decision to go to war, and that of the Athenians warning against war, Schwartz assigns to the late period (after the fall of Athens). According to Schwartz, the latter pair precludes the former and was to have replaced it in the final version of the work.[58]

The historian's 'development' which results from this—arbitrary, from a literary perspective—distortion of the text is clear. The 'war-guilt' is transferred from Corinth to Sparta's 'jealousy'; Athens (and, along with her, Pericles) is exonerated. 'Die geschichtliche Darstellung ist zur Apologie geworden' ('Historiography has turned into *apologia*.').[59]

The consequence of this spiritual biography of Thucydides probably represents the severest possible blow to the intellectual honesty of the man who made the struggle for unadulterated truth his life's work, a task of whose difficulty he was well aware (1.22). The historian is demoted from his *sine ira et studio* attitude to one of Athenian partisanship. In the words of Schwartz, after Thucydides' return from exile he became 'a *patriot again*' who now attacked Sparta with 'a *passion* which transposed itself into the *political* realm'.[60] In this way political partisanship is vigorously set in the biographical system.

According to Schwartz, the above-mentioned speech of the Athenians (which arrogantly tramples upon all that is just) is a plea on the part of the historian for Athens. It follows in his view that the Melian Dialogue, a model of Athenian brutality and similar in its argumentation to the earlier speech, must contain 'a barrage of attacks' on Sparta.[61] It is only logical, then, that Schwartz's Thucydides at last finds himself trapped into a 'bis zur antimoralischen Paradoxie gesteigerte Verteidigung der attischen Machtpolitik' ('a defence, raised to the point of anti-moral paradox, of Athenian power politics').[62]

The difficulties encountered by de Romilly in her book *Thucydide et l'impérialisme athénien*[63] (published around the beginning of World War II) may serve as an indication of the influence of Schwartz's politicizing interpretation upon later decades in precisely this context. Because she does not consider justified the anti-moral reading of the speech of the Athenians, she is at pains to distance the speech from both the related Melian Dialogue and the cruel behavior of a wantonly aggressive Athens. She does this by seeking to draw the speech close to the '*générosité*' of Periclean Athens as presented in the Funeral Oration.[64]

This would make Thucydides from a rigorous into a moderate defender of Periclean imperialism, i.e. still partisan in essence. De Romilly—unlike Schwartz, who seems never to have become conscious of the problem—sees the fateful implication of this reasoning and attempts to deal with it in the following way:

> Ce détachement d'homme de *science*, où se fonde l'*impartialité* de Thucydide, lui permet de comprendre, et par suite de *justifier*, mais *sans parti pris* comme sans illusions. ('The detachment of the man of science, on which the *impartiality* of Thucydides bases itself, allows him to understand, and, consequently, to *justify*, but *without taking sides* and without illusions.')[65]

By pointing out deliberate correlations and cross-references,[66] Schwartz's successors applied themselves methodically to understanding the text, which he had left in a shambles, increasingly as a unit. However, the reference to present-day politics, once vigorously foregrounded, remained largely intact—or became even more pronounced—in interpretations of the *content* of the work.

Pohlenz has Thucydides criticizing all those who after the war condemned the old imperialism:

> …wenn kleine Seelen sich nicht entblödeten, den Mann zu schelten, der Athen…für alle Zeit einen Platz in der Weltgeschichte gesichert hatte, so drängte es ihn, nicht nur zu zeigen, daß die Spartaner ihre Macht genau so rücksichtslos mißbraucht…hätten… ('…if small minds were not intelligent

enough to refrain from slandering the man who had secured Athens an ever-lasting place in world history, then he [Thucydides] felt driven to show not only that the Spartans had abused their power just as ruthlessly…'.)[67]

If Bismarck's era seemed to lurk behind Schwartz's Pericles, Pohlenz' representation is almost a reminder of the "Novemberverbrecher" of 1918. His conclusions are in the same vein: 'Und gerade heute empfinden wir wohl am besten, was in dem Vermächtnis liegt, das sein Perikles in seinen letzten Worten den Athenern hinterläßt…' ('And today especially we can sense the inheritance his Pericles bequeathed to the Athenian people in his final words'; the translation of Pericles' exhortation, 2.64, follows).[68]

In this way Thucydides was not only made to take sides in the politics of his own time, but became the patriotic defender and representative of power politics.

I may point out a mistake in logic at this point although in so doing I am looking ahead somewhat. Thucydides doubtless observed the human drive for power (and in far broader terms than can be expressed in narrowly nationalistic categories). However, it would be hasty to hypothesize that he identified his own attitude with what he found. Such a hypothesis would be taken from the interpreter's analysis—influenced as it is by his own time—and superimposed upon the analysis of the ancient historian.

It is perhaps good to mention here that—although more rarely—the opposite opinion has also been expressed. Abbott, in a book likewise inspired by contemporary events, could write of a Thucydides, 'whose courage in recording the vices of his own country is equaled by his generosity in recognizing the virtues of his country's enemies'.[69]

Indeed, the speeches which seem to be laudatory of Periclean Athens (especially the Funeral Oration) have seemed to some interpreters so incompatible with the rest of the work that they put them down to youthful enthusiasm[70] or the author's intention to unmask the speaker.[71]

The tendency to see the work as written 'for politicians by a politician'[72] dominates the nineteen-twenties and thirties. In 1933–4 three scholarly works appeared in German under the same title: 'Thukydides als politischer Denker'.[73] In these works the historian (after the collapse of Athens) is seen more or less as the 'spiritual executor of Periclean thought'.[74] There is likewise no dearth of references to contemporary issues[75] along the trail already blazed by Schwartz.

When at last, after the experience of the thirties and forties, scholars no longer saw fit to follow the power politics of a Pericles, it was time to be rid, not only of Pericles the power politician, but also of 'his' historian. Even in this, Schwartz's formula 'Pericles = Thucydides' remains intact.[76]

What is surprising is that the apologetic character of the work is found even in sections which do not deal directly with Athens. Bizer takes the view that the *Archaeology* was written to justify Athens' 'Gewaltherrschaft' as being a result of the course of early Greek history. Bizer writes:

> die Erhaltung dieser Herrschaft [war] ein ehernes Gesetz für jeden attischen Politiker, und der Vorwurf ungerechter Gewaltherrschaft und verbrecher-ischer Kriegspolitik, der nach Athens Sturz gegen Perikles erhoben wurde, war sinnlos. ('The retention of this hegemony was strict orthodoxy for every Athenian politician, and the charges of unjust rule by force and criminal war policy, which were leveled at Pericles after Athens' fall, were senseless'.)

Thucydides is once again identified with the law of power which he discovered: 'Thus, already in the *Archaeology*, he stands before us as an Athenian imperialist'.[77]

It scarcely needs to be explained in greater detail how closely related the biographical-political interpretation is to the positivist interpretation. It is therefore not surprising that both are united in a book—to which reference has already been made—which denies neither Cochrane's positivist influence nor the contemporary influence of present-day political experience (and the tradition of interpretation involving biography).[78]

In the *Archaeology* Finley sees on one hand 'the idea of progress'[79] (i.e. a linear concept of history) and on the other the key (the combination of democracy and sea-power) to Athens' power, of which Thucydides was (in Finley's view) a supporter: 'As a study of the remote past, it is undoubtedly coloured by the author's attitude to the present'.[80]

The shift from the linear to the cyclical view of history (1.22) was forced upon the ancient historian by the fall of Athens, when likewise his personal attitude toward the constitution changed: '…Thucydides forsook as a youth the outmoded conservatism of his family to become an admirer of Pericles and a believer in the imperial democracy that he had created…'; '…his personal misfortunes, as well as the natural tendencies of age, made him more conservative as he grew older…'; '…he became so hopeless of democracy that he expressly approved its limitation under the so-called Constitution of the Five Thousand briefly set up in 411'.[81]

Here again the limitations of the biographical-political interpretation become apparent. Thucydides no more went from being a 'democrat' in his youth to being a supporter of a mixed constitution 'as he grew older' (because of his supposed disappointment in 'the democracy'), than he praised tyranny as a constitutional form (this became clear in the previous chapter). His pronouncement on the subject (8.97.2) reveals the unchanging standard he applied at all times: the constitution of the Five Thousand was apposite to the historical situation because it at last permitted the city to *recover* from its inner turmoil. He clearly did not condone Andocides' denunciations in 415, but as an observer he had no choice but to recognize the resultant restoration of domestic peace (see Chapter 1). Even the Periclean democracy is evaluated—in terms of domestic policy—not as a democracy (in actuality it was, of course, the leadership of one man), but rather in terms of its moderation and the resulting relatively liberal relation between the individual and the state, a condition which prevented internal quarreling (2.65).[82]

Thus, if we are willing to drop the too-narrowly formulated presupposition of political engagement on the part of the historian, what seems at first to be a contradiction explicable only in terms of successive stages of the author's development can be understood as consistent judgment based on an identical standard, independent of any preference for the particular constitutional form in question.

Let us return to the *Archaeology*. De Romilly sees—in the later of her two books[83]—Thucydides' scholarly accomplishment here as 'le triomphe de la raison'; she, too, refers to the tendencies of the time:

> Les sophistes, avec leur logique et leur positivisme, les médecins, avec leur recherches du diagnostic, les Athéniens du Ve siècle en général, avec leur confiance dans les possibilités humaines, tous font à cette entreprise un entourage propice et stimulant. ('The sophists, with their logic and their positivism, the physicians, with their diagnostic researches, fifth-century Athenians in general, with their confidence in man's possibilities, all provide a favorable and stimulating environment for this enterprise.')

De Romilly also finds expression of the idea of progress, but in a narrower sense: 'La progression d'évolution (dans le sens de la richesse)' ('the progress of evolution [in the sense of wealth]').[84] Similarly, she observes that the Athenian Empire had furnished the model for the visualization of the great powers of the past: 'Une seule histoire l' intéresse: celle qui mène de la barbarie à l'empire athénien' ('One history alone is of interest to him: the one which leads from barbarism to the Athenian Empire').[85]

However, she soft-pedals the political involvement in favor of an elaboration of Thucydides' process of gaining insight and knowledge.

This shifting of emphasis seems to hold genuine promise. For if it turns out—and here the example of the *Archaeology*, being far removed from the Peloponnesian War both in time and content, is important—that the historian's categories of perception have possibly been formed through the shape taken by the political power-play of his own time, then his utterances can no longer justifiably be interpreted as subjective partisanship. As a consequence, an interpreter would have to allow Thucydides a certain limitation of perspective rather than insisting upon a conscious partisanship on his part.

Let us observe that in the *Archaeology* Thucydides expresses the view that financial reserves are necessary for the successful creation of a power base. If he further believes that this condition can be more easily achieved in Greece by a trade-based sea power than by a land power, it is possible that he has been influenced by his own experience of the sea-going Athenian Empire's superior strength. This is, however, no reason to ascribe to the historian a partisan intention.

On the other hand, both the belief in Thucydides' political engagement and the 'progress' view of the *Archaeology*—it is well to remember that both of the categories have been imported to Thucydides' work—characteristically limit one's ability to see the author's own intentions.

Let us admit that Thucydides sees a development of civilization from the beginning of Greek history. Let us admit that he also sees the greatest concentration of power up to his own time in the Athenian naval empire (the function of the *Archaeology* in the work as a whole is to demonstrate the relative insignificance of events before the Peloponnesian War). We should still not be deceived into thinking that the tendency to amass greater power brings with it any change in principle: the difference is gradual, relative to the extent of employed means.

It seems that Thucydides himself saw the value of the insight supplied by his *Archaeology* not in the concept of change ('progress'), but in the continuous, unchanging factor of power (or perhaps the desire for power).

He leads his reader time and again to this factor: '…also, one ought not to look so much at the visual impression made by a state as at its power…' (οὐδὲ [scil. εἰκός] τὰς ὄψεις τῶν πόλεων μᾶλλον σκοπεῖν ἢ τὰς δυνάμεις, 1.10.3). And why the tireless—almost exaggerated[86]—emphasis on the assertion that power is financial strength and money is power? Quite obviously because he believes to have distilled for himself a factor which till then had been hidden behind other categories.

Later, for instance, the Spartan ephor Sthenelaidas urges war against wealthy Athens with these words: '…others have a great deal of money and ships and horses, but we have good allies whom we must not betray to the Athenians…' (1.86.3). This contradicts the insight expressed in the *Archaeology* by the historian himself.

What, after all, are 'good allies'? According to tradition, Helen's suitors pledged their support to the man who should become her husband. Soberingly, and at the same time polemically, Thucydides denies the oath any real value. It was on the basis of his superior *power* that Agamemnon was able to induce the former suitors to follow him to Troy, not so much because they felt obliged by their oath.

Thucydides is so interested in this point that he inserts a report (stretching back for two generations) on the founding of Agamemnon's power (1.9). The result is surprising: Agamemnon's grandfather Pelops came to power in the Peloponnese because of his *money*. This is why he was able, 'though an immigrant', to give the peninsula his name. Agamemnon's father, too, consolidated his power 'by winning over to himself the population' (with money?) and by using the *fear* of external enemies.

The now-certain truth about Agamemnon is characterized as follows: in possession of so much inherited power, he was able to mount his expedition 'more because of fear than because of a sense of obligation'.

One further example. In ridding Greek waters of piracy, King Minos fostered a cultural advance in the resultant rise in trade and security. However, this advance was only a by-product. Minos' real intention was to secure his revenues (1.4). And what motive do the pirates have for their dangerous activity? They do it 'for the sake of their own profit and to support the weak' (1.5). Ironically, from a moral standpoint they come off almost better than Minos.

Thucydides, too, is aware that profits can be raised through the formation of economic blocs. This is, of course, why a man like Minos sought to expand his empire. But the historian does not by any means see this process as one-sided. He does not deny this realization to the politically and commercially weak. In fact he observes—one might almost say, to his surprise—that they are even ready to give up their freedom and make themselves politically dependent for the sake of commercial success. Their motive: 'Quest for gain' (1.8.3).

The larger motifs that remain unalterable in the course of history are therefore the desire for power (or for money, as the case may be) and fear. Both are objective factors which give impulse to political events.

It is worth bearing this result in mind, because Thucydides speaks *in propria persona* in the *Archaeology*. In terms of methodology it amounts to a preliminary indication for interpreting those passages in which the author seems to withdraw behind the curtain of his work, especially the speeches.

This is, however, also a confirmation of the tentative question posed at the end of the previous chapter, concerning the position of man in Thucydides. Even in the concise overview which the *Archaeology* provides—covering centuries in a few pages—the author does not miss the opportunity to look for the impulses of events in man himself.

The answer, pointing to the desire for power and to fear, seems at first oversimplified. But one should not forget that it is based upon (sometimes polemical) analysis, not upon the unquestioning adoption of pre-existing categories. Thucydides does not merely dismiss the real validity of an oath.

Rather, by means of an excursus into the past, he proves that Agamemnon had the power to insist that the oath be honored. It remains open, though unlikely, that the suitors would have kept their oath voluntarily.

On the other hand, the psychology of the weaker party is not as simple as is usually assumed. They can for special reasons freely enter into an agreement which would seem to an outside observer a forceful enslavement by the more powerful party. —And progress in civilization can be the result of a selfish motive.

This discrepancy between external appearance and true motive could actually be indicative of our author's conscious theoretical concern—if one is prepared to set aside the current categories of interpretation, or rather, to be open to questions that go beyond them.

We are at the end of our systematic retrospective of the problems of Thucydidean scholarship. Two kinds of caution are recommended: first, regarding the assumption of political partisanship on the part of the historian; second, regarding the question of the work's alleged practical goals.

On the other hand, if we set aside the idea of an *a priori* known or set goal, we regain the opportunity to ask questions about the factors that influence the course of events and about the position of man in relation to these factors. In other words, in what is often taken for granted in modern thought, we can discover what was problematic for the ancient author.

Still, one assumption must be made based upon our overview. We must in each case acknowledge the historian's subjective honesty in ascertaining and presenting the facts.

It is not admissible, when Thucydides gives only a brief notice about a certain period of time in a certain theater of the war, to claim that he 'had no knowledge of it' or, worse, that he is camouflaging his ignorance.

For instance, von Wilamowitz[87] believed that Thucydides had a good deal to say about the Sicilian theater in the first months of 425 (4.24 ff.), but gave only a brief concluding account (4.25.12) because he did not have detailed information (similar brevity at 4.48.6): having been exiled by this time, Thucydides was no longer receiving reports from Athens. To compensate for this disadvantage, according to von Wilamowitz, Thucydides inserts into his narrative of the following year (4.58 ff.) '*zum Ersatz* die grosse Rede des Hermokrates' ('*as a substitute* the great speech of Hermocrates').

This way of looking at an author who more than once advises his reader that he is not in a position to give absolutely accurate information on this or that point of his narrative[88] appears ill-advised. Regrettably, this attitude, which flourished at the end of the nineteenth century,[89] has not yet disappeared.[90]

A general remark from a historian's point of view: we can only bring a charge of historical distortion against Thucydides if we can prove— using other sources—that the fact in question is false *also from the angle at which Thucydides chooses to view it.* I cannot emphasize too much Jacoby's warning[91] that the path of 'indirect' argumentation on the basis of epigraphic material is risky because of its incompleteness in comparison to the sources available to the ancient historian, and especially in view of the context chosen by the historian.

If this is granted, then the philologist is not only justified but *obliged* to look for the viewpoints favoring a shorter or more detailed account in the *text itself.* We must seek to understand those aspects which guided the historian in his selection. 'Der Historiker hat das Recht zu fordern, daß er in diesem Punkte nicht anders beurtheilt wird als der Künstler' ('The historian has the right to insist that he be judged in this point no differently from an artist').[92]

If we are prepared to take this demand seriously, access to the work is opened in an essential aspect. If an act of artistic composition lies behind the selection and arrangement of material, then the reported events themselves are by definition interpretation, and the account (the presentation) of the events deserves the attention of modern interpreters.

This point of view may seem obvious. But when it comes to an assessment of Thucydides' own attitude, modern researchers have usually seen the narrative sections of the work in the light of the speeches (as providing the theoretical argumentation), in which Thucydides is supposed to have expressed his 'actual' views.[93] The narrative is considered self-explanatory because it describes 'mere facts'. However, this amounts to an unnecessary limitation of the already narrow basis[94] for discovering Thucydides' opinion.

We must also consider the fact that the speeches[95] (especially since they often appear in the form of antilogies) are always given from the point of view of actors in the chain of events (i.e. they are deliberately composed from a limited perspective). If this is the case, then the key to interpreting them should lie each time in the course of the events into which the historian places them and which he narrates *in propria persona*; the speeches should not rather be taken as the norm for interpreting the course of events. This entails a basic appreciation in value for the merely narrative portions relative to their function in the work as a whole.

Of course, I do not mean to deny that there are sections of the work which are limited to the form of a report as a means of communicating bare facts (in order to provide completeness of certain contexts). Nor do I dispute that on occasion Thucydides' detailed precision can be sufficiently explained in terms of an economic, strategic, medical, ethnographic, geographic or other technical aspect.

On the contrary, the fact that terse reportage is found in Thucydides is likely to be significant for the interpretation of the more detailed sections (insofar as the detail is not sufficiently explained by some specialized aspect).

In other words, when an author severely limits himself—to mention only the two most prominent characteristics—through a rigorous etiology and a strict simultaneous chronology (the latter principle working very much against continuity of presentation) specifically to stay as near as possible to the truth, it must be all the more striking if, in spite of this discontinuity, the facts come together in larger narrative units. And, vice versa, the structural elements inherent in such event-complexes must be all the more important to the historian because they stand on the foundation of the facts which he has ascertained so meticulously.

The interpreter's task is to seek out structural elements and narrative motifs in the individual course of events which go beyond the organizational principles dictated by causal and chronological considerations.

From the fact that the narrative is at least as important as the speeches in the work[96] it follows that we must orient our attempt to sketch Thucydides' view of man essentially according to the course of facts. That means we must look for and observe man in action in order to avoid the danger of taking the declarations of actors involved in the events for the declarations of the writer himself.[97]

Of course, the basis for our inquiry remains Thucydides' own testimony, in the chapter on method, to the effect that he is addressing readers 'who will wish to see clarity both of what happened and of what at some time again will be—*according to the human condition*—such and similar'.[98]

The general category 'the human condition', especially being mentioned at this important point in the work, serves as a warning against the frequent politicizing limitation to the 'Doric' and 'Ionian' or the 'Spartan' and 'Athenian' man.[99]

Yet another aspect appears from our retrospective of Thucydidean scholarship. The attempt has been made to relate the category of 'what is human' (τὸ ἀνθρώπινον) to the claim to 'immanent' causality on the part of the historian (making men, but no longer the divine, bring about the historical events) and to see this as polemic aimed at Herodotus.[100] We shall, following our review, approach this explanation with caution.

After our retrospective we must pose a preliminary question. Is the category 'what is human' (or, as we anticipatorily translated τὸ ἀνθρώπινον above and in the previous chapter, 'the human condition') limited to human *nature*? Or does it not rather include (bear in mind here the problem of chance, which lies outside the realm of human nature) the external circumstances affecting human existence, so that we should precisely translate τὸ ἀνθρώπινον by 'that which pertains to man', pointing to the human condition in a comprehensive sense?[101] This understanding is supported by the much maligned chapter immediately following the section on method (1.23).

After the *Archaeology* has sketched in negative the Peloponnesian War (all previous events were less momentous), this chapter presents the first direct characterization—and from a perspective which has surprised interpreters. The categories of the *Archaeology* retreat in favor of a wholly *unpolitical* point of view: this long war brought more *suffering* upon Greece than had theretofore been experienced in a similar length of time.

The nature of this suffering (παθήματα... τῇ Ἑλλάδι, 23.1) is elaborated in an excursus (23.2–3): the taking of so many cities, their devastation (through loss of inhabitants), internal conflict, banishment or flight (one thinks of Thucydides himself), murder.

But also—and here we are touching upon those *external* elements which are not caused by human agency but which influence the human situation—the earthquakes which occurred during this time, solar eclipses, droughts (and the resulting famines) and the horrors of the plague are being recalled.

In order to justify mentioning these events, too, which brought suffering independently of the war, Thucydides closes, 'for all this attacked (scil. the Greeks) together with the war', ταῦτα γὰρ πάντα μετὰ τοῦδε τοῦ πολέμου ἅμα ξυνεπέθετο (scil. τῇ Ἑλλάδι, cf. 23.1 end).

We should keep in mind, then, that at this decisive place—on the one hand after the end of the early history and the discussion of his methods, following the remark that the work is to be a possession for ever, and on the other hand coming immediately before the prehistory of the war (1.24 ff.)—Thucydides mentions a *characteristic* of the war period which looks at the war *uniformly from the side of suffering humanity*.[102]

Some have deplored the lack of reference to certain singular occurrences (esp. the lunar eclipse of 413), but we must respond (with Parry[103]) that the individual cases would not be consonant with the purpose of the excursus at 23.2–3, which aims at generality (i.e. in reference to our discussion of the literature on Thucydides, simultaneously a non-partisan perspective). The plague which carried off so many people—the only 'individual' event—confirms this. Thus the *literary* intention of this passage precludes any search for historical data.

However, critics have made numerous statements which simply do not do justice to this chapter. These range from the description, 'naiv-rhetor-ische Aufreihung der großen Vorfälle' ('naïve-rhetorical enumeration of the great events')[104] to 'Paradoxentafel' ('table of paradoxes'; a 'primitive' addition of the 'Herausgeber' ['editor']).[105]

As for our question of how to interpret τὸ ἀνθρώπινον, let it suffice to have shown that the historian, in the section just discussed, views the 'greatest upheaval for the Greeks and some of the barbarians' of 1.1.2 not only from the passive perspective of those affected, but also considers it under the double aspects of both the external causes and those originating in man himself.

It will be well to keep this characterization of the war in mind as we turn to its prelude and the optimistic plans of some of its advocates.

Notes

[1] Lord 1945, 216.

[2] German 'naturwissenschaftlich'; French 'scientifique'.

[3] In the inaugural lecture of J.B. Bury, Cambridge 1903; cf. Bury 1958², 123 ff.

[4] See Cornford 1907, 69 for his sharp disapproval of Gomperz (1896, 503).

[5] See esp. Cornford 1907, 59.

[6] e.g. Cornford 1907, 63; this criticism has been tirelessly repeated; cf. S.B. Smith 1941, 300.

[7] Cornford 1907, 242.

[8] Cochrane 1929; Abbott's book (1925) dates from the same decade.

[9] See Cochrane 1929, 17; it is in this context that Cochrane admits his 'distaste' for Herodotus (15).

[10] Atomist philosophy is seen as 'congenial' and 'preliminary' to the 'sciences of human behavior' (Cochrane 1929, 6).

[11] Cochrane 1929, 2; the same complex of defense against metaphysics, acknowledgement of positivism and identification with Thucydides is to be found in Abbott (1925, 76).

[12] We cannot here measure the influence of interpretations of fifth-century philosophy and sophistry on the modern image of Thucydides. One occasionally receives the impression that the enlightened philosophers of the fifth century staged the first rebellion against German Idealism.

[13] Littré 1839, vol. I, 474.

[14] Cf. partly the work of Weidauer 1954; also Schuller 1956, 984.

[15] Cochrane 1929, 3; cf. Patzer (1937, 97), who writes, 'Thucydides understood historiography in terms of its object, method and *goal*, in *perfect* correspondence to medical knowledge' (my italics; translated from the German).

[16] e.g. Wassermann 1954; cf. Schadewaldt 1929, 18.

[17] Cochrane 1929, 2 (my italics); cf. Wassermann 1956, 41; also Weidauer 1954, 68, 75.

[18] Kapp 1930, 92 ff.; cf. de Romilly 1956c, 41 ff.; also already Roscher 1842, 176 ff., 180.—Even the often-cited 'parallel' (as such *a priori* questionable since it is concerned not with the historiographic intention but with an extreme detail) 2.48.3 expresses no more than recognition (μὴ ἀγνοεῖν); any possibility of a utilitarian explanation (say, that the information Thucydides provides is intended to help steer clear of the malady or even to help find a way to provide help) is excluded by the words ἕν τε οὐδὲ ἓν κατέστη ἴαμα..., 51.2; σῶμά τε αὔταρκες ὂν οὐδὲν διεφάνη..., 51.3 (see below, pp. 78–80).

Also 3.82.2 only expresses the recognition of inevitability or absence of a way out of difficulty (see below, pp. 112 ff.). On this whole question see the salutary remarks of A. Parry 1981, 104 ff.

[19] Of course, I am not suggesting that *every* optimistic interpretation originates in positivism; I merely intend to show where the theoretical foundation behind such interpretation lies.

[20] For the instructive intention of the work see also Rittelmeyer (1915, 23 *et passim*), whose work takes its lead from the sophists; see also above n. 12.

[21] Cochrane 1929, 17, 19; Weidauer 1954, 40 *et passim*; Patzer 1937, 96 f.; Finley 1947², 70; Eberhardt 1954, 314.

[22] Heinimann 1945, 152; Finley 1947², 57; cf. also de Romilly 1951², 268 ff.; Cochrane 1929, 169; Schmid 1948, 33 f.

[23] Finley 1947², 109: '...that human nature...is subject to almost mechanistic laws'; Neu 1948, 178.

[24] Cf. Wassermann 1956, 41; Notopoulos 1945/6, 29 f.; one is reminded of Comte's 'savoir pour prévoir'.

[25] Cf. Herter 1950a, 150 ff; Schmid 1948, 36.

[26] Weidauer 1954, 40.

[27] Weidauer 1954, 37–40; Solmsen 1931, 54 n. 1, 50 ff.; Finley 1947², 46 ff.

[28] Finley 1947², 50 (my italics), cf. 48; cf. the exceedingly sharp criticism of Parry 1981, 107 f., 109.

[29] Wassermann 1930, 3.

[30] Weidauer 1954, 59; cf. Schadewaldt 1929, 29.

[31] Regenbogen 1933, 7.

[32] Herter 1953, 623 (my italics); examples could be multiplied.

[33] Finley 1947², 109.

[34] e.g. Schmid 1948, 30 ff.; 'People must know that they live under changeable fates' (32); war is something one ought 'to seek to avoid by negotiating beforehand' (34; cf. 117); 'He is to be praised who does not abuse his superior power' (34); cf. his remarks on the 'instructive value' (*Lehrwert*) of the work in the strict sense (40–1): the 'insight into the world of the past protects the historian as well as the politician against unfounded toying with possibilities' (quotations translated from the German).

[35] i.e. speaking mathematically: let this unknown quantity be eliminated. Many interpreters have actually taken this path, namely, to consider the course of events either under the aspect of ἀνθρωπεία φύσις (with τύχη neutralized) or under that of τύχη (with φύσις neutralized).

[36] Herter 1950a, 139: 'Ein Stein des Anstosses' ('a stumbling block').

[37] The three together in Herter 1953, 617 ff.; similar in attitude: Neu 1948, 98 f.; Ludwig 1952, 115; Bury 1958², 130; a different version of Thucydides' relationship to Democritus in Zahn 1934, 80 ff.; Schmid 1948, 112 (but cf. 32); cf. also in this context Cochrane's (1929, 6) reference to the title περὶ προνοίας, ascribed to Democritus by tradition.

[38] See above, n. 35.

[39] Herter 1953, 619.

[40] So Finley 1947², 191, cf. 313 (in the case of Pylos).

[41] Herter 1950a, 136 f., cf. 1954, 337 (on the events around Pylos); Zimmern 1928, 97 (on the plague).

[42] Patzer 1955, 153 (in the end Patzer refers to the 'limit of all penetrability'— predominantly from the angle of ἀνθρωπεία φύσις). Against this Strasburger (1954, 417) on chance in Thucydides, '...this is the indivisible remainder in the equation'; see also Zahn 1934, 82.

[43] Herter 1950a, 153.

[44] See above, n. 32, also the quotation in the text.

[45] Strasburger 1954, 399 ff.

[46] For this reason Finley's (1938) comparison of Thucydides with Euripides seems too limited in terms of its categories; cf. Bayer 1948, 42 n. 3.

[47] Ed. Meyer 1899, vol. II, 272.

[48] Patzer 1937, 1; cf. Strasburger 1957, lxviii: Schwartz expanded the question to a 'genuinely historical' problem; see also Rehm 1934, 133 *et passim*. In regard to the history of scholarship it must be pointed out that Schwartz (1929² [= 1919]) did not bring the notion of the historian's development into the discussion primarily by studying the person of the author, but rather because of the existence of an as yet unsolved problem (the 'Thucydidean Question')—which the further hypothesis of 'intellectual development' was intended to render usable again. For criticism of the notion of development, see Oehler 1963, 604 ff.

[49] Patzer 1937, 1 (my italics).

[50] Stenzel 1926, 206.

[51] Published in 1945, written during the war with vigorous political partisanship; cf. also Thibaudet's (1922) book, which appeared after World War I.

[52] In this regard Lord (1945, 11) is very much in step with the positivist interpreters despite his sharp attacks on 'scientific historians'.

[53] Cf. Abbott (1925, 5) for the England–Sparta identification; Abbott, by the way,—evidently influenced by the war—rejects the applicability of the concept of progress to human nature (74; this despite his confession of Positivism, 76).

[54] Gomme *ad* 1.22.4; examples can be multiplied.

[55] Stenzel apparently did not see the bias when he held up Schwartz' work as a "standard" (Maßstab) to Taeger's politicising – actualising interpretation (Stenzel 1926, 206)

[56] As an excellent example of how little the new philological armor was able to protect its wearer from poor literary judgment, we may point out that the Peisistratid excursus (dealt with in the previous chapter) is seen as an easy-to-excise (!)

'doublet' (because the same events are mentioned in 1.20), and an insertion of the 'Herausgeber'.

[57] Schwartz 1929[2], 137; cf. Pohlenz, whose categories are similar (1919, 115): '…but that, even without expansion, the inner growth of a nation can stimulate its neighbors' concern and lust for war,—that lesson the World War has sufficiently taught us' ('…aber daß auch ohne Expansion das innere Wachstum eines Volkes bei seinen Nachbarn Besorgnis und Kriegslust zeitigen kann, das hat uns doch der Weltkrieg zur Genüge gelehrt').

[58] Schwartz 1929[2], 108.

[59] Schwartz 1929[2], 133; for the exoneration of Athens from 'Kriegsschuld' see, among others, also Schmid 1948, 23, 52.

[60] Schwartz 1929[2], 142 (my italics).

[61] Schwartz 1929[2], 144.

[62] Schwartz 1929[2], 137.

[63] Even the title looks toward Schwartz; de Romilly thus adopted Schwartz' apologetic Thucydides (cf. 1951[2], 291).

[64] For example, de Romilly 1951[2], 228 ff.; cf. Bodin 1932, 94; against this see Wassermann (1947, 25), who, though emphasizing the relatedness, comes to the same conclusion as Schwartz (1929[2]).

[65] De Romilly 1951[2], 229 (my italics); this line of reasoning continues through to the present. Kakridis (1961, 113) defends the historian on account of his partisanship for Athens (in the Funeral Oration) as follows: 'Wie darf man es aber einem Liebhaber verargen, daß er das geliebte Wesen als in jeder Hinsicht vollkommen, ohne jeden Makel ansieht und verehrt?' ('How can one find fault with a lover because he views and worships his beloved as perfect in every regard, without any blemish?') It is this assumption (i.e. that Thucydides in the Funeral Oration 'for once went against his principle of impartiality') which necessitates Kakridis' plea on behalf of the historian, who through Kakridis' interpretation had become a potential defendant. According to Kakridis, Thucydides' 'warm heart' and 'pure heart' and 'strong soul' (all of which speak for Athens) are to be more highly valued than strict ascertainment of truth.

[66] This movement culminated in the works of Großkinsky (1936), Patzer (1937), and Finley (1940), who virtually demolished the foundation of the 'Thucydidean Question'.

[67] Pohlenz 1919, 136.

[68] Pohlenz 1919, 137:, cf. 21 n.56; Nestle (1934, 167) feels similarly that Pericles' words at 2.64.6 'are addressed to the German people of the present'. This attitude is basically quite similar to that of Taeger (1925, 298): 'Das übergewaltige Erleben, die Liebe zu Heimat und Volk, die Hoffnung auf neue Größe und der Kampf um den Geist, der allein sie heraufzuführen vermochte, zwangen Thukydides den Griffel in die Hand' ('The overwhelming experience, his love for country and nation, hope for new greatness and the struggle for the spirit that alone would bring it about—they all forced Thucydides' hand to seize the stylus'); Zahn (1934, 66) is more moderate; Gundert (1940, 114) sees Thucydides as 'himself prey to the charms of power'. 'November criminals' was the label under which conservatives

subsumed the German revolutionaries of November 1918.

[69] Abbott 1925, 149.

[70] Zimmern 1928, 81; Schmid 1948, 54 ff., 121.

[71] Strasburger 1957, 60; 1958, 29.

[72] Wassermann 1931, 249.

[73] Jaeger in *Paideia* I 1934; Regenbogen 1933; Dietzfelbinger 1934; cf. Nestle 1934, 'Thukydides als politischer Erzieher'; also Berve 1938, Ch. 3, 'Der politische Denker'.

[74] Regenbogen 1933, 16.

[75] e.g. Münch 1935, 26, cf. 65. On the 'Führerproblem' represented by the figure of Pericles and his successors cf. Dietzfelbinger 1934, 108 ff.; Großkinsky 1936, 72 f.; Bender 1938.

[76] Vogt 1956, 266.

[77] Bizer 1937, 41.

[78] Finley 1947[2]; cf. the quotation above, p. 16.

[79] Finley 1947[2], 82 ff.; see also Abbott's warning (1925, 74).

[80] Finley 1947[2], 93, cf. 24: 'Thucydides…appreciated this dynamic aspect of Athenian democracy to the full.'

[81] Finley 1947[2], 30, 32 f.; similarly (in reference to Thucydides' relationship to Pericles) Andrewes 1959, 233.

[82] Cf. also Pavan 1961, 19 ff.; further, above Chapter 1 n. 2, n. 13.

[83] De Romilly 1956a, 273.

[84] De Romilly 1956a, 271; Finley (1947[2]) also speaks occasionally only of 'material progress'.

[85] De Romilly 1956a, 285, cf. 261, 278; 1951[2], 63.

[86] Cf. de Romilly 1956a, 260 ff., esp. 267 f.

[87] Von Wilamowitz 1921, 311 (my italics).

[88] e.g. 1.24.4, 118.3, 138.4; 2.5.6, 57.1, 77.6, 93.4, 102.6; 3.94.5, 96.1, 113.6, 116.2; 4.104.2; 5.68.2, 74.3; 6.60.2; 7.87.4; 8.46.5; 94.2. On the (deliberately undertaken) selection, cf. 3.90.1; Ed. Meyer 1899, vol. II, 286.

[89] Here belongs also the fact—often repeated in reproachful tones—that Thucydides does not name his 'sources', with the result that the reader cannot check his information. This kind of question—originating from the ways of modern scholarship—misses the mark in not realizing that Thucydides vouches with his own person for the accurate representation of his witnesses' accounts. A question raised more recently concerns Thucydides' possible subjectivity when reporting on motives, thoughts, etc., of individuals. H.D. Westlake has in a special chapter (14) thoroughly investigated and vindicated the historian's practice: 'Thucydides was neither dishonest nor guilty of indulging in mere guesswork' (1989, 220).

[90] One need only consider the extensive Cleon-literature and its problem: 'Did Thucydides knowingly distort the picture of the man who (supposedly) was responsible for his exile or not?' Cf. Woodhead 1960, 289 ff.

[91] Jacoby 1929, 6.

[92] So the words of the historian Eduard Meyer (1899, vol. II, 378); cf. Strasburger 1958, 32.

[93] Cf. the quote from Finley 1947[2], 50; see above, n. 28. Finley blithely posits that the speakers in the *History* voice the author's own views on the predictability of future events.

[94] One can practically count on one hand those places in the work where Thucydides speaks in his own name. Those usually considered essential are 1.1–23; 2.47 ff., 65; 3.82 f.; 5.26; 8.97.

[95] Großkinsky (1936) may be considered to have rid us once and for all of the so-called 'Authentizitätsproblem' of the speeches, despite numerous attempts to revive it.

[96] Großkinsky had argued for the equality of λόγοι and ἔργα already in 1936 (77) on the basis of the section on method, 1.22.

[97] We must, however, begin with an interpretation of the speeches in Book 1 since they express the involved parties' speculations about the future course of events.

[98] 1.22.4 (my translation).

[99] Müri (correctly) 1947, 256 n. 6.

[100] Strasburger 1954, 417 n. 86.

[101] I consider ill-advised the traditional equation of τὸ ἀνθρώπινον (1.22.4) with ἡ ἀνθρωπεία φύσις (e.g. Topitsch 1943/7, 50).

[102] Ludwig (1952, 94) realized that the 'length' of the war manifested itself in an 'indescribable accumulation of suffering'; Parry, who likewise recognizes the significance of 1.23, finds that the ἀξιολογώτατος πόλεμος of 1.1 is explained in 1.23, not in Herodotus' terms by 'splendour', but rather by 'suffering and destruction' (1981, 94; cf. 114 ff. on 1.23: 'War as Pathos'); further Immerwahr 1960, 279.

[103] Parry 1981, 116: 'the universality of the disaster'.

[104] Schadewaldt 1929, 59 n. 1, quoted with approval by Bizer 1937, 50.

[105] Schmid 1948, 145.

3

PROJECTIONS AND PROSPECTS
Book 1

The considerations raised in the previous chapter suggest that our proper field of observation should be the actions and events of the war itself. These begin in Book 2 and come under Thucydides' very own topic, the 'war' of both camps, 'as they fought against each other' (1.1.1).

But first, a closer look at sections of Book 1 is indispensible, insofar as it is precisely a reading of this Book, which has always been of central importance to Thucydidean scholarship, that can guarantee a constant connection to the lines of inquiry presented in our systematic retrospective.

There is also another, perhaps even more cogent, reason. Book 1 provides, so to speak, the exposition for the entire work (one might include here those speeches from Book 2 which already fall into the opening period of the war).[1] In addition, since it is in the framework of this exposition that we first meet the actors of the later events and hear of their reflections and decisions about those events, Book 1 leads directly into our subject matter.

The teleological unfolding of the first conflict already stands, for the reader and the involved parties alike, under the sign of the approaching war.

After Thucydides has made his famous differentiation[2] between the openly stated accusations and differences on the one hand and, on the other, the 'truest' cause of the war, which was not openly acknowledged at the time (that fear of the rising power of Athens forced Sparta into the war, 1.23.6), he proceeds to the first of the 'αἰτίαι καὶ διαφοραί'.

It arises almost on the edge of the Greek political world in Epidamnus (24.1; the place is so remote that Thucydides first has to describe its geographical position). After years of internal struggle, the democratic party has driven the oligarchs from the city. When the oligarchs in turn threaten the city with force, the democrats seek the aid of their (democratically ruled) metropolis, Corcyra—without success. Next (on the advice of the Delphic oracle, as the historian does not omit to mention) they turn to the metropolis' metropolis, namely, Corinth. The Corinthians are right away ready and willing to help out 'κατὰ ... τὸ δίκαιον' (they consider Epidamnus as much their own colony as Corcyra's—Phalios, the founder, came from Corinth), 'but at the same time (ἅμα) from *hatred* of the Corcyreans' (25.3), who, they feel, have neglected them (Corcyra believes—as one of the richest cities in Greece—it can afford a condescending attitude towards the mother city).

Thus, right at the beginning of the conflict, there appears the split we encountered in the *Archaeology*: outward expression (justifiable aid to the endangered colony) and true motive (opportunity for revenge on the daughter city).

The Corcyreans react to Corinthian partisanship with partisanship of their own: they offer to help the oligarchs who had been driven from Epidamnus. This results in hostilities between Corinth and Corcyra; the first engagement (Leukimme in 435) ends favorably for Corcyra. The internal conflict of Epidamnus has thus provided the spark for a pre-existing, larger tension.

In turn, the larger (and much nearer to central Greece) area of tension, that between Corinth and Corcyra, has an activating influence on the still more or less dormant tension between Athens and the Peloponnesian League: when unallied Corcyra, anxious about further Corinthian measures, turns to Athens for help against Corinth, it (even before the actual aid of Athens, this prospect is manifest) pushes Corinth into setting in motion the Peloponnesian League, with Sparta at its head. Thus the third level would be reached: the opposition of the leading powers of Greece, Athens and Sparta.

Before the avalanche of the conflict attains these proportions, however, Thucydides places a pause at exactly the point where the decision is made whether the third level can be engaged or not. He gives the Corcyreans' speech at Athens requesting aid and the Corinthians' speech against such aid (1.32–43). This antilogy, then, comes *a priori* under the question of whether there is still a way out of the chain of cause and effect which Thucydides has described as so goal-directed.

Strasburger claimed that in these speeches' contrasting of right and usefulness Thucydides offers a 'general introduction to his thought':[3] the Corcyreans rely entirely upon the argument of advantage (= τὸ ξυμφέρον; in addition to the strategic importance of their island, they can offer one of the three largest navies in Greece); the Corinthians on the other hand work with the issue of justice (= τὸ δίκαιον; they harp on their previous favorable treatment of Athens).

There is of course nothing specifically Thucydidean in the simple antithesis of justice and advantage. Finley[4]—in his attempt to trace the historian's intellectual development to impressions received in Athens during the period before his banishment—adduces the example of Euripides' *Medea* (431 BC): in her argument with Jason, Medea represents τὸ δίκαιον (465 ff.; she refers to past good deeds), while Jason appeals to the notion of τὸ ξυμφέρον (522 ff.).

It must be pointed out that, in contrast to Thucydides' Corinthians, Medea is more credibly pursuing a claim which in itself is just because she has been injured with respect to a basic right through the unfaithful actions of her husband.

However, the Corinthians (cf. their attitude when helping Epidamnus at 25.3) appeal to justice for one reason only, namely, that they can place no advantage in the scales to counterbalance the Corcyrean offer. The only 'advantage' to which they can allude is the possibility that, in the event of a pro-Corinthian decision, the current tension between the two cities might give way to a 'friendly' relationship (41.3; 42.2–3; 43.2). The argument based on τὸ δίκαιον is itself then used entirely in the service of advantage: Corinth wants a free hand in dealing with Corcyra.

On the other hand the Corcyreans, in addition to offering a concrete advantage, do not fail themselves to lay claim to the 'just cause'[5] with which public prestige is always connected. The incensed Corinthians call it τὸ εὐπρεπὲς τῆς δίκης (39.2) and are of course well aware of its effectiveness.

Consequently, the degree of deliberateness in arranging the arguments, which is displayed in both speeches, seems too high to be accounted for simply by the antithesis of justice and advantage. The practice of manipulating normative concepts—which Thucydides later (3.82) presents as one of the devastating effects of the war—is in effect already evidenced here.

But if *both* sides view justice *per se* as a worthless and useless argument[6] (and one party is not portrayed as taking advantage of the good faith of the other), then the decision can only be based upon an evaluation of the advantages. Thucydides would then be concerned in this passage with the question of whether the Athenians have calculated their advantage correctly or not.

The Corcyreans are so convinced that they have recognized Athenian concepts of Athenian advantage that they take on an arrogance which is unusual for petitioners. By referring to Sparta's fear[7] and claiming that Corinth wants only to get Corcyra out of the picture (33.3) before the war with Athens, the Corcyreans are attempting to give the impression that Corcyra and Athens are in the same boat. 'However, it is the duty of us both to prevent this in that one [of us] *grants* (or *'offers'*) the alliance, but that you *accept* it' (33.4).[8] This arrogant confidence, however, proves to be a dangerous self-deception and the Athenian decision turns out not to be so easy to anticipate. Thucydides confirms this expressly in his description not only of the conclusion of the alliance between Athens and Corcyra, but also of how it came about.

In the subsequent assembly the Athenians vote 'nevertheless' for Corinth, the change of opinion coming only in a second assembly (44.1). In the first decision the prospect of détente offered by Corinth doubtless played a larger role than the feeling of dutiful gratitude (which we have assigned to the irrelevant area of τὸ δίκαιον).[9] This is evident from the explanation of the final decision (44.2): 'for' it seemed that the war was coming 'anyway'.

It is only under the impression of this (now firm) conviction that Corcyra's fleet and location astraddle the Italian trade route appear as genuine 'advantages'. But the question of whether the alliance was in Thucydides' own judgment 'the only reasonable decision'[10] must remain open.

For the conviction (which has determined the Athenian decision) that the war is inevitable, i.e. the intellectual *projection* of the further course of cause and effect, is what *creates* the *preconditions* in accordance with which the events proceed in the same goal-oriented direction and reach the third plane. It is unimportant whether the Corinthian offer of friendship was sincere at the time: Thucydides deliberately leaves this question open, and their attitude after the fact (1.68.4) cannot be adduced here. What matters is whether the Athenian decision has increased Sparta's existing fear to the extent that it is translated into action.

The Athenians believed they could avoid this possibility. This is expressed by the half-measure of the Corcyrean alliance, which is not a pact of aggression (under which Corcyra might, by attacking Corinth, force Athens to break its treaty with the Peloponnesian League), but rather a mutual defence agreement in the event that the island of Corcyra itself (or Athens) might be attacked.

Athens believes, then, that it can secure an advantage for the war which is coming 'anyway' without on her part hastening or provoking the actual outbreak of the war. In other words, a power of the 'third' level believes itself capable of limited engagement on the 'second' level such that the other third-level power is not drawn into the situation; it further believes that this engagement will *at the same time* bring additional security in the foreseeable event that its rival—for other reasons—becomes an active military opponent.

Actual events overtake this ingenious calculation. In the second clash between Corinth and Corcyra (Sybota in 433) the Athenian ships—present, in accordance with the treaty, only against the event of a direct attack on the island—are willy-nilly[11] involved in the sea battle. Athens and Corinth have thus crossed swords (49.7): the first 'αἰτία' has been established (55.2).

From this one the second follows of necessity: Potidaea, a member of the Athenian Empire, though inhabited by Corinthian settlers, defects when Athens demands certain securities out of concern over the quarrel with Corinth.

Since here already vital Athenian interests are at stake (the city is economically dependent upon the tribute of its 'allies'), there is a second clash between Corinth and Athens (62 ff.). Athens' siege of Potidaea forces Corinth to do everything it can to mobilize the Peloponnesian League (67 ff.).

From this vantage point, hindsight confirms that Athens' decision in favor of Corcyra has determined the subsequent course of events and that the plan for limited engagement has failed: the moment that Corinth turns to Sparta for help the third level is reached. By their decision, which was intended to avoid provocation, the Athenians themselves have provided the possibility of a trigger-conflict. It is now at the very latest that Thucydides' intention in reporting so fully the circumstances of the decision at Athens becomes clear.

The critical stage in the external prehistory of the war comes with the appearance of the Corinthian emissaries on the stage in Sparta. It is now up to Sparta to decide whether or not recent events constitute a rupture of the treaty (of 446) between the Peloponnesian League and Athens.

Since Sparta's answer is in the positive, the climax of the internal prehistory comes at the same time. Sparta's fear of Athens' growing power, the true cause of the war, has reached the point at which it is finally translated into action. Thucydides confirms this in his own words after the decision has been taken (1.88; cf. 1.23.6) and offers proof of his thesis in the ensuing *Pentecontaetia* (1.89 ff.).

How this decision comes about, entailing as it does the future suffering of Greece—the reader will recall the general description of the war at 1.23—and from what viewpoints the individual parties sketch out their own futures, all this the historian makes the agents themselves recite.

Under discussion is the great tetralogy mentioned in the previous chapter, further the so-called 'third Corinthian speech' (1.120 ff.) and the 'first speech of Pericles' (1.140 ff.). Even the Analysts have acknowledged that all six speeches represent an essentially unified complex,[12] so that we can presuppose a variety of correlations.

The Corinthians first allow other league members to present grievances against Athens before the Spartan assembly, skillfully arranging to take the floor last (67.5). In this way they can avoid the impression that they are in favor of the war merely for private motives involving their own city rather than in the interest of the League as a whole (68.2). However, their chief motivation is clearly immediate concern for their relatives who are trapped in Potidaea (67.1), and it is this concern which gives their speech its emotionally charged character.

In their excitement they even consider it necessary to assure the Spartans that they remonstrate not ἐπ᾽ ἔχθρᾳ ('to express hostility'), but merely ἐπ᾽ αἰτίᾳ ('to express a grievance') (69.6). To be sure, this does not prevent them from pressuring Sparta by threatening to seek allies elsewhere (71.5–6).

A substantial portion of their speech, whose purpose is to rouse Sparta from its inaction, is devoted to comparing Spartan caution and circumspection in maintaining existing possessions with Athens' utterly expansion-oriented spirit of enterprise (70). One might well ascribe this picture of Athens as *the* troublemaker in Greece to the tendentious nature of their harangue if Thucydides himself did not confirm (1.118.2; 8.96.5) the basic characteristics of the comparison.

On the other hand one should not, as has so often occurred, emphasize this 'Völkercharakteristik' to the extent that it becomes (along with the entire tetralogy) a merely political document through which Thucydides moreover wishes to contribute to the 'justification of Athens'.[13] One interpretation, originating with Schwartz, can understand the 'Völkercharakteristik' only as a pro-Athenian manifesto in which Athens 'auch von seinen Feinden des Lobes die Fülle erntet' ('earns an abundance of praise even from her enemies').[14] Apart from the fact that this 'Hohelied attischer Art aus feindlichem Mund' ('from the enemy's mouth the song of songs praising Attic character')[15] would be difficult for an unbiased reader to verify on the basis of the text itself, such interpretions block the ears to the admonition of King Archidamus. His speech, directed against the Corinthians,[16] warns that when it comes to making plans for the future 'one should not believe that one man differs much from another' (84.4).

This point cannot be overemphasized. A one-sided analysis of the Corinthian speech as a testament to Athenian superiority (which of course, *among other things*, it is) and possibly even a personal political statement of Thucydides clouds one's perspective for the remaining speeches. Already Schwartz found the response of Archidamus 'comprehensible only as a defensive complement of the agitational attack [of the Corinthians]'.[17]

One must exercise similar caution in regard to the following speech, given after the performances of the Spartan allies by an Athenian delegation which 'chances' to be in Sparta on other business (72.1). Scholars have, on the basis of the introduction of this speech, often concluded that it is a free invention of Thucydides.[18] But 1.87.5b makes it at least hard to deny the presence of Athenian emissaries in Sparta at that time.

Since this Athenian 'self-description' (or at least part of it) provides one of the last remaining points of departure for analysis à la Schwartz, it is worth a thorough investigation, which may also help to confirm observations made in the previous chapter.

De Romilly[19] believes that a speech delivered by Athenians is *a priori* not 'necessary' in the context of the debate, although some answer to the Corinthian reproaches is 'probable'; however, the Athenian speech as transmitted—at least partly—abandons the thematic material of the other speeches to the extent that it could be—at least partly—a later addition; but this addition 'ne modifie en rien l'explication donnée de la guerre'—it offers no correction at all. Thus far de Romilly.

One is tempted to ask whether the Corinthian speech modifies 'l'explication donnée de la guerre'. The answer is clearly no: the causes of the war (both internal and external) have already been established, and Thucydides himself adds expressly that the Spartans had not been so much influenced in their decision by the speeches of their allies as by their own fear of Athenian power (1.88).

And *vice versa*: is not the speech of the Athenian emissaries best suited to render Sparta's fear, the real cause of the war, understandable?

The basic question here is whether those interpretations which explain a component of this tetralogy as unnecessary, or even off the subject, perhaps have an unjustifiable notion of the theme of the debate, in other words, whether they might be applying a preconceived standard.

In the present case the answer to the question must be yes, if only because de Romilly's view that Thucydides uses the speech of the Athenians defensively to justify Athenian imperialism is an outgrowth of Schwartz's concept. According to this concept, Thucydides, in the speeches made at Sparta, is out to make the Spartans the scapegoat for the war. As is well known, however, Thucydides himself does not start with the moral question of 'war-guilt' when he sets out to explain 'whence so great a war originated for the Greeks' (1.23.5).

De Romilly supports her analysis of the speech in detail with the remark:

> tout le développement, qui…cherche des excuses à Athènes dans la conduite ordinaire d'hommes, déborde le cadre prévu et implique un but différent. ('The whole development, which seeks excuses for Athens in ordinary human behavior [i.e. the second part of the speech, 75.3–77.6], departs from the preconceived framework and implies a different goal'.)[20]

On the other hand, according to de Romilly, one of the two themes announced, 'l'importance de la puissance athénienne' ('the importance of Athenian power')(72.1 end; 73.1 end), never appears in the speech. Her inference: the section dealing with the power of Athens was replaced by the 'late' Thucydides with the second section now appearing in our text.

It is, I think, questionable whether *two* themes (to be handled separately) are announced at all, let alone whether one of them later drops out (or is replaced with 'excuses').

According to Thucydides' own words, the purpose of the Athenians' speech is to *warn* the Spartans not to be too quick (ὡς οὐ ταχέως αὐτοῖς βουλευτέον εἴη, ἀλλ᾿ ἐν πλέονι σκεπτέον, 72.1) to allow themselves to be pushed into war (...νομίζοντες [scil. ἡ τῶν Ἀθηναίων πρεσβεία] μᾶλλον ἂν αὐτοὺς ἐκ τῶν λόγων πρὸς τὸ ἡσυχάζειν τραπέσθαι ἢ πρὸς τὸ πολεμεῖν, 72.1; ~ 73.1: ...ὅπως μὴ ῥᾳδίως περὶ μεγάλων πραγμάτων τοῖς ξυμμάχοις πειθόμενοι χεῖρον βουλεύσησθε).

It is on the way to this goal that the speakers give *simultaneously* (evidently to give emphasis to their warning) an explanatory description of the Athenians' position of power:

72.1: καὶ ἅμα τὴν σφετέραν πόλιν ἐβούλοντο σημῆναι ὅση εἴη δύναμιν, καὶ ὑπόμνησιν ποιήσασθαι τοῖς τε πρεσβυτέροις ὧν ᾔδεσαν καὶ τοῖς νεωτέροις ἐξήγησιν ὧν ἄπειροι ἦσαν... ('and *simultaneously* they wanted to make clear how great the power of their city was, and to deliver a reminder both to the older ones of what they knew and to the younger ones a statement on what they had no experience of');

~73.1: καὶ ἅμα βουλόμενοι περὶ τοῦ παντὸς λόγου τοῦ ἐς ἡμᾶς καθεστῶτος δηλῶσαι ὡς οὔτε ἀπεικότως ἔχομεν ἃ κεκτήμεθα, ἥ τε πόλις ἡμῶν ἀξία λόγου ἐστίν ('and *simultaneously* wishing with reference to the entirety of what has been said against us to clarify that we possess not without good reasons that which we have acquired, and that our city is worthy of consideration (is to be reckoned with)').

According to de Romilly[21] both of these passages announce two themes (in chiastic arrangement): that already mentioned (and later replaced with 'excuses') concerning the significance of Athenian power (ὅση εἴη δύναμιν and ἀξία λόγου respectively), and a 'justification' through meritorious service in the Persian Wars of Athenian hegemony (ὑπόμνησιν ποιήσασθαι and οὔτε ἀπεικότως...respectively).

De Romilly sees the 'justification' in the first major section of the speech (73.2–75.1), where the Athenians describe their own accomplishments in the Persian Wars. However, in what sense a justification is involved in this passage is simply not to be discovered, especially since the Athenians emphasize, ῥηθήσεται δὲ οὐ παραιτήσεως μᾶλλον ἕνεκα ('but it will not be said so much for the sake of apology, 73.3); cf. 72.1: τῶν μὲν ἐγκλημάτων περὶ μηδὲν ἀπολογησομένους ('intending to make no apologies at all about the accusations').

There may be here an underlying misunderstanding of οὔτε ἀπεικότως,[22] which should be rendered 'not incomprehensibly' rather than 'not unjustly'. The emissaries wish 'with reference to the entirety of what has been said against us to clarify that we possess *not without good (comprehensible) reasons* that which we have acquired, and that our city is worthy of consideration (is to be reckoned with)'.

The presents ἔχομεν and ἀξία ἐστίν (as also the present perfect κεκτήμεθα) prove in addition that *both* 'announced themes' have reference extending *up to the present time* of the speakers. In other words, they do not indicate a dispositional division into 'événements anciens' (part one of the speech) and current power (the later addition/replacement of part two).

Moreover, the addition of καὶ ἅμα in both of the passages quoted above (72.1; 73.1) proves that only *auxiliary* topics are involved here, topics that come up incidentally during discussion of the main theme.

Decisive for the interpretation of the speech as a whole is the fact that Thucydides in the introduction—thus in his own name—after enumerating the individual points, states once more the main objective of the speech (to which the remaining points are therefore subordinate): ...νομίζοντες μᾶλλον ἂν αὐτοὺς ἐκ τῶν λόγων πρὸς τὸ ἡσυχάζειν τραπέσθαι ἢ πρὸς τὸ πολεμεῖν ('...believing that in consequence of the speech they would rather turn to keeping quiet than to waging war', 72.1).

The words ἐκ τῶν λόγων, which can only refer to the Athenians' arguments in their entirety, show that the other points are ancillary to this summary.

The introductory sentences of the exordium of the speech (73.1) correspond exactly. The main idea is clearly set off by the syntax: οὐ...ἀντεροῦντες...ἀλλ᾽ ὅπως μὴ ῥαδίως περὶ μεγάλων πραγμάτων τοῖς ξυμμάχοις πειθόμενοι χεῖρον βουλεύσησθε, καὶ ἅμα βουλόμε-νοι...δηλῶσαι...

The author has therefore twice (once in his own words, once in the words of his speakers) placed the complete speech under one unified main heading.

Thus there is no factual reason, on the basis of the introduction, to expect two sections of different intentions. At the same time, however, the statement that the speech is delivered οὐ παραιτήσεως...ἕνεκα ('not...for the sake of an apology', 73.3) must be considered valid for *both* main sections.

Another argument against the assumption that there are two main sections with *different* tendencies consists of the question of content: why should an explanatory reminder/presentation for the Spartans, a discussion of the importance of Athenian power, and the proof that it does not exist without good reasons not go together? It seems likely that these three points (for there are really three) are three aspects in terms of which the speakers wish their discussion of Athenian history, from the past up to the present time, to be understood, rather than that each aspect is assigned to a certain distinct epoch.

These considerations raise the question whether one *may* distinguish or separate Part 1 of the speech from Part 2 in terms of content. The very fact that Thucydides emphasizes *three* times (72.1; 73.1; 73.3) the non-apologetic intention of the speech makes it, in my opinion, natural to conclude that he wished to establish an unequivocal understanding (or possibly even to avoid a misunderstanding) of the attitude which the Athenians displayed. This makes for better logic than believing that the author later revised one section of his speech without changing the passages in which he had three times announced its content.

We must now attempt to understand also Part 2 in terms of this announcement.

Part 1 falls very clearly into the aspects announced: the Athenians show the Spartans how much Greece (and thus also proud Sparta herself) owes to their achievements during the Persian Wars. It is understandable that the speakers expect to be 'tiresome' to their Spartan audience (73.2): they want to ensure that their words are understood not as an apology but as a *demonstration of strength:* '…rather to bear witness and make clear what sort of city it is against which you will be fighting if you do not counsel wisely' (73.3).

There is little doubt that their demonstration succeeds. For instance, when they point out that the Athenians, even when their city had been taken by the Persians, did not give up (74.2 ff., with vigorous jabs at Sparta and its allies), but rather embarked in their ships and fought on to victory, this is nothing more than a veiled threat, which the Spartans are intended to understand: should Sparta decide to go to war, the Athenians will once again fight to the last.

In this section of the speech there are doubtless references to the greatness as well as the founding of Athenian power, but there is no thought of 'justification'.

These aspects become even more pronounced (since supported by theory) in Part 2 (75.1–77.6), where the speakers comment on the existing anti-Athenian *logos*. They explain how Athens could have become the most hated city in Greece.

The beginning was simple and peaceful: the Greeks, after Sparta had abandoned the battlefield (yet another jab), offered to transfer to Athens the leadership in the on-going conflict with Persia.

Thus the Athenians came upon their hegemony in the normal course of events and upon the expansion of their leadership to its present state, '... forced (first)[23]...especially by fear [scil. of the Persians, cf. Thucydides' description of the anti-Persian undertakings, 1.89, 100], then also by honor [scil. because of the position of leadership], later also by expediency [scil. through exploitation of the allies]' (75.2–3).

It is remarkable that the order of the three motives expresses both the historical sequence and the relative degree of urgency. The alteration of this order at 76.2 confirms this observation. There the change in the order of presentation of the motives corresponds to the change in the situation: there is no longer any fear of the Persians; this has been replaced by the new fear that Athens' now oppressed allies may revolt against her ἀρχή. Thus the order becomes: (1) honor (the leadership); (2) fear (of the subjects); (3) expediency (in the form of tribute from the ruled).

But addiction to honor and the urge for 'more'[24] (audible in ὠφελία) are for Thucydides himself impulses that lead to moral decline and the destruction of peaceful relations (πάντων δ᾽ αὐτῶν αἴτιον ἀρχὴ ἡ διὰ πλεονεξίαν καὶ φιλοτιμίαν, 3.82.8)—a development which in the Athenian speech is at least hinted at by the factor 'fear'.

That is, once the hegemony had developed into open domination (allies who 'defected' were subjugated: 75.4; 98.4; cf. further 99.1, οἱ γὰρ Ἀθηναῖοι ἀκριβῶς ἔπρασσον...προσάγοντες τὰς ἀνάγκας), there was no safe way to reverse the trend (75.4; 76.1–2; cf. Pericles on Athenian 'tyranny': ἣν λαβεῖν μὲν ἄδικον δοκεῖ εἶναι, ἀφεῖναι δὲ ἐπικίνδυνον, 2.63.2).

If under these circumstances Athens looks to its own advantage (τὰ ξυμφέροντα, 75.5), it behaves no differently from Sparta which likewise observes its ὠφέλιμον (76.1) within the sphere of its own hegemony. And, given a choice between giving up that hegemony at its own peril and forceful maintenance of its leadership, Sparta (had it not withdrawn after the Persian Wars) would decide just as Athens has—and incur as a consequence the same hatred from its allies as does Athens (76.1). Thus far the Athenian emissaries.

This last Athenian claim amounts to yet another provocation in the light of the fact that Sparta saw itself called upon to lead the fight against Athens under the banner '*Freedom* for the Greeks' (68.3, 69.1; cf. 2.8.4).

Now follows the theoretical explanation of why the Athenians possess their empire 'οὔτε ἀπεικότως'. 'Thus we have done nothing surprising, and nothing alien to human nature, either in accepting the hegemony that was offered or in refusing to let it go…' (76.2; cf. 5.105.2). The law of the dominance of the stronger over the weaker has always existed, and even the Spartans have considered the Athenians 'worthy' of their rule: '… until you, calculating your own advantage, now bring into the argument the idea of justice, which *no one*—when there was an opportunity to get something by force—*has ever preferred to force and thereby been dissuaded from acquiring more*'.

Even in the Melian dialogue (5.89, 105) there is no more reckless appeal to the right of the stronger. Here (as there) the Athenians are demonstrating that their power—in accordance with the introduction of their speech—exists 'not without comprehensible reasons'. The Athenians have 'comprehended' what it takes to acquire power; *they have recognized the eternal right of the stronger and acted in accordance with it.* This is the brutal sense of the second part of the speech. It is, just as Part 1, consonant not only with the announcement regarding Athens' power and its founding, but also with the main purpose of the speech as a whole, namely, to warn Sparta: this is a warning from the arrogant position of strength.[25]

That the same behavior is ascribed to the Spartans as to the Athenians is probably justified (cf. 1.88). Moreover, this fits well the tendency towards revelation of true motives which we observed in the speech of the Corinthians (and the *Archaeology*): one clings to justice not for the sake of justice but because it suits one's own present advantage. Anyone who claims not to understand this rule must either be a hypocrite or, if he truly does not understand, he loses the game (as is usually considered to be the case with the Melians).

In what follows, the tone of the Athenian speech becomes downright derisive: Athens rather deserves *praise* because, while 'adhering to human nature [i.e. the right of the stronger]', it behaves in its authority 'more justly than [necessary] according to the power it possesses' (76.3; for the actual situation, cf. 1.99.1).[26] As evidence for their 'μετριάζειν' the Athenians point to the legal relations which they maintain with their 'allies' (that this is an element of prestige the reader knows both from the speech of the Corcyreans and the first speech of the Corinthians). Other 'masters' behave less 'moderately' towards their 'subjects': βιάζεσθαι γὰρ οἷς ἂν ἐξῇ, δικάζεσθαι οὐδὲν προσδέονται (77.2).

The prefix προσ- indicates that the legal relations are something additional ('more just' than κατὰ τὴν ὑπάρχουσαν δύναμιν). Nevertheless, the cynical designation of these supposedly legal equals as 'ὑπήκοοι' ('subjects') underscores clearly the truth of the relationship. Athens, to the advantage of its own prestige, can afford the luxury of 'justice' *because it has firmly consolidated its power.* However, the emissaries (and Thucydides himself: 1.98.4, 99.1) leave no room for doubt that, as soon as important interests are at stake, the Athenians will resort to violence.

The subjects ought rather to be happy that they have not also lost their right to legal recourse. 'ἀδικούμενοί τε, ὡς ἔοικεν, οἱ ἄνθρωποι μᾶλλον ὀργίζονται ἢ βιαζόμενοι' ('when experiencing injustice, it seems men are more enraged than when exposed to violence', 77.4).

The Athenians freely admit that *they themselves have taken on the role of the Persians, the arch-enemy* of the Greeks (against whom their acceptance of hegemony was originally directed—for the freedom of the Greeks!): 'From the Persians, they [the subject-allies] suffered worse than this, and they bore it; but our authority seems oppressive, of course: for what is present is always burdensome to the subjects' (77.5).

This denigration of the free Greeks as Athenian slaves[27]—pronounced in Sparta!—is the climax of Athens' arrogance and at the same time a most vigorous humiliation of Sparta. With these words the Athenians would all but force the liberator's role on Sparta—except that Athens is so powerful, and therefore so secure.

Strasburger[28] has correctly observed that the attitude of the emissaries of Periclean Athens in no way differs from that of the Athenians on Melos, and that the interpretation of Schmid and others, who think they can trace a development from moderate Athenian imperialism (with which Thucydides supposedly identifies himself) to immoderation, is untenable. The facts as set down by Thucydides in the *Pentecontaetia* (and acknowledged by the Athenian speakers) militate against this sort of idealization. Naturally this is not to deny that, in unthreatened times, the system could function relatively smoothly (i.e. peacefully).

But what seems important to Thucydides here is not so much a temporary, relatively happy constellation as the basic underlying situation. The appeal to the natural laws of the exercise of power shows this.

In the previous chapter I referred to the key position of the Athenian speech. If we connect the attitude displayed here with the Melian Dialogue—correctly, as I think, based on certain more or less direct verbal echoes—the speech cannot be cited for the interpretation which views Thucydides more or less as the glorifier of Athenian power. If on the other hand we connect this speech to Pericles' Funeral Oration and its praise of Athens, then we find Thucydides' 'patriotism' confirmed.

In the previous chapter we saw that Schwartz *et al.*, on the basis of the Funeral Oration and the Athenians' speech in Book 1, attempted to see even the Melian Dialogue as a patriotic confession on the part of the historian.[29] The other path, to interpret the speech(es) of Pericles on the basis of the speech of the Athenians and the Melian Dialogue, has up to now scarcely been trodden.

Strasburger[30] took a decisive step in this direction when he observed that in the Funeral Oration 'freedom' is applied only to the life of the Athenians *within their own city*. Our interpretation of the Athenians' speech (this is obvious anyway in the case of the Melian Dialogue) provides a complement to this observation insofar as it shows that the Athenians in Book 1 are reflecting solely upon their relationship to their subjects. The Funeral Oration and the Athenians' speech thus have different perspectives and consequently one may adduce for comparison to the Athenians' speech only those points of the Funeral Oration which deal with foreign policy or policy involving the subject allies.

As I see it, we are essentially concerned with two passages.

(1) 2.41.3. Athens alone engenders no indignation in an aggressive enemy, 'on account of the sort of opponents at whose hands he suffers, nor grounds for reproach in a subject because he is not ruled by worthy masters' (…καὶ μόνη οὔτε τῷ πολεμίῳ ἐπελθόντι ἀγανάκτησιν ἔχει ὑφ' οἵων κακοπαθεῖ οὔτε τῷ ὑπηκόῳ κατάμεμψιν ὡς οὐχ ὑπ' ἀξίων ἄρχεται). This is cleverly expressed because the subject is not as likely to be concerned with whether he has a 'worthy' master[31] as he is with the fact that he has a master at all and must do without his freedom. And we were able to ascertain the relative nature of the term 'worthiness' already in the Athenian speech (1.76.2 and 3).

But when it comes to the absence of freedom, Thucydides' own words outweigh those of the Athenian speaker-of-the-day Pericles: 'But the goodwill of the people [scil. at the beginning of the war] tended by far towards the Spartan side, particularly because they claimed to be acting as the liberators of Greece' (2.8.4). '…So angry was the majority with the Athenians—the ones out of desire to be freed from their domination, the others out of fear of coming under their domination' (2.8.5).

(2) 2.40.4–5. 'Also in terms of virtue we are the opposite of most, since we gain our friends not by receiving favors but by conferring them… And we alone offer help without fear, *not* so much *out of calculation of our own advantage,* but rather *out of reliance* [or *trust*] [32] *on our freedom* (καὶ μόνοι οὐ τοῦ ξυμφέροντος μᾶλλον λογισμῷ ἢ τῆς ἐλευθερίας τῷ πιστῷ ἀδεῶς τινὰ ὠφελοῦμεν).

It has often enough been pointed out that this claim corresponds to nothing in the facts as Thucydides reports them.[33] Verification has therefore been sought in Athens' mythological past as found, for example, in the patriotic plays of early and middle Euripides; what is overlooked, however, is the fact that these parallels have absolutely no bearing on the personal attitude of Thucydides. The innumerable correspondences[34] prove only that Thucydides has captured the tone and self-image of Athens as the contemporary Athenians liked to hear it described by statesmen and poets alike. But can it be correct (or fair) to found an understanding of the mature Thucydides (the Athenian speech and Funeral Oration are after all, according to the Analysts, supposed to be 'late') on 'early' (or 'middle') Euripides, and thus deny him the intellectual development which is generally conceded in the case of Euripides?

No one would contest that the Funeral Oration's description of a free Athenian's life in his own city with its festivals and opportunities for leisure is not without beauty.[35]

But an interpreter must recognize that Thucydides has presented both sides, that of the rulers as well as the ruled. Thus we cannot consider the above remarks of Pericles, nor of the Athenians in Book 1, without also considering the remarks of the opposing side, especially since the first speech of the 'allies' (the Mytileneans, 3.9 ff.) deals with the same period as the Athenian speech in Book 1 and thus may be intended also as a complement to it.

We must not forget that the Mytileneans were still in a state of relative liberty because the Athenians had left them their autonomy—in name (3.10.5). This status as 'free allies' is of course precisely what gave the Athenians the external prestige (εὐπρέπεια λόγου) of justice and moderate exercise of power of which the Athenian emissaries in Sparta were boasting (3.11.3–4). From the Mytileneans themselves we hear that (because of Athens' superior forces) they are *de facto* unable to make use of their 'freedom'.

It is thus no wonder that the Mytileneans in revolt *quote* Pericles' remarks about the Athenian way of winning *friends* and about the πιστὸν τῆς ἐλευ-θερίας ('the reliance on freedom'). 'What sort of *friendship* or ἐλευθερία πιστή ('reliable freedom') was this in which we came together hospitably against our true feelings, and they out of fear treated us well in war, but we treated them likewise in peace? …we were their allies held fast more by fear than by friendship' (…δέει τε τὸ πλέον ἢ φιλίᾳ κατεχόμενοι ξύμμαχοι ἦμεν, 12.1).

These remarks of the Mytileneans, which serve to complement the picture of Athenian 'génerosité'[36] from the other side, provide confirmation for our assertion (in the 'Retrospective') that it is over-hasty to equate Thucydides' own attitude with that of one of his speakers.

When it comes to interpreting the Athenian attitude towards winning friends, it seems preferable to look for evidence in the text itself rather than to resort to the mythological past. If Pericles claims that Athens helps its friends without looking to its own advantage, then we must compare the only instance so far reported by the historian in which Athens has provided such assistance: the case of Corcyra. There, Thucydides repeated in his own words the 'advantages' which the Athenians intended to secure by means of this assistance (1.44.2–3). The author is justified in expecting that his reader will not have forgotten this case.

After this necessary detour we can now return to the Athenian speech and take it for what it is intended to be: an arrogantly recited description of Athenian power, combined with the demonstration that the holders of this power believe they have grasped the law underlying every kind of power and, as a result, are sitting as firmly in the saddle as is humanly possible; 'liberation of the Greeks' may be a good slogan, but as far as Athens is concerned it has no prospect of being realized so long as it is not combined with power—and power strives for advantage. There is in this condescending lecture a decisive correction of the second speech of the Corinthians (1.68 ff.). The Corinthians based their arguments upon emotion (cf. the slogan, 'liberation of the Greeks') without taking into account the relative power of the two sides wherein lie the preconditions for successful action.

It is only against this background that the main purpose of the Athenian speech, to warn the Spartans (1.78), acquires its full importance: 'Consider beforehand how unpredictable a thing is war before you find yourselves engaged in it. Should it prove to be long (!), the outcome usually depends upon chance occurrences from control of which we are (on both sides) equally removed; and how it will end remains a risk in the dark. At the beginning of a war people first devote themselves to activity (which they ought to do later); but when they have already experienced some disaster they cling to thought' (78.1–3). Do the Athenians realize how much this warning applies also to the powerful? The ambiguity and irony of this passage are surely the conscious intention of Thucydides (cf. Pericles' confidence, so justified by human standards).

Although the Athenians believe they have nothing severe to fear for their power in the event of war, their invitation to avoid war by legal means is surely a serious one (cf. 72.1 end): '...as long as the decision for the good is still a matter of free choice for both sides' (78.4). The word αὐθαίρετος ('self-chosen') here plays a part similar to that of ἀνήκεστον ('incurable', 'irreparable'), at 4.20.1 where Sparta announces its peace offer.

The question arises: did Thucydides, too, see here an opportunity to circumvent the war? Or, more cautiously expressed, did he see here the point at which—if at all—the events tending towards war could have been halted?

The introduction to the following speech suggests a positive answer. Thucydides dramatizes Archidamus' entrance to the extent that he reports the majority of the Spartans (after their allies and the Athenians had been shown out) to have been already in favor of a speedy beginning to the hostilities. The king's speech thus acquires the weight of *the last chance for peace*.

Wassermann[37] has shown that the historian was at pains to make of his Archidamus, in respect of personality and dignity, a worthy counterpart to Pericles.

Already the introductory characterizing remarks (ξυνετός 'sagacious' and σώφρων 'of sound mind', 79.2) hint that the voice of reason is about to get a hearing. There is no trace of the arrogance of the Athenians' speech, and the emotion-free tone of the speech lends a special dignity to the voice of the warner, speaking from the recognition of his own side's weakness. As far as the content is concerned, the significance with which the author has imbued this speech is underscored by the fact that Archidamus' reflections on the prospect of success fall into the same categories which directed *Thucydides himself* in the *Archaeology*.[38] Power (and success) must first of all be estimated in accordance with available resources both military and above all financial. '...ἔστιν ὁ πόλεμος οὐχ ὅπλων τὸ πλέον ἀλλὰ δαπάνης, δι' ἣν τὰ ὅπλα ὠφελεῖ, ἄλλως τε καὶ ἠπειρώταις πρὸς θαλασσίους' ('war depends not so much on arms as on spending money, through which arms have their usefulness, especially for continentals who fight a naval power, 83.2).

The last words show that Thucydides has also attributed to Archidamus a recognition of the superiority of sea power in Greek geographical circumstances (as likewise presented in the *Archaeology*).

We can see a connection between another aspect of the content of this speech and the words of Thucydides himself. Analysis has shown that Pericles (1.140 ff.) and Archidamus judge the prospects of the war in a similar fashion,[39] and Pericles' strategy (which builds on this judgment) is viewed by Thucydides himself as essentially promising (2.65).

To Archidamus' sentence quoted above one need only compare Pericles (1.141.5; cf. 142.1): αἱ δὲ περιουσίαι τοὺς πολέμους μᾶλλον ἢ αἱ βίαιοι ἐσφοραὶ ἀνέχουσιν ('it is the superiority of resources that keeps a war going rather than taxes exacted by force').

A further point which is in agreement with the historian's own judgment (1.23) is that Archidamus—on this point even closer to Thucydides than

Pericles—sees war primarily as something negative: 'I myself have experienced already many wars, Spartans, and I see my agemates among you in the same condition, so that no one will strive for war out of inexperience…or under the impression that it is something good or safe' (80.1).

I hope to be able to show in the next chapter that the relationship between anticipating expectation and concrete (correcting) experience is a genuinely Thucydidean problem. Let us here anticipate this much: that Thucydides seems to value more highly an opinion which takes account of earlier experience when considering the future because it is more seriously aware of the possible negative consequences.

After the enumeration of Athens' resources, Archidamus reasons that there is little hope of a brief war. 'I fear rather that we shall bequeath it even to our children' (81.6).[40] According to Archidamus the prospect of military success would come only after two to three years of preparation. Should the Spartans, persuaded by their allies, invade Attica at the present, Athenian retaliation would fall upon the—unprepared—Peloponnese. 'For we can settle the reproaches of cities and of private individuals. However, once we have all gone to war for the sake of certain individual parties [i.e. Corinth and Megara]—and it is impossible to know how it might turn out—then it will not be easy to withdraw from it with our prestige intact' (82.6; cf. 81.5).

To Corinthian allusions (69.5) to the fact that the Athenians have often foundered due to their own mistakes he poignantly replies with the previously cited argument that one man is not different from another (84.4).

Decisively different from Corinthian optimism (as from the Athenians' optimism, although they express similar ideas) is his conviction that the future does not unfold according to the dispositions of a human being making plans. 'But we should believe that the plans [or 'calculations'] of others are similar [to ours], and that *circumstances resulting from chance are not* [beforehand] *susceptible to rational analysis*' (οὐ λόγῳ διαιρετάς, 84.3).

Such are the basic elements of this warning speech at which Grillparzer was 'wahrhaft begeistert' ('truly enthusiastic'): 'Wenn das nicht Staatsklugheit ist, so gibt es keine' ('If that is not statecraft, then there is none').[41]

But we must still ask ourselves why Thucydides placed so much emphasis on a speech which, as the sequel shows, was in vain. Before answering this question we must have a look at the speech of Sthenelaidas and the final speech of the Corinthians.

Sthenelaidas' speech (1.86)—with the seeming simplicity of its short, well-targeted *cola* and the resulting easy comprehensibility—is a paradigm of refined rhetoric. The parody of Archidamus ('ἢν σωφρονῶμεν'),[42] the ambiguity (mentioned in the previous chapter) in the mention of the 'good' allies (where 'good' means 'loyal' or 'dear' but not 'capable'), the emotional appeal (e.g. 'worthy of Sparta' to vote for the war), the mention of the true cause of the war (Sparta's fear of Athens' rise to power)—all this is calculated to dispel as quickly as possible the effect of Archidamus' prudent speech.

In addition, the trick of using the 'division' method of voting (unusual in Sparta, 87.2) serves to single out visibly as cowards those who would perhaps vote for prudence and against the war.

The result: Sparta decides against reason.

When, thereafter, the Spartans call together their allies to vote on the decision to go to war at the alliance level, it is once again the irrational forces that have the last word. The Corinthians speak last *again,* and their speech is *again*[43] dominated by the emotion of fear for their relatives in Potidaea (1.119; the reader will recall how Thucydides, when describing the decision of the tyrannicides, likewise emphasized the *emotions* which led to the action).

It is not necessary to list here all the appeals to irrational sentiment (liberation of the Greeks, Athens as tyrant, etc.).

Of greater interest is the way the Corinthians justify their optimism vis-à-vis the impending war: 'For it is the business of prudent men, when they are suffering no wrong, to remain inactive; but it is the business of good [!] men, when they are suffering wrong, to go from peace to war, but then when a good opportunity presents itself [what optimism!] to return from the state of war to an agreement…' (120.3).

Not a thought is wasted upon the real imbalance of power. Instead we hear platitudes: one should not be drawn into ill-considered action by good fortune (!) in war (120.3a and 4b); the Corinthians are also conversant with the fact that people tackle a war with greater confidence at the start (120.5)—and coming from them this has a strongly ironic flavor.

The Corinthians deal glibly with facts brought up by Archidamus (and later by Pericles). While Archidamus warned that the war could last a long time, the Corinthians comment, '…and when we have taken vengeance upon the Athenians [!], we will end it again at the right moment [!]' (121.1; the historian will refer to this comment ten war-years later, 5.14.3).

A Peloponnesian victory is 'under many aspects' *'likely'* (εἰκός!): they have more people, more experience; they will doubtless build a fleet and lure away the 'allied' members among the Athenian crews with better wages (!)… (121.3); besides, it is *likely* (εἰκός) that Athens will be overwhelmed in a single (!) sea battle (121.4), etc., etc.

As for the basic question of managing the war, the problem of finances, they suggest applying to the oracle at Olympia for credit in addition to their own contributions. 'It would be unheard of if their allies untiringly finance their own enslavement while we…are unwilling to contribute funds to our own salvation…!' (121.5). It would certainly be 'unheard of', but indignation is not a substantive argument against the centrally administered Athenian tribute system (cf. Pericles' contemptuous remarks on the non-centrally administered Peloponnesian League, 1.141.2–7).

In general: 'But there are other paths of war available to us as well…' 'all kinds of other possibilities that cannot at the present be foreseen.' 'For war least takes its course according to a set plan: in the majority of cases, it invents its own means in regard to the circumstances as they happen to occur' (122.1).

The last sentence looks like a repudiation of any *a priori* conception, and yet the entire speech with its 'calculations of probability' purports to be a sketch of the prospects of the war.

The subsequent vote returns the expected decision to declare war, and here already Archidamus' warning proves valid: 'It was *impossible* for them to attack immediately after the decision *because they were not prepared for war*…'—they had to wait nearly a year (125.2). The irony of this passage is unmistakable.

One can easily imagine two ways of writing the history of a war. One way would be to observe the war in terms of the success or defeat of one side; this would consist of the history of a single empire or state during the war. Needless to say, such an account need not be 'subjective' in the sense that the historian writes as a partisan of the country in question.

The other way would be to observe the war *per se* during its course (this is how Thucydides formulates his theme, 1.1.1). This method demands that the historian maintain in his judgment an equal distance from both sides. Of course—and this, too, need scarcely be pointed out—this does not exclude the possibility that one of the sides, because (on account of its power, consolidation, impetus or the like) it represents the more significant political factor, may receive greater attention in the historian's presentation.

A regrettable trend (indicated in the previous chapter) in the development of the Thucydides-image is that interpreters have often not believed their author capable of adhering to his self-imposed objectivity when it comes to the warring parties. Accordingly, the Analysts have habitually directed their attention to the question of a phase-by-phase development of Thucydides' political attitude. In other words, Thucydides suffered a reduction in status from a historian of the second kind to one of the first kind. Moreover, since the war was also a piece of the history of his *native* city, interpreters believed it possible, if not necessary, to find in his presentation 'ardeur patriotique',[44] 'passionate love for Athens',[45] 'Liebe zu Heimat und Volk'.[46]

Unless I am much mistaken, what often accompanies the search for patriotic traits in this historical work is the secret fear that it might lose in educational value should it turn out that Thucydides was not an unconditional admirer of Periclean (which usually means 'classical') Athens and should he not identify himself in every particular with 'his' speaker Pericles.

This judgment overlooks two things. First, Thucydides does not for the most part describe a 'classical' or even a normative Athens, but rather the political Athens of his time. Second, the perceptiveness which allowed him to see not only the greatness but also the negative traits of his native city makes him *far more* representative of the 'classical' Athens than would have been the case if he had adhered to an unquestioningly patriotic point of view.

These considerations are necessary in view of the existing image of Thucydides, and they explain why the first result of our investigation of the pre-war speeches must be a negative one: without a polemical discussion of the traditional views of the debate in Sparta it is impossible to take a fresh look at the meaning of these speeches.

The Analysts of course were not capable of seeing the speeches in Book 1 as a complete compositional unit. Our own considerations have suggested that this failure resulted largely from an *exclusively* political reading of the speeches and from the insistence upon elucidating them through reference to the supposed partisanship of the historian. The question of how such partisanship could be combined with the work's intention to be 'a possession for ever' was not addressed.

But if Thucydides is what he claims to be, a historian of the second kind mentioned above, then the notion of partisanship for one or the other of the warring parties must yield to his overarching theme, namely, the war itself. To this level of the 'possession for ever', the opposition of the two sides is strictly subordinate, and if it is necessary to look for a definitive opposition this could only be *war* and *peace*.

This is no mere theoretical demand but the result of our reading of the first Book: The pre-history of the war contains two points at which the agents, through their decisions, determine the as yet undecided course of events to come. First, Athens' intervention on the side of Corcyra (emphasized by the first Corinthian speech and the speech of the Corcyreans); and second, the decision of Sparta, and then of its allies, to go to war (highlighted by the tetralogy of speeches in Sparta and the third Corinthian speech). The consequence of the first decision is that the conflict does reach what we termed above the 'third' level; the second shows that the partners on this third level accept the conflict as final. (In the context of the decision to go to war Pericles' first speech, which we did not review in detail, has a rather complementary stamp insofar as it shows—after Sparta's decision—that Athens too is ready to undertake the war.)

The speeches, then, accentuate those points at which the movement from peace toward war is decisively promoted.

Thus we hold the key to interpreting the speeches we have investigated last: they show the *attitude of the individual parties to the impending decision.* I believe that our interpretation has shown that Thucydides was here thinking not so much about blaming a first aggressor (or about the inevitability of the war) as about *how* the individual parties *justified their ideas about the course of the war.* All the speakers, the warners as well as the warmongers, attempted to support their suggestions with a *sketch of the future.* And it is likely that the historian's problem lies precisely in these sketches (the mere fact that he devotes so much space to them is evidence for this).

First a word on Thucydides' own position. It should be clear that he is in agreement with the weighing of the balance of power and prospects for success as set forth by Pericles and Archidamus. Consequently, he too considers the Spartan/Peloponnesian decision to go to war as at least hasty and premature. I say nothing of the question of whether the war represented for him a 'solution' of any kind to the conflicts. The latter problem stands outside the historic course of events he describes, from which his presentation does not stray.

But what is probably essential for Thucydides himself is not primarily the unmasking or 'exposing' quality of the speeches (often strongly emphasized by interpreters), for in his view this is merely a precondition for understanding the political events (however often this quality may surprise the reader). For instance, if one does not know that in the political sphere considerations of advantage generally take precedence over considerations of justice, one neither has access to the real motives of the actors nor insight into the actual occurrences and the calculations which bring them about. This is one reason that the Athenian emissaries present so clearly the 'principles' of Athenian policy.

It is what in each case lies behind the prestige-carrying façade of 'justice' that primarily interests the historian.

For instance, when one and the same fact, the unpredictability of war, is used by the Athenians (78.2) as a ground for a warning and by the

Corinthians (122.1) as a ground for optimism, the Positivist assertion that history can be rationally comprehended becomes a genuine problem.

Another example: the method of argument (mentioned in the previous chapter)[47] based on the εἰκός is applied by Pericles (141.5) and Archidamus (81.6) within reasonable limits, but is abused *ad absurdum* by the Corinthians (121.2, 4).

We have seen,[48] on the other hand, how Thucydides himself could use this form of argument in a convincing way in order to leave the sphere of the subjective. What protection is there against the inappropriate use of a method which, within certain limits, is serviceable?[49]

The problem appears to spread from the comprehensibility of events to the capacity of human beings to comprehend, but this is mere appearance. To the extent that human incompetence is a political-historical factor, it contributes decisively to the incomprehensibility of events. (Remember that even a man like Pericles, confident in his ability to cope with the range of human fickleness from initial enthusiasm to a later change of heart [1.140.1], comes to the brink of personal ruin: 2.65.3).

A look at the complete group of speeches gives us the following: the first pro-war speech of the Corinthians (emotional in inspiration, anything but rational in execution and purpose); the warning of the Athenians (arrogantly confident in their own superiority); the warning of Archidamus (characterized by experience and recognition of the League's weakness); the warmongering speech of Sthenelaidas (employing emotional excitement in order to destroy the rational arguments of Archidamus); the final pro-war speech of the Corinthians (derisive of the results of any serious reflection).

As many contradictions as speeches: for Analysts, sufficient opportunity to find 'doublets'—for Thucydides, just enough to permit the presentation of a diverse reality.

And what does this reality look like? *The prudent (and for that reason warning) voices are, in the final result, simply outmaneuvered by those which excite emotion.* Sthenelaidas (*emotionally* excited by the fear of Athens' rise to power) wins the Spartan decision to go to war; the Corinthians (*emotionally* driven by concern for their relatives in Potidaea) carry the day with the Peloponnesian League.

One last example from the analytic position. Pohlenz[50] was loath to admit that the historian had composed the speech of Archidamus and the final Corinthian speech at the same time because the ideas in the former refute *in advance* the ideas in the latter.

One must ask whether this refutation in advance is not *precisely the fact which Thucydides wished* (or had) to *sketch*. The success of the illogical

Corinthian arguments is *more striking after* the voice of reason has already been heard.[51]

Moreover, is it not the case that the warner (a well-known feature of Greek literature)[52] is felt most emphatically when his warning goes unheeded? It is significant in the case of Archidamus that he delivers his warning not on the basis of the relative strength of the two opposing sides alone, but also on the basis *of his own experience of previous wars.*

If this is so, then the deeper significance of this complex of speeches lies in the demonstration of the fact that the war, which (in accordance with the description at 1.23) brought so much suffering upon Greece, was set in motion by irrational forces—against reasonably calculated prospects of success and without consideration for the experience of previous disaster.

But here we have arrived at an aspect which—in similar fashion—came to light in the first chapter:[53] it would naturally be hard for a 'rationalist' to grasp that human nature, even when being acquainted with the causes that will determine a future development, allows its decisions to be determined by emotional judgments (though they have been previously refuted). But it is precisely this that Thucydides so insistently demonstrates.

We then seem to have been correct in characterizing Thucydides' own attitude as one of regret for the *de facto* inevitability of what appears avoidable to rational hindsight.

But this regret evidently springs from a historical realization which transcends the Positivist image of the confident rationalist. Once it has been seen that prudent, fact-oriented planning is subject to severe limitations, this is not merely a negative realization, for simultaneously *emotion* (or the side of human nature which is inaccessible to reason) has been *recognized* as an *objective, operative factor* in political and historical events.

The historian's realization is the more remarkable in that it contains the further realization of a *limitation*: contemporary methods (such as prognosis according to the εἰκός) cannot readily be applied to *future* historical developments, whereas they can be of use in understanding the unalterable past.[54]

The result of Book 1 is that, in the decision about war and peace, the powers of reason were defeated while those that in human estimation (or in accordance with the author's own categories of observation) had no prospect of success were victorious. This places the reader—who of course knows the outcome of the war—before another paradox: the Peloponnesian League decides against reason—and in the end is the victor!

It is worthwhile to ask the question: does the course of the war (contrary as it is to the original presuppositions) not present essentially the same problem which Thucydides' description of the domestic situation in

Athens in 415 suggested? Must not the historian's fundamental interest increasingly have been directed toward those factors which defied rational understanding and systematization, rather than toward the foundation of a functional system which would see fit to ignore the incalculable factors as insignificant remainders?

The only way to answer this question is to observe the literary emphases in Thucydides' presentation of certain complexes of events.

Notes

[1] Finley 1947[2], 112; Strasburger 1954, 412.

[2] On this see Schuller 1956, 971 ff.

[3] Strasburger 1954, 416.

[4] Finley 1939, 51; cf. 1938, 32 f.

[5] 33.1; 34.1; see Calder 1955, 179.

[6] Cf. the Corinthians' desperate attempt to lend more weight to their use of the term 'right' by the implication of an alleged advantage, 42.1–2. Pearson (1957, 232) gives too positive an assessment of the value of τὸ δίκαιον in this context.

[7] It is characteristic of the freedom of Thucydidean speeches that the true cause of the war (according to 23.6 the one least admitted in public) appears as argument already in the *first* speech of the work (cf. 86.5).

[8] Cf. 33.2; 35.5; 36.3.

[9] This is why I cannot agree with Calder's judgment (1955, 180): '…the Corinthians spoke of past favors while the Corcyreans intimated future benefits.' Calder equates the Athenians' judgment with that of the Corcyreans.

[10] Calder 1955, 179.

[11] This is the *narrative*-oriented motive for the *detailed* description of the battle whose climax is that the Athenians are drawn into the fighting against their will.

[12] Substantial credit for this goes to the dissertation of R. Zahn (1934). (The Analysts searched for layers of composition allegedly conceived at different times by the historian.)

[13] Schmid 1948, 174; cf. Walter Schmid 1947, 47 f.; further Parry 1981, 136 ('splendid compliment…of Athens'); among others.

[14] Schmid 1948, 174.

[15] Wassermann 1931, 253; Ludwig (1952, 40) is able, on the basis of the antilogistic structure of the speeches, to demonstrate the inappropriateness of analyses based solely on one side or the other.

[16] Müri 1947, 256 n. 6.

[17] Schwartz 1929[2], 103. '…nur als defensives Komplement des agitatorischen Angriffs verständlich' ('understandable only as a defensive complement of the agitational attack').

[18] Cf. Schmid 1948, 174; differently, Adcock 1951, 6; Rohrer 1959, 48.

[19] De Romilly 1951[2], 35 f., but cf. 224; similarly Gomme, vol. I, 252.

[20] De Romilly 1951[2], 226.

[21]   De Romilly 1951², 225 f.

[22]   The alleged parallel passage ὑπόμνησιν ποιήσασθαι… has nothing to do at all with a justification. Walter Schmid (1947, 14 f. and *passim*) makes the same mistake (with the same consequences: 'Apologie der attischen Herrschaft'), also unmistakably following in the footsteps of Schwartz (1929²). It is impermissible to base the interpretation (as does Bodin 1932, 96) on the restorative tendencies of an Isocrates (*Paneg.* 20), in whose language Thucydides' 'οὔτε ἀπεικότως' is consistently recoined as 'δικαίως' and 'οὐκ ἀδίκως' (referring to his own time). Reich's remarks (1956, 18 f.) are too vague despite his correctly connecting οὐ…ἀπεικότως with 76.2. For the meaning of οὐκ ἀπεικότως, cf. Thucydides 6.55.2; 8.68.4; but especially 2.8.1: …ἀλλ' ἔρρωντο ἐς τὸν πόλεμον οὐκ ἀπεικότως· ἀρχόμενοι γὰρ πάντες ὀξύτερον ἀντιλαμβάνονται…

[23]   The difficult position of τὸ πρῶτον seems to me (with Steup *ad loc.*) to point to corruption. One would normally expect τὸ πρῶτον in the place where we now find μάλιστα. De Romilly's (1951², 212) and others' assumption that this represents two superimposed dispositional systems (τὸ πρῶτον : οὐκ ἔτι and μάλιστα : ἔπειτα : ὕστερον) is not very convincing. Alberti (1959, 44 f.) does not discuss this passage. Drobig's (1958, 331 ff.) interpretation is too much colored by his word study of δέος.

[24]   Cf. the πλέον ἔχειν of the Athenian speakers at 76.2 end.

[25]   Warning and arrogance can indeed go together. I cannot share Gomme's (vol. I, 253 f.) objection to the apparent contradiction between the frame (the call for peace) and the content of the speech (Gomme finds it so provocative as to be intended to sweep the Spartans into a hasty declaration of war).

[26]   It is upon this passage and the word ἄξιοι at 76.2 (as a value term highly suspect) together with the 'Periclean ideal' of τιμή (75.3; 76.2) that de Romilly (1951², 214 f.) bases her notion of a moderate Athenian imperialism which does not abandon 'principes moraux'. Cf. Finley 1947², 127 f.: 'this moderation which crowns and accompanies the creativity of Athens'; similarly Topitsch 1943/7, 59 *et. al.*

[27]   Cf. Hermocrates the warner at 6.76.4: καὶ οὐ περὶ τῆς ἐλευθερίας ἄρα οὔτε οὗτοι τῶν Ἑλλήνων οὔθ' οἱ Ἕλληνες τῆς ἑαυτῶν τῷ Μήδῳ ἀντέστησαν, περὶ δὲ οἱ μὲν σφίσιν ἀλλὰ μὴ ἐκείνῳ καταδουλώσεως, οἱ δ' ἐπὶ δεσπότου μεταβολῇ… (6.76.3 f. ~ 1.99).

[28]   Strasburger 1958, 29 n. 5.

[29]   One example will suffice: 'The very fact that the assertions of the Athenians [scil. in the Melian Dialogue] expressly or implicitly recur in speeches made by Pericles or his envoys, is a weighty argument against those who see in the Melian Dialogue an indictment of Athenian policy' (Wassermann 1947, 25). In my view, these recurrences are a 'weighty argument' against the equation Thucydides = Athens.

[30]   Strasburger 1958, 31 n. 1; cf. Eberhardt 1954, 324; Strasburger further adduces 7.69.2; one should add Nicias' attempt to create a feeling of commonality among the allies before Syracuse (7.63.3); on the Funeral Oration's essentially domestic theme see also de Romilly (1951², 116).

[31] On this see de Romilly 1951², 117 and above, n. 26.

[32] 'Aus dem Vertrauen, das die Freiheit in uns erzeugt' ('from the trust which freedom engenders in us') (Diller 1962, 201).

[33] Cf. already Steup, *ad loc.*; further Michaelis 1951, 77; Strasburger 1958, 30.

[34] The most thorough treatment is in de Romilly 1951², 120 ff.

[35] But of course one must not forget here the remark of the Corinthians: '... δι' ὅλου τοῦ αἰῶνος μοχθοῦσι καὶ ἀπολαύουσιν ἐλάχιστα τῶν ὑπαρχόντων διὰ τὸ αἰεὶ κτᾶσθαι, etc. (1.70.8–9). Cf. the sarcastic remark of the oligarchs on the 'Five-thousand': on account of their campaigns and foreign business ventures the Athenians had never before encountered an issue for deliberation so important that 5000 people had bothered to assemble for it (8.72.1).

[36] De Romilly 1951², *passim.*

[37] Wassermann 1952/3, 193 ff.

[38] Finley 1947², 130; cf. *op. cit.* 28, 29.

[39] These are the basic points of agreement between the two speakers (cf. de Romilly 1951², 33 f.; Zahn 1934, 41 ff.): Athens' naval superiority (the Peloponnesians will not even have a chance to *drill* in the event that they can build a fleet at all); i.e. no Peloponnesian influence (such as support for revolt) in Athens' island empire; Athens itself unassailable (because it is not dependent upon Attic harvests), as opposed to a relatively exposed Peloponnese; the Peloponnesian League's money shortage as opposed to Athens' full coffers (and continuing payments of tribute by its subjects), etc.

[40] This remark can hardly refer to the fact that Archidamus will die after five years of war and 'bequeath it' to his son (de Romilly 1951², 127); cf. Adcock 1951, 7.

[41] Tagebücher 19/2/1829 (*Hist. krit. Gesamtausgabe* of A. Sauer, Abt. II, Bd. 8, p. 333), cited in Wassermann 1952/3, 193.

[42] Compare also οὐδὲ ... λόγοις διακριτέα μὴ λόγῳ ... βλαπτομένους (86.3) with Archidamus' τύχας λόγῳ οὐ διαιρετάς (84.3).

[43] Pohlenz' objection against the fact that in both cases the Corinthians are the *last* to speak is, in my opinion, as unfounded as his assertion that the two Corinthian speeches are contradictory (the first inflammatory, in the second the Corinthians as 'prudent, coolly calculating speakers') in the context of this 'tournament of speeches' (1919, 98; again 1936, 283).

[44] De Romilly 1951², 220.

[45] Martin 1930, 53, cf. 46.

[46] Taeger 1925, 298; citations can easily be multiplied; for 'modern Pericleanism' see Chambers 1957a, 80 f.

[47] See above, pp. 15 f.

[48] See above, p. 4 with n. 3.

[49] As soon as one realizes that the inappropriate use is deliberately portrayed as such by Thucydides, such passages lose their usefulness for purposes of analysis (e.g. Danninger 1931/2, 16 ff., cf. his chart, 29).

[50] Pohlenz 1919, 109; Zahn (1934, 44) fails in her attempt to find in the final Corinthian speech an argumentation which goes beyond that in Archidamus'

speech. Zahn's purpose was—in opposition to Pohlenz—to preserve the compositional unity of the complex. Similarly de Romilly 1951², 33; cf. Walter Schmid 1947, 51, 62 ff.

[51] The objection that the Corinthians could not have heard Archidamus' speech directly does not, of course, apply in the case of Thucydidean speeches; see the Athenian general's response to the arguments of the Peloponnesian generals at 2.89 (Chapter 5 below).

[52] On this subject see Wassermann 1952/3, 194.

[53] See above, p. 10.

[54] See above, pp. 4, 15 f.

4

PRELUDE TO WAR
Book 2.2–6

In the spring of 431—still before the general eruption of hostilities—ca. 300 Thebans launch a surprise attack on the city of Plataea. The raid is, however, a failure and the invaders are killed almost to a man.

Thucydides has shaped this event—insignificant as it seems for the course of the great war—into a narrative account (2.2 ff.) which has often been admired but scarcely investigated in terms of its embedded goals.

In the unfolding of the event, the historian familiarizes his reader with all the details, not only of the action, but also of the motives and plans:[1] the Thebans, exploiting the still-existing state of peace (2.3), wish to settle an old score with Plataea by violent means; their collaborators within the city (who open the gates for them) are concerned with the personal acquisition of power (ἰδίας ἕνεκα δυνάμεως) and the annihilation (διαφθεῖραι) of their political opponents (2.2). Under Theban rule these men would enjoy a much more privileged position as oligarchs than in the democratic city dependent on Athens.

The planning of this undertaking appears to be exemplary. A relatively small strike force of slightly more than 300 men is to enter a gate which has been opened from the inside—because it is still peacetime, no watch has been posted (2.3); the main army, as security against failure, follows later (5.1). The collaborators want to use the strike force to capture their opponents (obviously, the leaders of the democratic party) in their own houses (2.4). A moonless night is chosen (new moon, 4.2) and, in addition to the fact that the Plataeans suspect nothing, there is the significance of the appointed time for the raid: 'around the time of the first sleep' (2.1).

However, the execution soon deviates from the plan: after entering the city without incident, the Thebans decide to induce the townspeople by public proclamation to surrender peacefully (2.4). This goes against the earnest advice of their Plataean friends who urge taking their chief opponents into custody without delay. Thucydides intimates that the Thebans are here depriving themselves of a decisive strategic advantage, namely, the sense of orientation offered by their collaborators and the information regarding the whereabouts of the leading democrats. The Thebans, however, 'opine' that they will more easily win the town over by this 'peaceful' proclamation.

But opinion is deceptive (for the majority of the population is not interested in changing the existing conditions, 3.2).

Here again the author's psychological interest is noticeable. He now gives the reaction of the Plataeans (3.1): the sudden capture of the city frightens them (the element of surprise from the original Theban plan still has its effect) and they in turn 'opine' that there are many more enemies in the city than are actually present ('for they could not see *at night*'—this element of the plan also remains effective).

On the basis of these two considerations—fear due to surprise and overestimation of the enemy's numbers—the Plataeans agree to a treaty with the invaders—not, however, because of the 'friendly' (cf. φιλίαν 2.4) attitude which the Thebans intended to display.

Eventually the inevitable comes to pass: after the initial fright, the Plataeans discover the enemy's real number and arrive at the 'opinion' (νομίζοντες 2.4 ~ νομίσαντες 3.1 ~ ἐνόμισαν 3.2) that they can easily overpower the invaders. In consequence they decide to attack.

Their counter-plan, in addition to such preparations as roadblocks and cutting passages through the walls of adjoining houses, takes up some of the elements of the *original* plan of the *Thebans*: familiarity with the city (...ἐμπειρίας τῆς κατὰ τὴν πόλιν, 3.4) now of course favors the Plataeans; but also the new moon (4.2) and the night (ἔτι νύκτα καὶ αὐτὸ τὸ περίορθρον, 3.4) are deliberately appropriated from the Theban plan as well as the impetus of surprise (ὡς ἔγνωσαν ἐξηπατημένοι, 4.1).

In the subsequent description of the fighting (4.1–7) we leave the—so far actionless—sphere of plan and counter-plan, i.e. the sphere of bloodless events.

This change is likewise reflected in the narrative. There is a plethora of concrete occurrences, the seemingly smallest details are related significantly, and double expressions intensify the salient emotional element: it is not only the men of Plataea who attack 'with great noise' (πολλῷ θορύβῳ), but *also* 'the women and the slaves' take part by 'screaming and howling' (κραυγῇ τε καὶ ὀλολυγῇ) and by throwing from the roofs not only stones but 'λίθοις τε καὶ κεράμῳ' ('stones and tiles'); the surprised Thebans can find no exit 'ἐν σκότῳ καὶ πηλῷ' ('in darkness and mud'). The gate by which the Thebans had entered is closed by a Plataean, 'using a spearshaft as a bar in place of the pin' (such detail!); some of the Thebans try leaping from the wall (and nearly all fall to their deaths); others open an unwatched gate by cutting through the bar ('…a woman gave them an axe…') but they are soon discovered; still others die in various other ways; one large group escapes into a house which is part of the city wall, taking the house-door for an inner gate of the wall; the Plataeans already consider whether they should fire the house: the disaster for the previous night's victors is complete.

Why the detailed description in this passage? The answer is evidently that Thucydides wishes his reader to visualize the reversal (the μεταβολή)[2], the complete *disorientation* of those who had at first been so *well oriented*. He expresses this paradox by using paronomasia to suggest a comparison between the fleeing Thebans in their 'ignorance' (ἄπειροι μέν) of an escape route and the pursuing Plataeans who 'know their way' (ἐμπείρους δέ, 4.2).

The unexpected result is that the 180 (of more than 300) Thebans who remain alive must surrender *unconditionally*. They have thus ended up in a significantly worse situation than the Plataeans when, the night before, they had struck an agreement with the invaders.

What of the main Theban force, the 'security' in the original plan, 'in case something might go amiss for the invaders' (5.1)?

The same heavy rain which had unexpectedly aided the Plataeans by turning the streets of their town to mud and hindering the invaders also impeded the arrival of the army, which was to have arrived 'while it was still night'.

The river Asopos, which the army had to cross on its way to Plataea, was swollen with the heavy rainfall. 'On account of marching in the rain and of the arduous river-crossing they arrived *too late*: some of the men had already been killed, the others captured alive.'

The result seems once again paradoxical. The Theban plan had included the main army as a reserve force, yet it is precisely this element, intended as a provision against *unforeseeable* circumstances, which is *itself* eliminated by an *unpredictable* event. The original plan thus collapses.

Can the Thebans still salvage something from this situation? Yes: since the attack took place during peace time, many Plataeans were on their lands outside the city (surprise during peace time is also an element that comes from the original plan, 2.4). As a result of this situation the main force decides on a substitute plan, i.e. to take at least these Plataeans prisoner and to exchange them for their own people.

But the Plataeans inside the city arrive at this possibility independently (i.e. plan and counter-plan cross once again). Under oath[3] they assure the Thebans that they will release the prisoners on the condition that the Theban army withdraw without violence from Plataean territory.

For the second time the Thebans give up their advantage (although they have been informed of the Plataeans' breach of the first agreement: 5.1.4) and comply with the Plataean demand.

At this the Plataeans swiftly bring their people and property into the city—and kill the 180 prisoners.

One might expect the story of the unsuccessful attack to end with the Plataeans' second breaking of a treaty.

But Thucydides appends one last detail. Two messengers set out from Plataea to Athens, the first at the beginning of the attack, the second after the Plataean victory. In response to the second message the Athenians send a messenger of their own with the command to await further deliberations of the Athenians and take no action with respect to the Theban prisoners. Thucydides points out twice that the Athenians were not informed of subsequent events (6.2–3). Then, with pointed brevity, the messenger (at his arrival) 'found the men killed' (ηὖρε τοὺς ἄνδρας διεφθαρμένους, 6.3).

The author's interest in these errands stands in stark contrast to the curt, summarizing tone of the immediately following final sentence (6.4). 'And after this the Athenians marched with an army into Plataea, brought in grain, and left a garrison there; and they evacuated the men least fit for military service together with the women and children (καὶ μετὰ ταῦτα οἱ Ἀθηναῖοι στρατεύσαντες ἐς Πλάταιαν σῖτόν τε ἐσήγαγον καὶ φρουροὺς ἐγκατέλιπον, τῶν τε ἀνθρώπων τοὺς ἀχρειοτάτους ξὺν γυναιξὶ καὶ παισὶν ἐξεκόμισαν).' There is no particular emphasis, no especially detailed description in the presentation of these events though they must be thought of as taking place over a period of many days, at least. Bare, sober facts are all that is necessary for a full account of the remaining events at Plataea.

Is this description of the messengers' errands important for the subsequent course of the war (or even for the later fate of Plataea)? Scarcely: the factor that is decisive for future events, the murder of the prisoners, had already been related (5.7).

Is it possible—one might imagine this question being raised—that Thucydides the 'Athenian' wishes to cleanse his countrymen of the charge of acquiescing in the murder of the prisoners? This too can be eliminated, since it would be an isolated case.[4]

If the account of the messengers and their errands has no significance for our understanding of the original historical context, then we must look elsewhere for its function.

From the description of the unsuccessful attack there first arises the impression that Thucydides is primarily interested in describing the causes for the failure of a well-conceived plan. We began by pointing out the significance of the non-factual side of planning for Thucydides' account, and we discerned in the description of the course of events a detailed comparison of plan and execution.

This interest seems justified in itself, because the defeat must come as something of a surprise to any outside observer, not merely to the attackers who were so well prepared. It is understandable that the relation between theory and practice has here become a problem for Thucydides.

We can pick out from his careful analysis those factors which caused the failure. The Thebans themselves make the first mistake in believing both that they can reach 'peace through understanding' in a city which has just been seized, and that the co-operative attitude of the Plataean negotiators is a result of this very Theban conduct rather than of surprise and fear. It is precisely the resulting deception, which is of course primarily self-deception, that makes possible the sequel.

The second factor (the rains) is obviously unforeseeable—because it lies outside the realm of human causality—although the Thebans had intended to account even for the unforeseeable.

A third point—now after the defeat—is that the Thebans, though already once deceived, spoil also the last chance of at least saving those of their people that have survived the attack.

These factors, together with the elements of the original plan (and their surprising appearance in the Plataean counterplan), would suffice as a causal explanation of the unexpected events that result. But the author does not confine himself to the causal context.

Together with the actual events the reader receives an impression of the parties involved and of their attitudes towards the events. This impression is produced by the depiction of motives (long-standing enmity, personal ambition) and human behavior (the inconsistency of the Thebans, reactions and counter-reactions, responding to the breaking of the peace with two breaches of treaty and murder). From the interweaving of the tiniest details (psychological as well as concrete) the reader also has an impression of a complexity which in its dimensions seems to transcend an orientation according to mere facts and an organizational schema.

The narrative emphasis is concentrated on three points: the desperate situation of the attackers under attack; the late arrival of the relief force hastening to the rescue; the late arrival of the messenger whose message would have meant salvation for the prisoners. This is a climactically arranged series of pictures showing the progressively hopeless situation of the invaders. The messenger who arrives 'too late'—who seems practically superfluous from a historical perspective and would be more at home in the realm of Tragedy—makes the essential point clear: something 'irreparable', an ἀνήκεστον—to use Thucydides' own word[5]—has happened. Moreover, as closer inspection reveals, this is true for *both* sides. For the Thebans the result of their high-flown plan is something far worse than mere (even though entirely unexpected) failure: even more unexpected is the experience, connected with the failure, of the loss arising from the death of 300 of their men. This is an experience which will later become transformed into an argument *against* any form of mercy or compassion (3.67.3). This in turn touches the other side: the murder of the prisoners must make the Thebans hate the Plataeans irreconcilably (which would not have been the case in the event of a simple military defeat), i.e. it will produce a backlash for the Plataeans' own situation by eliciting further bloodshed.

It is therefore the irrevocable character of the event, which can never be cancelled out or reversed, that most interests Thucydides, and it is the function of the account of the messengers to give this feature prominence.

The question arises why the author chose precisely this point in the work, a point relatively far removed from the larger events of the war, to expand upon the perspective of irrevocable failure, a perspective which is certainly evident in the factual sphere as well. In other words, it is a question of the compositional context of the Plataean narrative.

The interpretation of the attack on Plataea has always been connected—to little advantage—with the chronological problem of the beginning of the war.[6] Scholars have repeatedly found it necessary to speak of a contradiction in Thucydides' account: does he consider the attack on Plataea or the first invasion of Attica as the beginning of the war?[7] Since the literary perspective has yielded so completely to the discussion of chronology, it will be well to remember Jacoby's admonition not to speak of late (in the Analysts' sense) 'Überarbeitung' ('revision') when the historian seems to speak of different dates for the beginning of the war, but rather to look for compositional reasons for the special place held by the attack on Plataea (between the account of events prior to the war and the account of the war proper).[8]

This way of putting the problem seems promising: the story of Plataea belongs neither to the war nor to its prehistory, but has characteristics in common with both.

In Book 1 we saw the great projections and warnings as well as optimistic plans. On both sides those in favor of war carried the day, and—at least as far as was humanly possible to calculate—it was the Athenian prospects and hopes for victory that seemed on the surest footing. And *immediately before* the story of Plataea stands Pericles' strategy with its proud enumeration of Athenian reserves (1.140–4).

A connective thread is easily drawn. The Thebans, too, have prepared their surprise raid as thoroughly as humanly possible and included reserves in their plan (and this calculation, which precedes the undertaking in terms of time, plays a large role in the narrative). Nevertheless—because of their own shortsightedness and external circumstances—they fail in such a way that the original deliberating categories of plan and success (or failure) are no longer sufficient for describing the debacle.

The general relation to the subsequent history of the war is simple: Plataea is the first military action. Thus the second part of the narrative, that which describes the fighting, forms a natural introduction to the events of the war.

Moreover, in the factual realm the attack has a kind of releasing effect.[9] A striking rupture of the existing state of peace, it vigorously stimulates the efforts of both sides to arm themselves.

And finally, the matter-of-fact brutality of the event stands in stark contrast to the subsequent description of the war-happy mood throughout Greece (2.8). 'Neither side had anything small in mind' (8.1), each individual believed it his duty to do his part (8.4). It is emphatic (and sounds rather like bitter irony) when the author confirms from his own later perspective the judgment of the optimistic speakers in Book 1 (Athenians 78.3; Corinthians 120.5; Pericles 140.1): 'For when starting out everyone strives more keenly.' He adds by way of explanation: 'There was also at that time a large number of young men in the Peloponnese, a large number on the other side in Athens who went into the war *not unwillingly because of their inexperience*' (8.1).

We have grasped an element of Thucydides' compositional technique when we recognize that this last thought also comes from Book 1. This is the same attitude with which the cautioner Archidamus opens his speech: 'I myself have *experienced* many wars already…and I see that my agemates among you are in the same position, so that none of you is eager [ἐπιθυμῆσαι] for war as a result of *inexperience,* as is doubtless the case with the *multitude…*' (80.1).

Evidently one can start a war lightheartedly only out of inexperience. For the best strategist—as a result of his limited perspective—can miss important factors because they are either unpredictable or unimaginable. And the real consequences of such a neglected factor can in turn surpass all imagination.

We are probably justified in saying that the author has deliberately juxtaposed the costly (for the Thebans) first experience of this war with the inexperienced eagerness of the youth of Greece. (Consider also the fact that at 2.8 the catalog of states entering the war follows immediately upon the description of the mood in Greece: Chapters 7–9, as it were, describe the deployment for war.)

This result, I believe, speaks to the artistic (and intellectual) goals of Thucydides. Between the prehistory and the history of the war (one might also say, between theory and practice, between blueprints and concrete execution) he finds—without abandoning the self-imposed order of strict chronology—a point in time where he can *in nuce* hint at the broad variation and complexity of the courses of events (together with the irrevocability of their results) as they fall out in this war. In so doing he at once looks backwards and forwards and creates a kind of frame.

Thus, the significance of the Plataean episode is to be found in its exemplary quality. Even a small, apparently marginal event can—at least for a time[10]—become for Thucydides representative of that dimension which lies beyond the merely factual, beyond what is determined by mere causality and chronology, in that realm where we find the most telling effects for humanity. The story of Plataea anticipates an experience of which the rest of Greece has no premonition, and into which it is, in its lack of premonition, plunging.

Notes

[1] See Ludwig's (1952, 43 f.) fine remarks on this.

[2] On this term, cf. the events around Pylos and Sphakteria, 4.3 ff. (the second series of events investigated in Chapter 7) as well as the reversals in the Sicilian War (Chapter 10).

[3] This is according to the version that Thucydides received from Theban sources. Plataean witnesses assured him, as he adds, probably not without irony, that the Plataeans had sworn no oath and had agreed not to the release of the prisoners but only to 'negotiations'. Is it likely that the Theban army would actually have given up its human collateral in exchange for the mere prospect of 'negotiations'?

[4] See, for instance, his candid report on the Athenian generals' complicity in a massacre on Corcyra (4.47 f.).

[5] In a comparable context the Spartan ambassadors at Athens warn against an ἀνήκεστον: 4.20.1 (Chapter 7).

[6] Schwartz 1929², 36; Pohlenz 1920, 60; Jacoby 1929; Gomme *ad* 2.1, 19.1, 22.1.

[7] Even the latest contribution (Lendle 1964), characterized as it is by perceptive and penetrating analysis, takes this contradiction for granted.

Some considerations on this point: Thucydides' τεκμήριον for the beginning of the state of war is that point in time when contact between states takes place exclusively through the medium of κήρυκες, agents whose persons are sacrosanct according to international wartime law. A war thus ceases with the conclusion of a treaty ending this state (σπονδαί, 5.20.1, etc.).

At 1.146 Thucydides implicitly disagrees with the theoretical objection that the period of αἰτίαι καὶ διαφοραί could scarcely be called peacetime. His answer: ἐπεμείγνυντο δὲ ὅμως…ἀκηρύκτως μέν, ἀνυπόπτως δὲ οὔ. Mere suspicion is not equivalent to a state of war.

The attack on Plataea puts the state of war into effect everywhere and is thus the factor which triggers the war: οὔτε ἐπεμείγνυντο ἔτι ἀκηρυκτεί (2.1).

The fact that general campaigning (the πόλεμος in the larger sense) does not begin at this moment does not alter the date of the beginning of the war, as set according to practices of international law.

On the other hand, the first clash between the great powers (the Peloponnesian invasion of Attica) has the same incisive significance for the factual course of the war. The Spartans feel that this invasion means τὸν πόλεμον ἄρασθαι φανερῶς, 1.125.2—just as the cessation of peace-time diplomatic forms was the *legal* beginning of the war.

Thucydides carefully distinguishes and points out the actual outbreak of hostilities and the legal beginning of the war, 2.1:

(a) legal: relations from here on maintained exclusively through heralds;

(b) factual: after the (chronologically later) initiation of campaigning (καταστάντες, scil. ἐς τὸν πόλεμον, = invasion of Attica, cf. 2.13.9: ὅτε ἡ ἐσβολή…ἔμελλε…ἔσεσθαι καὶ ἐς τὸν πόλεμον καθίσταντο) no interruption of hostilities.

(a) is chronologically specified at 2.2.1;

(b) is solemnly marked at the appropriate place in the factual account (ἡγεῖτο δὲ Ἀρχίδαμος ὁ Ζευξιδάμου…, 19.1).

Similarly, the text distinguishes between the legal and the factual *end* of the war:

(a) factual: 5.12, 13: cessation of hostilities 14.1: ὥστε πολέμου μὲν μηδὲν ἔτι ἅψασθαι μηδετέρους…

(b) legal: 5.18–19: the treaty
        20: the moment of the conclusion, reference to 2.1.

Must this distinction between the legal state of war (= crucial point in the chronology, i.e. the scientific-methodological perspective) and the factual course of hostilities (= theme— cf. 1.1.1 ὡς ἐπολέμησαν πρὸς ἀλλήλους—or content to be understood through the methodological system of coordinates) signify a discrepancy or even force us to assume the existence of two conceptions of the writer?

[8] Jacoby 1929, 4; Berve (1938, 26) had already seen in the detailed description of the attack a relationship to the larger developments of the war.

[9] Cf. Ludwig 1952, 47.

[10] I once again draw attention to the sudden descent from the stylistic highpoint (after 2.6.3) into the sphere of the bare chronicle.

5

PLAN AND REALITY
Book 2

It is not only the Thebans who are surprised in Book 2 to learn that things do not always add up as expected.

King Archidamus, now field marshal in a war he did not want, likewise must have the experience of action which only brings *near* success. His original suggestion (1.82.4; cf. 2.18.5) had been to spare Attica (i.e. the only point in Athens' defenses vulnerable to attack) as a 'hostage' so as not, by devastating the countryside, entirely to deprive the Athenians of any interest in a peaceful settlement. Accordingly, he now attempts negotiation one last time before giving his troops the signal to invade. Thucydides, recalling 1.23 directly before the beginning of the action, lets the rebuffed Spartan envoy pronounce the fact that the die is once and for all cast as he crosses the Attic border. 'This day will be the beginning of great misfortunes for the Greeks' (2.12.3).[1]

However, Archidamus hesitates once more—this is evidently where the mistake in his calculations occurs—to proceed into the Attic heartland and as a result is criticized by his own men (18.3, 5). For his hesitancy gives the Athenians the opportunity meanwhile to remove the populace and all their moveable property from the fields (18.3; cf. 14.1), a fact which decisively weakens a key element in his plan.

For when the Spartan king at last takes action, he relies on provoking the Athenians to a pitched battle (the superiority of the Peloponnesian troops in land engagements is always considered a given) by ravaging, practically under the very eyes of the Athenians, the territory of that *demos* which supplies the strongest contingent of the Athenian army (2.20).

Quite consistently with his earlier expression of confidence in his own age and experience, he now counts upon the restlessness and inexperience especially of the numerically strong youthful contingent of the Athenian army (20.2 ~ 21.2). He also reckons that because the Athenians are more accustomed to giving than to receiving blows (11.8) they will lose their nerve. As he had said already with clear reference to the Athenians in his speech at the beginning of the campaign, καὶ οἱ λογισμῷ ἐλάχιστα χρώμενοι θυμῷ πλεῖστα ἐς ἔργον καθίστανται ('and those who under the influence of emotion use reason least turn to action most', 11.7).

It clearly is the historian's opinion that this plan, skillfully based as it is on the psychology of the Athenians, would have had a devastating effect on the warplan of Pericles at an earlier point of time when people and possessions were still out in the fields. This view is communicated by Thucydides' brilliant description of the mood inside the city (21–2).

The Athenians' attitude is anything but rational. At first they had entertained hopes for the safety of the territory nearer the city for the absurd reason that fourteen years earlier the Spartan king Pleistoanax had halted just inside the Attic border (21.1). Now, when events fall out just as Pericles had predicted (2.13.2; 1.143.5), they consider him an incompetent general (2.21.3) because he alone insists upon keeping to the plan as laid out previously. The picture of the general mood is rounded out with a description of oracle mongers and their willing listeners as well as of unofficial gatherings that spark heated debates over the pros and cons of a sortie. Grotesquely, Pericles can accomplish his intention only by attempting to prevent assemblies of any kind, i.e. by completely avoiding public appearances. He allows the people to vent their frustrated anger only in the previously planned retaliatory excursion against the Peloponnese (23.2; cf. 1.143.4).

As Thucydides represents the situation, there is no doubt that Archidamus' plan comes very near to succeeding and that its failure is at least partly due to his own hesitation.[2]

On the other hand, Pericles can hardly claim for himself a brilliant success merely because the Athenians, in the end, do not actually take the field.

This inference is important because Thucydides deliberately suggests it to his reader. He does not give so thorough a representation of anti-Periclean feeling in Athens merely to show the effects of Archidamus' plan, but also because this situation constitutes the first *test case* for Pericles' plan.

Pericles had lobbied for war with confidence *even though* he had been aware (καίπερ εἰδώς, 1.140.1; cf. 144.1) that men's mood during wartime differs from its initial enthusiasm, and he had from the first held out the possibility of Attica's being ravaged (143.5). But if people abandon their plan under circumstances that have been foreseen (καὶ ὧν παρήνεσε πρότερον ἐμέμνηντο οὐδέν, 2.21.3), what will they do when the unexpected happens?

Pericles had advised his Athenians that events in the factual realm can move just as unpredictably (or 'foolishly') as the fluctuations of human attitudes.[3] 'This is also why we tend to blame chance whenever something turns out contrary to our expectation' (δι' ὅπερ καὶ τὴν τύχην, ὅσα ἂν παρὰ λόγον ξυμβῇ, εἰώθαμεν αἰτιᾶσθαι, 1.140.1). One has understood this last sentence—in the sense of Democritus fr. 119—as a rejection of the 'vulgar habit of thought' which makes excuses by equating subjective human miscalculation (παρὰ λόγον) with objective chance (τύχη).[4] This, of course, helped to retain that other well-known equation Pericles = Thucydides and could be explained to mean that in this passage Thucydides was *a priori* excusing or perhaps exonerating Pericles from responsibility for certain misfortunes because he had planned for them in such a way as to be safe from chance.[5]

However, Pericles' enlightening metaphor merely makes clear to his audience the fact that, besides the disruptive element of human senselessness, there is also a kind of 'senselessness' in the course of events which is normally called chance. In other words, he at this point is *not* attempting to cancel out the problem of chance in the same sense as Democritus.

It is, however, clear from the subsequent speech (1.141.2 ff.) that he *does* believe he has armed himself with certain contingency plans against political or military accidents caused by chance, but it is also quite clear that he has in mind only accidents of the type explicitly mentioned in that speech.

But it is part of the very nature of the accidental that it does not confine itself to the realm of the expected or of previous calculation, and Thucydides, unlike many of his speakers, is fully conscious of this. The chance in question here is the appearance of the plague-like epidemic in Athens.

It is important to realize at the outset that the epidemic in the end represents more than merely the test case for Pericles' second consideration (the one touching upon the behavior of human beings in unforeseen circumstances, i.e. in a 'senseless' turn of events). The fact alone that the detailed description of the plague and its demoralizing consequences follows immediately upon the Funeral Oration, in which Pericles develops his ideal picture of Athens and its citizens, is compositionally important and gives the so-called plague chapters a broader scope, if not the character of a corrective. Moreover, it has never been doubted that Thucydides found the disease and its effects worth describing for their own sake.

There is a sentence from Pericles' Funeral Oration which is of particular interest to us in the present context. The inconsistency of the Athenians' reaction to the Peloponnesian invasion would seem to confirm Archidamus' judgment.[6] But Pericles states that his Athenians are capable of making sound political decisions and do not consider preliminary speeches (i.e. consideration) detrimental to action, but on the contrary believe it harmful to act without first being properly advised (2.40.2).

This means that Pericles is still, *after* the recent experience brought on by the first Peloponnesian invasion, attempting to maintain a view that characterizes the Athenians' attitude as rational. It must therefore prove the more dangerous should an accident 'strike' (cf. ἐγκατασκῆψαι, 2.47.3), which might transport the viewpoints of action and preliminary advice into a completely different arena.

Then there occurs what Pericles (1.140.1), like the other speakers of Book 1, believed he had taken into consideration and what, under the changed circumstances (αἰσθάνομαι γὰρ τὰς αἰτίας, 60.1), he would even have to expect: the Athenians ἠλλοίωντο[7] τὰς γνώμας ('changed their minds', 59.1). In conjunction with the two expected disadvantages of war and invasion (59.1), the plague creates a situation in which the people now *actually abandon their plan* and *even undertake peace negotiations* with the enemy (59.2).

Despite Pericles' efforts to comfort and reassure his audience by interpreting the plague as the 'only' factor disturbing to the original calculation (πρᾶγμα μόνον δὴ τῶν πάντων ἐλπίδος κρεῖσσον γεγενημένον, 64.1), even as an act of the gods (2), he cannot restrain the effects which this chance occurrence has on human nature. The Athenians do not rest until they have fined and removed him from office (65.3f.; cf. 59.3; Plato, *Gorg.* 516a2).

One might also express the result in terms of familiar categories of interpretation, thus: the ἀνθρωπεία φύσις, which up to now seemed controllable, through one single case of unpredictable τύχη has itself become an unpredictable 'factor'.

Thucydides himself had already remarked that during the course of the war it (ἀνθρωπεία φύσις) would display behavior (one could also say 'react' to circumstances) different from that at its beginning (2.8.1). The question of 'when' must apparently remain open since the answer depends on incalculable elements.

It should be worthwhile to look at certain statements in the so-called plague chapters from this perspective. In my opinion it is not sensible to dismiss the importance of this passage by arguing that the disease was not 'decisive for the war's outcome' (on the grounds that the city had recovered from it by 415,[8] 6.26.2), or that Pericles was soon re-elected. Against these objections—both of which have more to do with Pericles' military considerations than with Thucydides' own categories—one may ask why Thucydides might have given such weight to his description, which goes far beyond what is specifically of medical interest.

A remark such as πρῶτόν τε ἦρξε καὶ ἐς τἆλλα τῇ πόλει ἐπὶ πλέον ἀνομίας τὸ νόσημα ('and for the city the disease for the first time started lawlessness on a wider scale also in all other areas', 53.1) by itself shows that the effects of the plague are by no means neutralized by biological and military recovery alone (in a new generation's coming of age). On the contrary, this sentence suggests that the disease saps Athens' strength from a perspective which had not found a place among the original planning categories of military and financial power or potential numbers of men at arms, namely, the human factor.

This is precisely the kernel of Thucydides' description and where he proves himself once again a brilliant observer of human behavior. In Chapter 51, directly after the medical report describing the plague's pathology, comes the description of human behavior and suffering.

This is where we find the frivolous and unfounded hope of those who have recovered that, having survived such a disease, they would never succumb to any other illness (51.6); the foolish interpretation of the old oracle which, taking the present for its only standard, prefers λοιμός over λιμός (54.2–3); similarly, the meaning imputed on the basis of the current situation to the Delphic pronouncement that the god himself would enter the war (54.4).

Thucydides also sees how those affected reinterpret the moral situation on the basis of the altered circumstances (e.g. ...κρίνοντες ἐν ὁμοίῳ καὶ σέβειν καὶ μὴ ἐκ τοῦ πάντας ὁρᾶν ἐν ἴσῳ ἀπολλυμένους, 'they judged worshipping and not worshipping the same when they saw all equally perish', 53.4). The ἄγραφοι νόμοι ('unwritten laws'), to which Pericles had referred as the pride of Athens (37.3), are no longer honored on the grounds of amounting to 'τῷ δόξαντι καλῷ' ('what seemed to be noble').[9] But those who feel shame and an obligation to help are bound to die exactly because of their sense of duty (51.5).

Next to statements such as these, which (except for the last one) emphasize the subjectivity and illogicality of human behavior, we find others that seek to explain the capitulation of human beings before the force of events, because the disease simply overwhelms all human resources: ...χαλεπωτέρως ἢ κατὰ τὴν ἀνθρωπείαν φύσιν προσέπιπτεν ('...(it) befell people with a force too great for human nature', 50.1); τελευτῶντές τε αὐτῶν ἀπέστησαν ὑπὸ τοῦ κακοῦ νικώμενοι ('and in the end they discontinued them (i.e. supplications, etc.) *defeated by the disease*', 47.4); δεινότατον δὲ παντὸς ἦν τοῦ κακοῦ ἥ τε ἀθυμία ὁπότε τις αἴσθοιτο κάμνων... ('but the most terrible part of the whole disease was *the despondency* whenever someone realized that he was sick...' 51.4); ὑπερβιαζομένου γὰρ τοῦ κακοῦ οἱ ἄνθρωποι, οὐκ ἔχοντες ὅτι γένωνται... ('for, since *the disease was overpowering*, the people, not knowing what was to become of them...', 52.3).

79

From all this it is not only clear that the unexpected plague brings unspeakable suffering to the people it affects; rather *it changes the situation as a whole*—in a manner similar to the attack on Plataea—*such that the situation is no longer defined by previously conceived calculations but rather by the unforeseen element.* Here the unexpected even alters the effects of pre-existing conditions (overcrowding of the city due to refugees, 52.1; the Peloponnesian invasions and the general conditions entailed in being at war, 59.1) so that they join its thrust and help to break the last restraints controlling behavior: οἱ Ἀθηναῖοι ἠλλοίωντο τὰς γνώμας.

Seen from a general perspective, then, the plague—which had been the only individual fact mentioned at 1.23 and then primarily with reference to the suffering it had caused—is also an eminently political factor: its effects for the first time undermine the social order even in the area of the ethical norms that constitute the foundation of that order.

Here for the first time are unleashed the forces (πρῶτόν τε ἦρξε καὶ ἐς τἆλλα τῇ πόλει ἐπὶ πλέον ἀνομίας τὸ νόσημα, 'and *for the city* the disease *for the first time started lawlessness* on a wider scale also *in all other areas*', 53.1) of an egoism which is no longer willing to subordinate personal goals to those of the community. In his last speech (cf. 2.60.2–4, 62.3, 63.3, etc.) Pericles tries in vain to rein these forces in (...ἰδίᾳ δὲ τοῖς παθήμασιν ἐλυποῦντο...οὐ μέντοι πρότερον...ἐπαύσαντο...πρὶν ἐζημίωσαν, scil. Περικλέα, '...but *privately* they were troubled by their sufferings...however, they did not stop...until they had imposed a penalty, scil. on Pericles'; simultaneously: removal from office, 65.2–3).

Once set free, this private egoism (κατὰ τὰς ἰδίας φιλοτιμίας καὶ ἴδια κέρδη...τοῖς ἰδιώταις τιμὴ καὶ ὠφελία, 'according to their *private* ambitions and *private* profits...for the *private* persons honor and benefit' 65.7; ὀρεγόμενοι τοῦ πρῶτος ἕκαστος γίγνεσθαι, '*each* striving to become first (in rank)' 65.10; κατὰ τὰς ἰδίας διαβολάς, 'according to their acts of *personal* slander' 65.11) has such a decisive effect on the later course of the war that it constitutes a considerable portion of the explanation for the greatest ἀπροσδόκητον of all, the fall of Athens (...αὐτοὶ ἐν σφίσι κατὰ τὰς ἰδίας διαφορὰς περιπεσόντες ἐσφάλησαν, '...they *themselves*, falling upon each other according to their *personal* quarrels, succumbed' 65.12).

We can follow still further the tension that arises between the projections of Book 1 and the developments that result in Book 2 (the book division seems apt in this case). Through constant references back to the speeches in the first book, Thucydides forces the reader to compare plan with execution, to measure the perspectives of planning against those of the course of events.

This becomes quite clear in the military operations of 429 in north-western Greece. However, even a case such as the Peloponnesian attempt to take Plataea sticks closely to this framework, as is shown by the emphases of the historian's description. To be sure, the narrative of events at Plataea again proves to have details that point far beyond the military action itself.[10] From the formal perspective, the fact that Thucydides employs the rare device of a dialogue (between King Archidamus and the Plataean envoys) underscores this observation.

Wassermann[11] has shown that Archidamus is depicted here in a manner quite consistent with the characteristics that appeared in Book 1: he looks upon the use of force only as a last resort and personally attempts to avoid it for as long as possible.

Accordingly, he first seeks a solution based on Plataean neutrality (71.1), and later (because of the Plataeans' fear of Theban revenge) he suggests a treaty stipulating the surrender of Plataean territory for the duration of the war (72.3).

However, this accommodating offer is *a priori* doomed to failure because the Plataeans *no longer have a free choice:* their women and children are after all (2.6.4, cf. 72.2) in Athens—originally for protection but now as potential hostages. Thucydides further develops this genuinely tragic dilemma by *yet again* adding an account of *messengers* whose efforts, the reader by now must expect, are to prove futile. Archidamus grants an armistice for the time it takes the Plataean envoys to travel to Athens ('ἢν πείθωσιν αὐτούς', 73.1) and back.

The Athenian answer points out for the Plataeans that Athens has never failed them before and will continue to help 'as much as possible' (73.3). Accordingly, the Plataeans decide 'not to betray the Athenians' (74.1)—and thereby assent to their own destruction. There is no doubt that Thucydides, in describing the grounds for their decision, is looking ahead to the non-appearance of the promised Athenian help.

In this way the events at Plataea too have attained a dimension beyond the purely factual realm, a dimension which the historian is at pains to set forth in detail. This small town, which has become a bone of contention between the two great powers, will afford each of them the opportunity to lose face. Athens will not send the help it has promised, and one might ask Sparta how this attack on Plataea, famous for its heroism in the Persian Wars (71.2), is compatible with the slogan 'freedom for Greece'.[12]

But in the middle stand the Plataeans who *in any case,* no matter whose side they take, must lose. If they side with Sparta they expose their women and children to Athenian retaliation; if they side with Athens, they invite the immediate attack of the vastly superior Peloponnesian force. The tragic character of their situation is intensified by the fact that both great powers would for the moment like to avoid the use of violence.

In the following highly detailed description of the Peloponnesian attempts to storm the town, scholars have usually resorted for explanation to military-technical interest on the part of the historian. But here, too, there appear structural elements already familiar to the reader.

Thucydides places the course of events in the light of the Peloponnesian expectation that the united allies, with their unusually powerful[13] army, will take the town in short order (ἐλπίζοντες <u>ταχίστην</u> αἵρεσιν ἔσεσθαι αὐτῶν στρατεύματος <u>τοσούτου</u> ἐργαζομένου, 75.1).

After constructing a palisade wall (75.1), the allies, working forced (ἠνάγκαζον, 75.3) shifts day and night under Spartan leaders, throw up a mound running towards the town. The Plataeans react swiftly by increasing the height of their fortifications at the appropriate place (4), and then devise in addition (ἐπι-νοοῦσιν, 75.6) a means of carrying away the growing mound from beneath by passing through a hole in their fortification wall. But when their opponents make this impossible (through the use of clay and wattle), they undermine the mound itself (76.2). When even this does not seem sufficient to them, being 'few against many' (76.3), they 'devise yet another' measure (προσ-επ-εξηῦρον): they build a second wall, in the shape of a crescent, directly behind the threatened area of the fortification wall (76.3). They are even able to deal successfully with the siege machinery which the Peloponnesians simultaneously bring to bear, with the result that the latter despair of a swift victory—despite the powerful means (cf. ἀπὸ τῶν παρόντων δεινῶν, 77.1) at their disposal. The Peloponnesians thus decide to undertake a complete circumvallation of the town (77.1).

But before this they make one last attempt, fire: πᾶσαν γὰρ δὴ ἰδέαν ἐπενόουν, εἴ πως σφίσιν ἄνευ δαπάνης καὶ πολιορκίας προσαχθείη ('for they were trying to think of any mode if somehow [the city] might be brought under their control without expense and siege' 77.2). Thucydides here refers in a flashback to the initial Peloponnesian hope (cf. ταχίστην, 75.1).

While this last attempt provides the dramatic high point (the greatest fire ever set by human agency), it nonetheless fails—by a hair's breadth—of success: '...and it came very near to destroying the Plataeans, who had survived the earlier attempts.' A rising wind (for which the Peloponnesians were hoping) *would have* sufficed (the past contrary-to-fact construction highlights the critical situation) so that 'they *would not have* escaped'. But instead of wind 'there is said'[14] to have been a storm, which rained out the fire (77.5–6).

82

Only when the Peloponnesians have failed 'in this, too' (78.1), do they abandon their attempts to storm the town and set about laying a proper siege—a project for which they need only 'a portion' of the force they have been using up to now (78.1).

The category in which Thucydides would like the series of unsuccessful storming attempts and successful Plataean countermeasures to be understood is again evidently that of the course of events παρ' ἐλπίδα (though on a smaller scale than the Theban attack). The assembled Peloponnesian army, vastly superior in manpower and material (there are five references to the power discrepancy: 75.1; 76.3; 77.1, 2; 78.4), contrary to expectation fails to storm a relatively small (οὐ μεγάλην, 77.2) town, even though it contains only 480 men-at-arms: 'Altogether there were this many…, and no one else, slave or free, was within the walls' (78.4), records the penultimate sentence of the account, at once looking backward to the unexpected failures of the Peloponnesians and forward to the coming siege.

Another proper test case for the strategic projections described in Book 1 first appears, as mentioned above, during the course of the fighting in the year 429 in north-western Greece. Here is another instance—just as in the description of the Epidamnian conflict and its consequences in Book 1—of Thucydides' ability to give a complete, synoptic picture of a course of events. This conflict too begins on the margin of the Greek world, to some extent among barbarian tribes, and ends, as it were, before the gates of Athens, in the Piraeus.

The prelude is as follows (2.68). The inhabitants of Amphilochian Argos, being in a difficult situation, had taken in their neighbors, the Ampraciots, and the newcomers had subsequently forced the Amphilochians out of their own town. The Amphilochians turned for help to the Acarnanians and these two groups turned together—this phase of the development corresponds to the appearance in Athens of the Corcyreans in Book 1—to Athens. An Athenian naval force under Phormio helped them to regain their town.

The enslavement of the captured Ampraciots by the victorious allies is what brought about the irreconcilable nature of the hostility between the two sides (68.9, perhaps comparable to the Plataeans' execution of their prisoners). Late in the summer of 430 the Ampraciots, together with the Chaonians and joined by some other local, non-Greek tribes, attempted—and failed—to retake Argos.

The next year (2.80 ff.) these two tribes desire to subdue not only Argos but all of Acarnania. Logically enough they ask for Spartan support, using as bait (or, to use the terminology of Book 1, ξυμφέρον 'advantage') the prospect that, in the event of an attack by both land and sea *simultaneously*, there was a good chance of taking not only Acarnania but also Zacynthos, Cephallenia and even the Athenian base at Naupactus (from which Athens was controlling the Corinthian Gulf, and which was useful both for sailing round the Peloponnese and launching attacks on the Peloponnesian coast). The Spartan assent once again escalates the conflict, as in Book 1, to the 'third level'.[15] Corinth, too, is by its ties to the Ampraciots again very much involved (ξυμπροθυμούμενοι μάλιστα, 80.3).

Thucydides' characteristic powers of analysis are in evidence: 1) in the description of how this basically sound strategy disintegrates piece by piece into its component parts; 2) in the tracing of the entire campaign in its sometimes overlapping phases; and 3) in bringing the reader to an understanding of how each of the originally unified parts of the undertaking becomes distinct and independent, developing its own individual impetus and direction.

One of the very first forays violates the decisive condition of the plan, namely, the simultaneity (ἅμα, 80.1) of the land and sea attacks. While the Peloponnesian fleet at Leukas is awaiting the arrival of the contingent from Corinth and vicinity, Knemos, the Spartan commander, manages to transfer his land force across the gulf[16] and join the allied troops without attracting the notice of the twenty Athenian ships patrolling at Naupactus. But now, instead of waiting for the Corinthian ships (or the whole fleet) to arrive (οὐ περιμείνας τὸ ἀπὸ Κορίνθου ναυτικόν, 80.8),[17] he invades Acarnania with the troops at hand and passes Argos by with the intention of making an immediate attack on Stratos, the largest of the Acarnanian cities.

Even so, the situation is not entirely unfavorable, because the coast-dwelling Acarnanians (out of fear of the expected simultaneous (!) invasion, cf. ἅμα, 81.1) do not come inland to help, and because the Athenians (on account of the expected arrival of the ships from Corinth) cannot afford to expose Naupactus.

But the next stage in the splintering of the undertaking follows quickly. The midsection of the army, composed of Chaonians and other barbarians, makes the self-confident (σφίσι τε αὐτοῖς πιστεύοντες, 81.4) decision not to build a camp like the other sections but to march on and win for itself the glory of the conquest (καὶ αὐτῶν τὸ ἔργον γενέσθαι, 81.4).

The Acarnanians, seizing the unexpected opportunity (μεμονωμένων εἰ κρατήσειαν, 5), ambush their opponents. The beaten and fleeing section of the Peloponnesian force, it is true, is received into a united single camp by the remaining two contingents, but there can no longer be any thought of launching an attack. Knemos leads his troops back *southward* κατὰ τάχος ('as fast as possible') and in the end finds himself in Oiniadai—before the invasion has even begun (πρὶν τὴν ξυμβοήθειαν ἐλθεῖν, 'before the allied assistance arrived'). The result: κἀκεῖθεν ἐπ᾽ οἴκου ἀπῆλθον ἕκαστοι ('from there each left for home', 82).

But the invasion never even takes place, due this time to the splintering of the naval force. The Corinthian contingent, ὃ ἔδει παραγενέσθαι τῷ Κνήμῳ, ὅπως μὴ ξυμβοηθῶσιν οἱ ἀπὸ τῆς θαλάσσης ἄνω Ἀκαρνᾶνες, 'which *was to be there* at Knemon's side, lest the Acarnanians from the sea come inland to assist' (it is important to Thucydides that the reader see how the undertaking as a whole falls into single phases), οὐ παραγίγνεται *'was not there'* (83.1).

In the meantime the 47-ship fleet on its way from Corinth and vicinity has been decisively defeated by the 20 Athenian patrol ships stationed at Naupactus, although the Corinthians (their admirals are specifically named) had not thought the Athenians daring enough to attack them (οὐκ ἂν οἰόμενοι πρὸς ἑπτὰ καὶ τεσσαράκοντα ναῦς τὰς σφετέρας τολμῆσαι τοὺς Ἀθηναίους εἴκοσι ταῖς ἑαυτῶν ναυμαχίαν ποιήσασθαι, 83.3).

There should be no doubt that Thucydides intends the disappointment of Corinthian expectations to be understood in the context of the last prewar speech of the Corinthians (μιᾷ τε νίκῃ ναυμαχίας κατὰ τὸ εἰκὸς ἁλίσκονται, scil. οἱ Ἀθηναῖοι, 'and they are likely to be ruined by a single victory in a naval battle', 1.121.4; cf. above p. 55). There is a certain irony in the events arising from the fact that in their prewar speech the Corinthians were speaking of a sea battle delivered by themselves, whereas when the fight actually takes place they are not prepared (οὐχ ὡς ἐπὶ ναυμαχίᾳ...παρεσκευασμένοι) and would gladly have stolen past the Athenian ships under cover of darkness (83.3).

The reference to the last speech of the Corinthians in Book 1 is likely to have provided the motive for the highly detailed description of the battle itself. This description shows—as de Romilly has demonstrated[18]— that the Athenian attack is carried out without the slightest deviation from Phormio's plan. Even the wind that rises regularly just before dawn (and is unknown to the Corinthians) forms a definite element in his plan (84.2–3).

Here, then, Athens' superiority on the sea seems clearly demonstrated, and Pericles' expectations[19] about the course of the war seem justified in practice.

But it is precisely this *clear-cut* case that (similarly to the way in which the Poteideatika arise from the Kerkyraika)[20] becomes the *occasion* for the development of a *complex* series of events.

The impulse arises from the *incapacity* of the Spartans to recognize that the loss of the sea battle is due to the experience and technical superiority of the Athenian fleet (85.2).

It is exactly their inexperience in matters of naval warfare, however, which gives the Peloponnesians the courage to make a second attempt. They see the cause of their defeat as a lack of energy (γεγενῆσθαι δέ τινα μαλακίαν) and angrily (ὀργῇ) send Knemos two 'advisors' to prevent this lack of energy from recurring.

The first measure undertaken by the advisors is an enlargement of the fleet, which now, after all, does constitute a serious threat for the small Athenian force.

Phormio, expressing his concern that he must reckon *daily* with the possibility of a Peloponnesian attack, requests immediate reinforcements from Athens (85.4). The Athenians provide the reinforcements but send them first on a special mission involving a detour to Crete. The delay allowed for by the Athenians as a result of this mission (which does not produce the desired result) is lengthened by a *chance* occurrence: unfavorable weather around Crete keeps the squadron *'for no short time'* (85.6). This is the point at which—similarly to 83.1 above—the course of events starts to become independent, i.e. gets out of control. Thucydides again emphasizes the 'hinge' in the events (86.1): the Peloponnesian fleet leaves unmolested from Kyllene to its battle position at Panormos on the Achaean coast ἐν τούτῳ, ἐν ᾧ οἱ Ἀθηναῖοι περὶ Κρήτην κατείχοντο.

Moreover, both fleets lie opposite each other for *six* or *seven* days with no sign of the reinforcements for Phormio and they use the time to make preparations for the coming battle: they *practice* maneuvers (which of course applies especially to the Peloponnesians) (μελετῶντές τε καὶ ...παρα-σκευαζόμενοι, 86.5).

Thucydides has very likely emphasized this freedom of movement for the Peloponnesians because it is here that a situation arises which Pericles had thought impossible: πῶς δὴ ἄνδρες γεωργοὶ καὶ οὐ θαλάσσιοι, καὶ προσέτι οὐδὲ μελετῆσαι ἐασόμενοι διὰ τὸ ὑφ᾿ ἡμῶν πολλαῖς ναυσὶν αἰεὶ ἐφορμεῖσθαι, ἄξιον ἄν τι δρῷεν; ('How could men do something worthwhile who farm the land and don't go to sea, and who furthermore *won't even have a chance to practice* because of being *blockaded by us at all times with many ships?'* (1.142.7). Later on (§ 8) Pericles allows that the Peloponnesians might pluck up the courage of inexperience in order to face a small blockading fleet (cf. 2.85.2), but insists that, under pressure of the superior number of Athenian ships, they would remain inactive and, due to lack of practice, they would be clumsier and therefore more hesitant to engage.

But it is precisely this premise of numerical superiority which is lacking in the present circumstances—due to bad weather in Cretan waters. Thus Pericles' statement (1.142.6 f.), which seemed confirmed by the first clash, is rendered dubious by a subsequent development—one, in fact, which is a result of the first case.

The Spartans want to provoke battle quickly, πρίν τι καὶ ἀπὸ τῶν Ἀθηναίων ἐπιβοηθῆσαι ('before some aid arrived from Athens', 86.6). The two speeches which Thucydides inserts before the description of the second battle[21] show to what a point of crisis the situation has escalated since the outbreak of hostilities in Amphilochian Argos (which has now quite disappeared from the account).

Speakers on both sides have difficulty encouraging their crews to fight. The Peloponnesians are afraid because of their recent defeat, the Athenians because of their current numerical inferiority.[22]

The close relationship (as indicated by verbal allusions) between the speeches and the subsequent battle description has been demonstrated by de Romilly.[23] However, her conclusion ('grâce à elles [scil., les harangues militaires] le récit de bataille, reposant sur un certain nombre de grands thèmes plus ou moins connus antérieurement, se dégage…avec l'évidence d'une démonstration' ['thanks to them (scil. the military speeches) the narration of the battle, based upon a certain number of grand themes which are more or less known beforehand, emerges…with the clarity of a demonstration'])[24] seems debatable, since the categories of observation employed by the speakers on both sides (even of both sides taken together) fall short of those of Thucydides' narrative account.

This is particularly clear in the case of the explanation given by the Peloponnesian generals for the first defeat (87.1–3). They still now repeat reasons which Thucydides himself has already invalidated through reference to the Athenians' long-time practical experience (85.1–2).

According to the Peloponnesian generals, the battle had not been properly prepared for (τῇ…παρασκευῇ ἐνδεής 87.2 ~ ἄλλην ναυμαχίαν βελτίω παρασκευάζεσθαι 85.1); chance, too, (τὰ ἀπὸ τῆς τύχης) had been against them. The latter can only refer to the wind that Phormio had made a part of his plan and which had thrown the Peloponnesian fleet into such confusion.[25] In other words, the Spartans *interpret an element of the opponent's plan*, which is not recognized as such, *as objective chance*. It would scarcely be possible to express more clearly the limited perspective of a human being attempting to analyse events in which he is himself involved.

This is also true of the ensuing admission that lack of experience had 'presumably somewhat contributed' (καὶ πού τι καί) to the defeat. Thucydides himself had presented this as the *main* reason (…ἡ ἀπειρία πρῶτον ναυμαχοῦντας 87.2 ~ οὐκ ἀντιτιθέντες τὴν Ἀθηναίων ἐκ πολλοῦ ἐμπειρίαν… 85.2).

The Peloponnesian generals thus base their confidence on numerical superiority and on improved preparation (87.4–6) for the second battle (in addition to routine assumptions about the courage and bravery of Peloponnesian troops). 'Thus we cannot find one single point in which we are likely (εἰκότως!) to lose. Even all our previous mistakes will now, by being factored in, themselves be a lesson' (7).

Readiness to learn from mistakes is something rarely found in Thucydides' personages. In this case the trait is made dubious by the problem of whether the speakers have accurately assessed the situation (that is also, their mistakes).

On the other side, Phormio attempts to raise Athenian spirits by refuting the arguments of the Peloponnesian generals[26] and by developing his own strategy. He believes it important not to be lured into the narrows, because this would prevent the kind of maneuvering which forms the basis of Athenian naval superiority (89.8). But it is this very plan which the Peloponnesians will foil.

Of course in one point Phormio's speech does do the situation justice: he recognizes the enormity of the risk. In other words, Thucydides is here announcing that a test situation for the plans of Book 1 is imminent: ὁ δὲ ἀγὼν μέγας ὑμῖν, ἢ καταλῦσαι Πελοποννησίων τὴν ἐλπίδα τοῦ ναυτικοῦ ἢ ἐγγυτέρω καταστῆσαι Ἀθηναίοις τὸν φόβον περὶ τῆς θαλάσσης ('But the struggle is of great consequence for you: *either to end the Peloponnesians' hope for their navy* or to bring closer to the Athenians the fear for the sea', 89.10). This phrase shows where the apparently marginal conflict over Amphilochian Argos has led: the Peloponnesians are now primarily aiming at a sea victory against Athens rather than an attack on Argos or Acarnania.[27] This battle (quite different from the first, and from the Corinthian point of view, undesirable engagement) is essentially a challenge to Athens' claim to be undisputed mistress of the sea. In other words, this is an appropriate situation to serve as a touchstone both for Pericles' overall strategy (1.142.7–8)[28] and for the Corinthian assessment of probability (1.121.4).[29]

It may be difficult for the modern reader to view an engagement of 77 Peloponnesian ships against 20 Athenian ships as a true test of Attic naval superiority. But one would do well to keep in mind first Pericles' claim (1.142.7) that every Peloponnesian fleet would *at all times* be facing a numerically superior Athenian blockade, and second, that still 17 years later a single defeat would rob the Spartans of all confidence in their own ability to fight at sea (8.11.3). Thus the success which is at issue here is largely also a psychological one, in which questions of number and strength play a smaller part than a 'victory' of whatever stamp.

The battle itself causes deviations from the plans of *both* sides.

Phormio is forced (by a Peloponnesian feint in the direction of the exposed Naupactus) into the dreaded narrows. Thucydides thus shows how the plan, set out previously in such detail (89.8–9), is turned on its head (τὸν δὲ ἀγῶνα <u>οὐκ ἐν τῷ κόλπῳ ἑκὼν εἶναι</u> ποιήσομαι <u>οὐδ' ἐσπλεύσομαι</u> ἐς αὐτόν 89.8 ~ ὁ δὲ…φοβηθεὶς περὶ τῷ χωρίῳ ἐρήμῳ ὄντι…<u>ἄκων</u>…ἔπλει παρὰ τήν γῆν 90.3, cf. ἐντὸς τοῦ κόλπου, 4).[30] Eleven of his ships do escape the Peloponnesian encirclement and reach the open sea, but the others are driven ashore and put out of action. Some are even towed away by the victorious Peloponnesians (90.5–6).

All but one of the remaining eleven escape their 20 swift pursuers into Naupactus' harbor and lie there at anchor near the temple of Apollo, bows facing outward, with the intention of fending off a possible landing attempt of the enemy (ἢν ἐς τὴν γῆν ἐπὶ σφᾶς πλέωσιν, 91.1). In other words, the battle at *sea*, as far as they are concerned, is over (and of course lost).

But now comes an amazing turn of events (91.3–92.2) which amounts to a complete *metabole* of the situation and which is somewhat comparable to the reversal suffered by the victorious Thebans in Plataea. As chance would have it, there is a merchant vessel lying off Naupactus (ἔτυχε δὲ ὁλκὰς ὁρμοῦσα μετέωρος, 91.3; the reader observes the emphasizing first-word position of ἔτυχε ['it "chanced" to be lying off…'] cf. 6.102.2b; 7.2.4). The last of the fleeing Athenian ships sails around this vessel and rams and sinks its nearest pursuer, a ship from Leukas.

The suddenly detailed account—as in the description of the attackers under attack in Plataea or the depiction of the confusion caused by the wind in the first sea battle—indicates to the reader the arrival of a *critical point* in the course of events. This event, which was 'unexpected *and* contrary-to-calculation' (γενομένου…ἀπροσδοκήτου <u>τε καὶ</u> παρὰ λόγον, 91.4),[31] puts fear into the Peloponnesians as they sail up in victorious mood (ὡς νενικηκότες, 2) and thus in poor order (ἀτάκτως διώκοντες διὰ τὸ κρατεῖν, 4), which causes some to halt (to wait for those who follow), others to run aground out of ignorance of the area (αἱ μὲν…αἱ δέ).

The Athenians—as usual, Thucydides highlights the reaction and counter-reaction—take renewed courage from this turn of events and drive towards the momentarily unprepared foe. The latter, 'on account of the recent wrong turns *and* their present disorder' (92.1), put up a short resistance and soon flee towards Panormos. The Athenian victory is complete when the Athenians not only capture six enemy ships but regain their own as well.

The Peloponnesian fleet—fearing the arrival of the Athenian reinforcements—even withdraws under cover of night as far as Corinth (except for the ships from Leukas). 'And the Athenians from Crete, with the 20 ships that should have arrived for Phormio *before* the battle, arrived not much later than the retreat of the ships at Naupactus' (92.7).

With this last sentence the author has followed the fragmentation of the whole undertaking to its final individual action. What is emphasized is that the squadron arrives *shortly* after the battle and thus could 'almost' have joined the attack. In literary terms this statement is a reference to 85.6–86.1 and the observation at 86.5 that the two fleets lay at anchor opposite each other for six or seven days without engaging. At the end Thucydides thus once again underscores the difference between 'what should have happened' and 'what really happened'—an aspect of the whole course of events which has been essential since Knemos' first move.

It seems useful, in the light of this distinction, to look again at the second sea battle in which both Phormio's plan and the Peloponnesian commanders' probability-calculations (εἰκότως, 87.7) are brought to nothing by the actual course of events. De Romilly's[32] interpretation runs thus: a slight element of chance (ἔτυχε, 91.3) restores the 'normal' state of affairs (i.e. Athens' experience-based naval superiority and Peloponnesian incapacity to fight at sea), thus justifying after the fact Phormio's plan, which had been based upon 'normal' battle conditions: '(Thucydide)...donnait le résultat final comme plus nécessaire que fortuit' ('[Thucydides]...presents the final result more as necessary than as accidental').

I can hardly agree with this interpretation. If one considers the battle in the larger context of events after the fighting in Argos and the developments—unforeseen by any of the persons involved—proceeding from that occurrence; if one in addition traces Thucydides' interest in 'hinges' and crisis points in the course of events; if one further thinks of the limited perspective evident in the Peloponnesian generals' analysis of the situation; and finally if one adds the references to the forecasts of Book 1, then in my opinion everything points in the same direction (and with this result fits well also the discrepancy between Phormio's plan—described in detail at 2.89.8—and the actual events of the battle): the relationship of plan to success is problematic for this historian, and he *wants* (partly through stylistic means, at least by sharper focus on certain decisive details) *to make his reader aware of this problem*.

In addition, chance (being among those factors which are decisive for this course of events as a whole) performs a distinct function in the narrative of the second naval engagement (I remind my reader of the emphatic syntactical position of ἔτυχε at 91.3). If we do not limit our interpretation of the events to the last engagement and the speeches directly preceding it, but rather observe the chain of cause and effect prevailing between the individual phases as worked out by the historian, then to the chance event which makes possible the turning point of the battle falls the role of cancelling out the effect of a previous chance event (the fact that bad weather had kept the Athenian reinforcements at Crete so long that they arrived just a little too late for the battle). In other words, *a chance occurrence here neutralizes the consequences of another chance occurrence.*

This is essentially the same result in the realm of facts that we obtained in the introductory chapter in the realm of human nature. There, ignorance neutralized the effects of ignorance.

One might object (and such opinions have in fact been expressed) that this sort of neutralization actually argues *for* a rationally comprehensible series of events. In mathematical terms, the sum of two odd integers must be an even integer. One answer would be that the number of odd integers contributing to the sum cannot be known in advance by a human being: it could just as easily be three (or only one). Another kind of answer would point to the high price which human beings have to pay to have their calculations balanced (or 'evened') out (and the illustration of this price is one of Thucydides' main objectives in the case of the events of 415).

A third answer is the historian's own continuation of the action: 'But before they disbanded the fleet after its return to Corinth and the Crisaean Gulf, Knemos, Brasidas and the other Peloponnesian generals wanted…on the advice of the Megarians, to attempt an attack on Piraeus, the port of Athens' (93.1).

One may doubt that Thucydides wished the incident introduced by this sentence to be understood in the context of the previous action. Against this objection is the fact that the responsible parties (the Peloponnesian generals) are the same.[33] Besides, the phrase 'before they disbanded the fleet…[they] wanted', seems to indicate a *psychological* connection to what preceded: after two failed ventures in one summer, they would at least like to score a victory somewhere else. One should then identify this as a *substitute action,* a psychological phenomenon often observed by Thucydides.[34]

The fascinating thing about this action is that now the Peloponnesians really do hold all the cards but—one might say out of fear of their own courage—they cannot bring themselves to take advantage of the opportunity.

The port is completely unguarded because the Athenians do not expect any sort of attack (especially a surprise attack, 93.3). The Peloponnesians on their part have the element of surprise entirely at their disposal. They march their crews across the Isthmus of Corinth to Nisaea and embark them in 40 ships which happen (!) to be available in the dockyards. In other words, this undertaking requires no lengthy preparations (cf. εὐθύς, 4) which might become known at Athens and cause alarm.

But, having set out under optimal conditions (arrival in and departure from Nisaea by night), 'they sailed for Piraeus—no more[35]...for fear of the danger (and a wind of some sort is also supposed to have hindered them), but rather for the tip of Salamis which lies towards Megara' (93.4).

While the Peloponnesians are busy themselves scaling back their objectives, events proceed on the other side *as if they had stuck* to their original intention. Beacons from Salamis cause alarm in Athens, 'and there was a panic *inferior to no other during the war*' (94.1). The people in the city imagine the enemy already in the Piraeus; those in the harbor town believe that Salamis has been taken and that an attack on the port is imminent (ὅσον οὐκ).

'This is precisely what would easily have happened if they had really wanted to go ahead (not to hesitate); and no wind would have hindered them.' In addition to the emphasis on the panic, the contrary-to-fact statement again—as at 2.77.5—contributes to bringing to the fore 'what *almost* happened' and thus highlights the critical moment when events might just as well have taken a different turn.

The potential, but unrealized (and this may be one reason for Thucydides' vivid and colorful description), alternative would in this case have had *decisive* influence on the course of the war. Despite Pericles' insistence on the absolute invulnerability of Athens as a sea power, at this stage it was *objectively possible* to take *the harbor town itself* by a surprise attack—a possibility not countenanced in any plan.

It is only when here, too, one takes into account this relationship to the plans of Book 1 that one grasps why the historian has made the spread of the actual panic from the lower to the upper town, and that is the 'as-if' (or 'almost') situation, into the climax of his description.

That the 'point' of the story is to be found in the neglected—on the Peloponnesian side—opportunity is shown by 94.1. Further evidence is found in the final sentence, which returns once again, after an account of the Peloponnesian withdrawal from Salamis, to the (unattained!) goal of the expedition, the Piraeus (94.4): the Athenians also return home from Salamis, 'and after this (μετὰ τοῦτο) from now on (ἤδη) in the future (τὸ λοιπόν) they kept better watch over the Piraeus by closing the harbors and taking the other precautions'.

Such an emphatic statement that future surprise attacks are prevented must refer back to the singularity of the attempt just reported in the narrative. Thucydides, then, is here developing—parallel to his concept of chance— *the idea of the 'missed opportunity'*.

This category is ideal for establishing the historian's interest in the critical points of a given series of events. In other words, the deeper he looks into occurrences, the more the *potential* turns of events in a situation leap out at him and force him to ask two questions. What factors bring about the actual course of events out of an originally open-ended development; and on the other hand, what conditions prevent a sequence of events from proceeding in an original, and at first apparently viable, direction?

With this perspective we can gain an entirely different appreciation for Thucydides' often praised (and blamed) 'detail' (or precision).

In the most recent case, it was the Peloponnesians' unexpected fear which prevented the undertaking from achieving the success to which it seemed all but predestined. In other cases other factors have similar effects. For example, the next episode (2.95–101), as if serving as a pendant to the most recent Peloponnesian failure, offers an example of a decisive opportunity neglected by the Athenians. The subject is the campaign of the Thracian king Sitalkes, who intends both to avenge himself on the Macedonian king Perdiccas for breaking a promise (this king had proven himself untrustworthy to Athenians as well) and simultaneously to keep a promise of his own (2.29.4 f.) to the Athenians, namely, to free them from the war against the Chalcidians on the Thracian coast (95.2).

That Sitalkes was capable of accomplishing this objective—whose success would be most welcome to Athens—is quite clear from the immensity and power of his realm, about which Thucydides must first inform his reader.[36] 'Being king of *so great* an empire, Sitalkes prepared to march' (98.1); his total army is even supposed (λέγεται) to have been 150,000 strong. The terror which his invasion of Macedonian territory caused even in central Greece is evidenced by the rumor, current among Athens' enemies, that they themselves might be its ultimate goal (101.4).

On the other hand, the Athenians—instead of the fleet they had promised—merely sent envoys with presents, *'because they did not believe he would come'* (101.1)!

This gigantic undertaking, to whose preparations Thucydides devotes several chapters, bursts in the end like a soap bubble. Even without the Athenians Sitalkes campaigns (with little success, regarding his original intentions) against the Bottiaeans and Chalcidians (who had soundly defeated the Athenians that same spring, 2.79), and against the Macedonians, until he is persuaded by his nephew Seuthes to beat a hasty retreat (ἐν τάχει 101.5 ~ κατὰ τάχος 101.6). But Seuthes only advises this course because he has been bribed by the Macedonian king Perdiccas (101.5).

A campaign which might have completely freed Athens from involvement in one theater of the war thus collapses without producing any effect remotely proportional to the expenditure of effort.

We have looked at Book 2 from the point of view of the plans and hopes of the involved parties as expressed in Book 1 prior to entering the war. Behind this approach, which compares and contrasts the books as *Plan and Reality*, there stood also the methodological question of whether the categories applied in Chapter 3 were adequate to Thucydides' conceptual universe.

We can now answer the question in the affirmative since it has become clear on a broad basis[37] that the plans set forth by the advocates of the war in Book 1 were composed with a view to the greater event-complexes of Book 2. The first Peloponnesian invasion and the Athenians' reaction to it stand in direct relation to Pericles' prediction of this very event in Book 1. The plague is an example of what Pericles had referred to as a 'senselessness' in the course of events. Finally, the chain of occurrences beginning at Amphilochian Argos leads—particularly in the second naval battle—to a military situation whose result both the Corinthians in their last speech and Pericles in his first speech believed they could forecast. In every case the actual *course* of events (even when the result was similar to original expectations) signified an unmistakable *correction* of the planners' expectations.

This *opposition of plan and execution* which we have observed in the connections between the first two books returns in miniature in the smaller event-complexes. One thinks of the Theban attack on Plataea, so well planned and so utterly unsuccessful (Chapter 3); of Archidamus' only 'nearly' successful attempt to lure the Athenians into making a sortie; of the disappointment of the assembled Peloponnesian army which expected to take tiny Plataea in short order; of the failed Peloponnesian attack on Amphilochian Argos and Acarnania; of the opportunities calculated for their advantage by the generals on both sides before the battle at Naupactus; finally, of the Peloponnesians' attempt to carry out a surprise attack on Piraeus.

The large number of instances in which a (never-to-be-realized) plan is consciously set forth very likely points to a particular interest on the part of the historian in the relation between plan and reality. Consonant with this is the tendency to greater detail in those passages of the narrative where the reality begins to grow independent from the plan. The search (fostered by the details) for the conditions that determine a course of events also points in this direction. The fact that Thucydides is willing to label even seemingly 'insignificant' circumstances with a 'by chance' or 'nearly' bespeaks the keenness of his analysis. It is only in this way that he can make it clear, e.g. that the result of the second naval battle (at Naupactus), which on the surface might be taken as a triumphant confirmation of Pericles' predictions, was in reality dependent on factors fundamentally beyond human control, but that in this particular case those indeterminable factors happened to cancel each other out.

However, the increasing 'independence' of occurrences, whether in general or in the individual phases of smaller undertakings, is meant by Thucydides as a serious response to the decision to go to war as described in Book 1.

It is true that the immediate decision lay with Sparta and that Sparta allowed itself to be influenced much more by its own fear of the rising power of Athens than by its allies (1.88). Nonetheless, now the Corinthians and Pericles also find themselves in the company of those against whose designs the war maintains its own course, refusing to go along with theirs.

The further Book 2 progresses, the less one can help thinking of the ἄλλαι ὁδοὶ τοῦ πολέμου, which according to the Corinthians (1.122.1) are supposedly so easily at their disposal; or of the unpredictability of war—much emphasized by the Corinthians—which never proceeds according to a set plan but 'generally itself creates from itself ways and means in relation to whatever comes about' (*loc. cit.*).

The war as an active subject looks different from its personification in the speech of the Corinthians. Thucydides describes the independent development of the war not merely in the exemplary pictures of the expectation-shattering disaster for the Thebans or of the plague, which is πρᾶγμα…ἐλπίδος κρεῖσσον γεγενημένον ('a matter that…has developed beyond what was expected'); rather he documents it even in the small details, e.g. in the progressive brutality of the individual naval engagements. In the first clash, the Athenians make prisoners of 'most' of the crews of captured ships (84.4); in the second, the Peloponnesians kill all Athenians 'who did not swim to safety' (90.5); in the last, 'the Athenians killed one part of the men, *but some* (τινάς) they *also* took prisoner' (ἄνδρας τε τοὺς μὲν ἀπέκτειναν, τινὰς δὲ καὶ ἐζώγρησαν, 92.2).

If we wanted to give a *brief summation of Book 2*, we might say that Thucydides, after the prelude and projections, at last begins to present his very own theme, namely, 'the war of the Peloponnesians and Athenians, how they fought with one another' (1.1.1). We might add that as he does so *the war takes on its own face* by emerging gradually from behind the plans of the people involved and revealing itself as an independent entity.

Before we turn to individual occurrences of the war, let us look at the causes which so far in the eyes of Thucydides produced the discrepancy between plan and reality. They fall into two main areas: human error and chance occurrence.[38]

If we wish to use 'the accidental' as a category for interpreting Thucydidean event-chains it is not sufficient merely to look for synonyms in the Greek text which correspond to the English word 'chance'. Of course it is true that the word τύχη (e.g. 1.84.3) generally represents what we call 'chance' (or 'accident'); and such phrases as the 'ἀμαθῶς χωρῆσαι' ('foolish course') of facts or 'πρᾶγμα…ἐλπίδος κρεῖσσον γεγενημένον' ('a matter that…has developed beyond what was expected') can certainly point to chance.

However, we must always bear in mind that Thucydides does not catalog events or assign them to preset categories; rather he narrates every situation individually, highlighting the critical elements of its development in a manner appropriate to the situation.

What is called for, then, is not a word study but an interpretation of content, based upon a reading of entire event-complexes, which seeks to recognize and clarify those factors looked upon by the historian as relevant. Only in this way is it possible to see that Thucydides wants his reader to understand certain elements as conditions which shape situations but are outside the realm of human control: e.g. the rain that delays the Theban relief force, or the Cretan storm that prevents the timely arrival of the Athenian auxiliary fleet, or the unexpected rain that puts out the fire threatening Plataea. The same may be said of the type of occurrence which we designated above as 'the missed opportunity'.

Our approach, which takes its standard from the narrative portions of the work, leads to this consideration: from the events of Book 2 it is clear that the accidental is by no means as irrelevant for Thucydides as scholars have sometimes represented. On the contrary, detailed interpretation shows that this concept is useful for an understanding of Thucydides insofar as it seems to open our eyes to a genuine concern of this author.

We may attempt one further step. The fact that chance (as defined above) plays a part not only in the narrative sections but also in the speeches (e.g. of the Corinthians and Pericles), and the fact that these very speeches can be corrected by the events described in the narrative, indicate that Thucydides *is consciously presenting the limited perspective* in which a planner is up against factors of which he is ignorant and over which he has no control.

This statement is diametrically opposed to the attitude—found, e.g. in Democritus, fragment 119—which attempts to explain chance away as a pretext invented by human beings to excuse their intellectual shortcomings. Moreover, if Thucydides sets human optimism next to chance and subsequently provides a corrective for that optimism in the concrete experience of chance, then we are entitled to conclude that *the kind of attitude represented in this fragment is known to the historian and that he rejects it or is at least critical of it.*

In this context the speech of Archidamus (who himself bases his judgment on the *experience* of previous wars) goes far to serve as evidence. While its warning is being ignored, the gist of this speech is confirmed by the experience of the first years of the war. When the Spartan king observes that the fortunes of war *cannot* be analysed with the mind beforehand (…τὰς προσπιπτούσας τύχας οὐ λόγῳ διαιρετάς, 1.84.3),[39] this signifies a direct response to and rebuff of an optimism which imagines the course of events to be under the sway of human reason.

The fact that the Thucydidean concept of chance was developed in conscious opposition to another existing view has additional significance for our interpretation. The category 'chance' has been freed from a system of classification in which it was relegated to being a (negligible since calculable) remainder in the equation[40] and has become an issue which the author, in his analysis of events, tracks down as structurally significant.

These last observations perhaps permit a look at the place of Thucydides in intellectual history. From the fact that his notion of the human relation to the accidental is deliberately opposed to a more optimistic view of this relationship it follows that such terms as 'Sophistenschüler' or 'enlightened rationalism' do not apply to him. Rather one must allow him a kind of 'rationalism' which—and this is of course a more genuine sense for 'enlightened'—finds its fulfillment in the recognition of the limits of rational activity.

Such a conclusion fits well with the result of our introductory chapter, where Thucydides the enlightened know-it-all had to make way for Thucydides the observer *a posteriori,* for whom the limits of rational influence on human nature become a genuine problem.

We have thus arrived at the second of the two factors out of which grew the discrepancy between plan and reality: human error.

The cause of the error is often a faulty assessment of the real situation. This was true of the Thebans when they counted on a peaceful reaction from a threatened populace, of the Theban relief force who let the Plataean hostages slip away, and similarly of the Athenians who did not trust Sitalkes. It was also a case of inaccurate assessment, combined with overconfidence, when the barbarian tribes separated from Knemos' forces in an attempt to win the victory for themselves alone. The cause of the error may also be sudden fear as, e.g., in the case of the abandoned attack on Piraeus (one also thinks of the sudden fear of Harmodios and Aristogeiton). Excessive hesitation may be the cause, as in Archidamus' attempt to provoke the

Athenians (where one might also speak of a 'missed opportunity'). Knemos' single-handed action (for which Thucydides gives no motive) is among the mistakes with the heaviest consequences.

In almost every case we can also observe a human being deviating, on irrational motives, from a preconceived plan. Thucydides works this out most broadly, as we have seen,[41] in the reaction of the Athenians to the plague and to the Peloponnesian invasion: *here the inconsistency of human behavior actually becomes an independent theme.* It is (to cite even a case where unpredictability is somewhat limited) when reading the author's remarks, hard to escape the conclusion that in a different Dorian war— one in which famine rather than plague played a role—people would probably read λιμός instead of λοιμός in the famous pronouncement of the oracle.

Even this sentence, given as the view of the historian and pointing to the probability of future behavior (κατὰ τὸ εἰκός, 2.54.3), completes Thucydides' other observations in a manner which runs contrary to that of modern interpreters who would see in Thucydides' work the 'constancy' and 'predictability' of human nature. It is true that human nature reacts to circumstances, but the circumstances are not predictable, nor is the *timing* or—except for a rare case—the *direction* of the human reaction. A general prediction about behavior can apparently be made at most in the negative: human beings will in all likelihood depart from their plan, or to overstate the case: *a constancy of human nature is only found in the inconstancy of its behavior.*

This conclusion also requires further evidence. For now, let it suffice to say that in this case, too, what is today generally ignored as unproblematic has by the ancient historian been acknowledged as a problem.

Finally, let us once again ask whether the meaning of the historical work as such can be limited to the problem of how to guarantee freedom of action to *statesmen* (and this means the training of future politicians). Already in light of what we have so far observed the question seems too narrow. The tension we have traced between plan and experience does affect the statesman, too, but not him alone; rather it emerges as a general problem in the course of any war. It affects not merely Pericles but all the Athenians who first voted for the strategy he suggested and then departed from it. According to 2.8 it affects all the people involved.[42]

Pericles'—according to 2.65 very promising—strategy is a good gauge of the type of problem that interests Thucydides: there exists a plan whose reserves of strength will actually endure until the collapse decades in the future (2.65.13)—but what does not exist is the group of people who would be willing to follow this plan. The situation is similar to that in which Archidamus finds himself during the discussion of war and peace.

We have already hinted that the eventual fall of the power which was in every way the stronger must appear unexpected and paradoxical.[43] Because of the unexpected course of the war, the historian's investigation and his desire to understand must of necessity have been increasingly directed toward the unpredictable factors—this seems only too understandable and at the same time explains why Thucydides' *History* must be read in terms of the *intellectual insight* for which it strives (and which it attains) rather than as a manual for future practical use.

Proceeding in this direction we can also come to see that Thucydides does not stop at political analysis, rather 'the human' (1.22.4), i.e. human beings in terms of their internal and external conditions, becomes for him the guiding category in observing the war.

Of course these conditions are partially visible also in the statesman when he is deprived of his sphere of influence whether by deposition or death (Pericles), by exile (Themistocles and Hermocrates), or by any other circumstances.

But the problem of the statesman remains firmly embedded in the larger issues, which show human beings planning and acting in situations they have been brought into both by their own plans and by factors outside their control.

The extent to which such situations are important for Thucydides' view of humanity has been made clear in the outcome of the attack on Plataea; in the description of the mood resulting from the Peloponnesian invasion; in the suffering caused by the plague, whose demoralizing effects for the first time gave free rein to selfish impulses; and finally in the highly significant and exemplary tragic choice forced upon the Plataeans which—though the fact would admittedly be a marginal event in relation to the main action—foreshadowed the bloody destruction of the besieged.

In the next chapter we will devote our attention to such climactic structuring of event-complexes towards a final extreme situation.

Notes

[1] Cf. Herodotus 5.97.3

[2] I cannot agree with those who would make Pericles' superior 'γνώμη' responsible for the fact that things have gone favorably for Athens up to this point.

[3] ἐνδέχεται γὰρ τὰς ξυμφορὰς τῶν πραγμάτων οὐχ ἧσσον ἀμαθῶς χωρῆσαι, 1.140.1—for the connections between Books 1 and 2 see especially Zahn 1934, 54f., de Romilly 1951², *passim*.

⁴ Herter 1953, 617 ('die vulgäre Denkgewohnheit' ['the vulgar way of thinking']); cf. Ludwig 1952, 115.

⁵ Herter 1953, 621, adducing 2.65 ('deutlich die Absicht einer Apologie *ex eventu*' ['clear intention of a defense *ex eventu*']); cf. 1950a, 140; further (and earlier) Zahn 1934, 13 f.

⁶ 2.117; see above, p. 75, cf. Luschnat 1942, 19.

⁷ For the pluperfect see Gomme *ad loc.*

⁸ Schadewaldt 1929, 64; Herter 1953, 620; *et al.*

⁹ 'What *had* been thought honourable'? (Gomme *ad loc.*, cf. Müri 1947, 261).

¹⁰ Müller-Strübing (1881, 70 ff.) finds in the Plataea episodes (insignificant as they are for the war at large), with their 'loving attention to even the smallest details', confirmation of the 'epic', even of the 'Homeric', quality of Thucydides' *History*.

¹¹ Wassermann 1952/3, 198.

¹² On this point see Diller 1961, 194 f.

¹³ Cf. Gomme *ad* 78.1.

¹⁴ λέγεται: even at the literary climax of his account the historian does not abandon his critical attitude towards his sources—not even when it means compromising the dramatic effect. This observation argues against a hyperbolic narrative style on the part of Thucydides (Dow 1962).

¹⁵ See above, pp.38, 40.

¹⁶ On the landing site see Gomme *ad* 2.80.8.

¹⁷ His behavior throughout is similar to that of the Thebans after their lucky entrance into the city of Plataea.

¹⁸ De Romilly 1956a, 125 ff.

¹⁹ πλέον γὰρ ἡμεῖς ἔχομεν τοῦ κατὰ γῆν ἐκ τοῦ ναυτικοῦ ἐμπειρίας ἢ ἐκεῖνοι ἐκ τοῦ κατ᾽ ἤπειρον ἐς τὰ ναυτικά, 1.142.5.

²⁰ See above, p. 41.

²¹ On both speeches, cf. especially Luschnat 1942, 21 ff., 26 ff.; de Romilly 1956a, 140 ff.

²² 86.6; 88.1–3; Phormio is even said to fear 'the fear of his soldiers'. The passage at 88.1–3 alone contains eight expressions regarding fear and courage.

²³ De Romilly 1956a, 140 ff.

²⁴ De Romilly 1956a, 150.

²⁵ 2.84.3; this section is the climax of Thucydides' account, emphasized by pleonasm (cf. βοῇ…ἀντιφυλακῇ…λοιδορία…οὔτε τῶν παραγγελλομένων οὔτε τῶν κελευστῶν), and even assonance and equality of syllables in the emphatic pronouncement: ἀδύνατοι…ἀναφέρειν ἄνθρωποι ἄπειροι…ἀπειθεστέρας τὰς ναῦς παρεῖχον.

²⁶ For details see de Romilly 1956a, 141; Luschnat 1942, 26 ff. Phormio seeks refuge in some rather forced ideas, such as the notion that the very fact of Athenian resistance to greatly superior numbers must terrify the enemy (89.5; see Classen-Steup *ad loc.*).

²⁷ Cf. Gomme *ad* 2.86.5.

[28] Cf. Luschnat 1942, 28.

[29] See above, pp. 55 f.

[30] Cf. de Romilly 1956a, 145 f.

[31] For the doubled expression see above, p. 66.

[32] De Romilly 1956a, 147 ff.

[33] In similar fashion the person of Alcidas forms the connection between the Mytilene complex and the Corcyra complex (cf. 3.69).

[34] Cf. for instance the substitute action of Harmodios and Aristogeiton when they imagine their political goal to be unattainable (6.57.2–3, above p. 5 n. 4), or the secondary plan made by the Thebans when their first plan comes to nothing (2.5.4; above, pp. 67 f.); further, see the suggestion of the Ionian and Lesbian refugees 3.31.1 (cf. ὡς τῆς Λέσβου ἡμαρτήκεσαν, 3.69.2), below, p. 107.

[35] The irony (a device seldom employed by Thucydides) is plain (cf. Steup *ad loc.*). Thucydides is incidentally using the same means exploited on the stage by Euripides, e.g. in *Medea* 83 where the Nurse, stunned by Jason's attitude, cries out: 'That he should perish (!)—I do not wish (for he is my master)...' For further examples see Page *ad loc.*

[36] Cf. esp. 97.5–6; Münch (1935, 37) has emphasized (in opposition to those who see Thucydides' interest as primarily geographical and ethnographical) that in the so-called 'Odrysian Excursus' (a term strictly applicable only to Ch. 97) 'all the details are for the sake of military and political interest; even the geographical material serves this purpose'.

[37] I would like to emphasize again that many of these cross-connections between Books 1 and 2 were discovered not by me but by the Analysts; the present work is merely an effort to uncover the unified intention behind these connections.

[38] This brings us close to Müri's (1947, 262) conclusion that human planning is limited externally by τύχη and παράλογος, internally by the passions (ὀργή).

[39] There is a parallel in the attitude of Hermocrates, whose warnings also go unheeded (a fact overlooked by Landmann 1932, 61; 63). His realization that chance is removed from the realm of human control (ἧς οὐκ ἄρχω τύχης, 4.64.1) is more than once emphasized by Thucydides (cf. 4.62.4; 6.78.2).

[40] See pp. 16 f. above.

[41] Above, pp. 76, 78 ff.

[42] Above, p. 71.

[43] Above, p. 60.

6

ENDPOINTS OF SERIES OF EVENTS
Book 3.2–85

The series of events that comprises the defection of Mytilene from the Athenian League (3.2 ff.) stands in contrast to the developments so far investigated inasmuch as the 'actors', even before they begin to act, lose the initiative. Something planned as action unfolds in reality as reaction.

This is remarkable since we are dealing with a second attempt to break away from Athens—one which, with respect to an earlier failure, is supposed to be better prepared. The groundwork is to be laid in general by blocking the harbor, constructing fortifications, laying in provisions, bringing in troops from abroad and taking measures to consolidate power on the island of Lesbos itself.

But at an early stage news of these preparations reaches Athens, and so in the end the Mytileneans are 'forced to carry out this revolt, too, earlier than they intended' (2.1). Preparations are nowhere near complete when the military action begins, and the initiative seems to have slipped from Mytilenean into Athenian hands.

However, there is ample time between the arrival of the news at Athens and the beginning of hostilities. One would expect the Athenians to take advantage of the premature revelation of Mytilenean intentions. But the opposite is the case: the Athenians, oppressed by plague and war, prefer not to believe the reports and close their eyes to the danger (Lesbos did after all represent an intact sea power): μεῖζον μέρος νέμοντες τῷ μὴ βούλεσθαι ἀληθῆ εἶναι ('allotting a greater part to *wishing it were not true*', 3.1). In other words, *what they wish to be true wins out over a reality* vouched for by numerous informants (Tenedians, Methymnaeans and people from Mytilene itself).

In the end they do send an embassy to talk the Mytileneans out of their revolt. It is only when this course does not bring the desired success that the Athenians become fearful (δείσαντες) and desire, even at this late date, to 'get the drop' (προκαταλαβεῖν, 3.1) on the Mytileneans: now they suddenly do send out a fleet of 40 ships (3.2) which just happens to be ready to sail (it had been assembled for another purpose), because they see an opportunity for a surprise attack during a festival of Apollo which the people of Mytilene normally celebrate outside the city walls (3.3). The motive for sending out the ships, therefore, is precisely the same as that for mistrusting the original reports of a revolt: the hope of avoiding a full-scale war complete with siege.

But this 'sudden' action is robbed of its element of surprise. The Mytileneans learn of the approach of the Athenian fleet *shortly before its arrival* (cf. οὐ πολλῷ ὕστερον, 4.1), with the result that they are able to cancel the celebration just in time. The messenger, meeting with (cf. ἐπιτυχών) unusually good travel connections, has made the journey from Athens to Lesbos in three days (3.5).

Refusing once again to negotiate, the Mytileneans put to sea, unprepared though they are (Thucydides repeats: ἀπαράσκευοι…καὶ ἐξαίφνης ἀναγκασθέντες πολεμεῖν, 'unprepared…and suddenly forced to fight', 4.2), for a battle which they lose. The result: λόγους ἤδη προσέφερον τοῖς στρατηγοῖς, 'they *already opened negotiations* with the generals' (to persuade the fleet to withdraw). Despite their victory, this suggestion is all too welcome to the Athenian generals: καὶ αὐτοὶ φοβούμενοι μὴ οὐχ ἱκανοὶ ὦσι… '*being for their part, too, in fear* lest they be not sufficient' (4.3). In this way the fears of both sides, each ignorant of their opponents' apprehension, lead to a truce.

Mytilenean envoys (among them, by shrewd design, one of the informants who 'by now regretted' his actions) travel to Athens to persuade the Athenians to withdraw their ships and to convince them that Mytilene's intentions have been harmless.

Simultaneously, a secret embassy sets out for Sparta to ask for aid against Athens (it is this embassy, upon whose success depends the entire subsequent action, that has difficulty making the crossing: ταλαιπώρως, 4.6).

Following a negative response from Athens, the Mytileneans appear to regain the initiative with an attack on the Athenian camp; but this is mere appearance: οὐκ ἔλασσον ἔχοντες οἱ Μυτιληναῖοι οὔτε ἐπηυλίσαντο οὔτε ἐπίστευσαν σφίσιν αὐτοῖς, ἀλλ᾽ ἀνεχώρησαν ('*though proving not inferior, the Mytileneans neither encamped outside nor trusted their own strength, but withdrew*', 5.2). From now on they behave *passively*, merely waiting for Spartan aid. The arrival of messengers requesting a further embassy to Sparta strengthens their hopes in this direction.

This absurd game, in which each side out of fear of the other dares only to react but not to act, now turns in favor of Athens: οἱ δὲ Ἀθηναῖοι πολὺ ἐπιρρωσθέντες διὰ τὴν τῶν Μυτιληναίων ἡσυχίαν ξυμμάχους…προσεκάλουν ('but the Athenians, *much encouraged because of the Mytileneans' inactivity*, summoned allies…', 6.1). In other words, they have the impression that the Mytileneans are unaware of their own power (which was the cause of Athens' original apathy), or are simply not willing to use it.

The members of the Athenian alliance—who, in the event of a general uprising of the allies, might have sided with Mytilene—behave in the same way: …πολὺ θᾶσσον παρῆσαν ὁρῶντες οὐδὲν ἰσχυρὸν ἀπὸ τῶν Λεσβίων, ('…they were on location much faster, *because they saw no strong action coming forth from the Lesbians'*, 6.1). Athens is free to create a blockade and to build two forts on the island itself. By their passivity, the Mytileneans have *missed the opportunity* most feared by the Athenians.

While the situation is beginning to worsen in this way for the rebels on Lesbos, the envoys 'sent out on the first ship' (8.1—i.e. those who, according to 4.6, reached their destination 'ταλαιπώρως') manage to secure both Mytilene's acceptance into the Peloponnesian alliance and the promise of immediate military assistance. They win their point in part by reference to the plague and the financial burdens of Athens: 'καιρὸς δὲ ὡς οὔπω πρότερον' ('a chance like never before so far', 13.3); '…ὥστε οὐκ εἰκὸς αὐτοὺς περιουσίαν νεῶν ἔχειν…' ('…so that it is *not likely* that they have an abundance of ships', 13.4).

The limited perspective of these assertions is evident from the fact that the Athenians *in the meantime* have already overcome the passivity (13.3 ~ 3.1) arising from their troubled circumstances. Indeed these claims become a concrete factor in the war (in ways the speakers could hardly expect) the moment that they reach Athenian ears. The latter are indignant διὰ κατά-γνωσιν ἀσθενείας σφῶν ('because of contempt for their weakness', 16.1) and, stung to even greater activity than before, demonstratively launch a show of raids on the Peloponnesian coast (in reality they must expend nearly their last resources on this dubious operation),[1] δηλῶσαι βουλόμενοι ὅτι οὐκ ὀρθῶς ἐγνώκασιν (scil. οἱ Πελοποννήσιοί τε καὶ Μυτιληναῖοι), 'wishing to demonstrate that they (scil. the Peloponnesians and Mytileneans) had not judged (scil. the situation) correctly' (16.1).

The feint has the desired effect. The Spartans had already been forced to see their call for a second invasion of Attica that same summer sabotaged by their allies' lack of enthusiasm for anything beyond bringing in the harvest (15.2). Because of this unexpected (cf. πολὺν τὸν παράλογον, 16.2) show of Athenian strength, they consider the *Mytilenean claims false* (οὐκ ἀληθῆ καὶ ἄπορα, 16.2) and cancel operations. At this, the seeming success of the Mytilenean embassy turns to failure because Athens, encouraged by Sparta's reaction, now has a free hand for the war on Lesbos. Rein-forcements solve the still pressing problem of Mytilene's and her allies' numerical superiority on the island itself, and as winter begins the city is invested with a circular wall (18.3–5).

Thus, the fate of the rebels seems sealed, and the Mytileneans themselves have this impression. But then, towards the end of the winter, the Spartan Salaithos makes his way through the Athenian blockade undiscovered, bringing the inmates news of an immanent Spartan relief operation (25.1).

Once again the situation seems to change direction: καὶ οἱ μὲν Μυτιληναῖοι ἐθάρσουν τε καὶ πρὸς τοὺς Ἀθηναίους ἧσσον εἶχον τὴν γνώμην ὥστε ξυμβαίνειν ('and the Mytileneans were encouraged and *less inclined to come to an agreement* with the Athenians', 25.2).

With the arrival of summer, the Peloponnesians send 42 ships under the Spartan Alcidas to Lesbos and undertake the *worst* (except for the second) invasion (26.3) of Attica in an attempt to pin down Athenian forces at home (26.1). The invasion is drawn out over so long a period of time because the invaders are waiting for news of success on Lesbos—in vain, of course.

This is another example of the splintering, familiar to the readers, e.g. from the Peloponnesian campaign against Argos and Acarnania,[2] of a comprehensively planned undertaking into component theaters: οἱ δὲ Μυτιληναῖοι ἐν τούτῳ, ὡς αἵ τε νῆες αὐτοῖς οὐχ ἧκον..., ἀναγκάζονται ξυμβαίνειν πρὸς τοὺς Ἀθηναίους... 'But *during this time* (i.e. while the Peloponnesians were in Attica, waiting, cf.2.86.1), when the ships did not arrive for them..., the Mytileneans *were forced to come to an agreement* with the Athenians' (27.1).

When the starving *demos*, armed by Salaithos, turns against the authorities, the latter decide upon surrender in order to avoid becoming isolated (28.1). Once again Mytilene's fate seems sealed, and, as events proceed, it proves to be for the last time.

But the historian adds a coda (as in the description of the unsuccessful attack on Plataea): Alcidas' troops, οὓς ἔδει ἐν τάχει παραγενέσθαι ('who were supposed to arrive speedily', 29.1),[3] linger so long at sea that they are still under way when they receive news of Mytilene's fall. ἡμέραι δὲ μάλιστα ἦσαν τῇ Μυτιλήνῃ ἑαλωκυίᾳ ἑπτά[4] ὅτε ἐς τὸ Ἔμβατον κατέπλευσαν ('but for Mytilene it amounted to about seven days after its fall when they landed in Embaton', 29.2).

During the deliberations over what to do now, there enters an (otherwise unknown) man from Elis by the name of Teutiaplos who suggests (*oratio recta*!) a surprise attack[5] on the but recently occupied Mytilene.

> κατὰ γὰρ τὸ εἰκὸς ἀνδρῶν νεωστὶ πόλιν ἐχόντων πολὺ τὸ ἀφύλακτον εὑρήσομεν, κατὰ μὲν θάλασσαν καὶ πάνυ, ᾖ ἐκεῖνοί τε ἀνέλπιστοι ἐπιγενέσθαι ἄν τινα σφίσι πολέμιον...εἰκὸς δὲ καὶ τὸ πεζὸν αὐτῶν κατ᾽ οἰκίας ἀμελέστερον ὡς κεκρατηκότων διεσπάρθαι (30.2).

For, since the men are holding the city only recently, we shall in all probability find much that is unguarded, and especially at sea where they least expect that an enemy would attack them…further it is likely that also their army is scattered in houses rather carelessly since the men feel they are victorious.

According to Teutiaplos, they might even expect help from inside.[6]

That the speech represents the historian's own opinion[7] is indicated by the subsequently related facts (32.3; 33.2), which prove Teutiaplos' analysis of the situation right. Further evidence is the consonance with our earlier observation[8] that planning in accordance with the εἰκός, on the rare occasions when it is being conceived of reasonably, can fall on deaf ears (οὐκ ἔπειθε τὸν Ἀλκίδαν, 'he did not persuade Alkidas', 31.1).[9] Thucydides creates a climax here by reporting a second case,[10] which, though promising success (ἐλπίδα δ᾽ εἶναι· οὐδενὶ γὰρ ἀκουσίως ἀφῖχθαι, '[they argued] that there was hope, for they [scil. Alkidas and his fleet] had arrived unwelcome to no one' 31.1) and possibly decisive for the war at large (ὅπως…τὴν Ἰωνίαν ἀποστήσωσιν, 'in order that…they might bring Ionia to defect [scil. from Athens]') is likewise rejected (ὁ δὲ οὐδὲ ταῦτα ἐνεδέχετο, 'but he rejected *even this* proposal', 31.2). Indeed, Alcidas even squanders the sympathy of the potential allies (ἀπέσφαξε τοὺς πολλούς, 'he butchered the majority [scil. of his prisoners]', 32.1) until someone points out to him that this is 'not the proper way to liberate Greece' (2).

It is quite clear, then, that Thucydides has used the speech of Teutiaplos to make a characteristic 'missed opportunity' the preliminary climax of his narrative, and we must ask why.

One answer may be that Alcidas' actions not only cheat the Peloponnesians out of a probable success, but actually help the Athenians. The mere presence of the Peloponnesian fleet in the Aegean frightens the Athenians (μέγα τὸ δέος, 33.2), and the Athenian general on Lesbos feels relief (κέρδος δὲ ἐνόμισεν, 3) when Alcidas flees right away after his ships have been sighted.

But the essential reason for the presentation of Teutiaplos' advice— which *in no way influences* Alcidas' decision[11]—must of course be sought in the immediate context of the fate of Mytilene. The possibility, offered by Teutiaplos' plan, of rescuing the Mytileneans can perhaps be compared to the situation familiar from tragedy when the chorus, just before the unexpected catastrophe, sounds a song of joy in the belief that the impending danger has been averted.[12]

The *consequences* of the Peloponnesian relief action confirm that this comparison—made with all due caution[13]—is not inappropriate. Thucydides expressly emphasizes how much the Peloponnesian fleet—though remaining entirely inactive—contributes by its mere presence to Mytilene's misfortunes. The angry (cf. ὑπὸ ὀργῆς, 36.2) death sentence at Athens (to kill all Mytilenean men and sell the women and children into slavery) is handed down not the least *because of the Peloponnesian aid* to Lesbos:

καὶ προσξυνελάβοντο <u>οὐκ ἐλάχιστον</u> τῆς ὁρμῆς <u>αἱ Πελοποννησίων νῆες</u> ἐς Ἰωνίαν ἐκείνοις βοηθοὶ τολμήσασαι παρακινδυνεῦσαι. οὐ γὰρ ἀπὸ βραχείας διανοίας ἐδόκουν τὴν ἀπόστασιν ποιήσασθαι (36.2).

and not the least contributed to their rage the fact that the ships of the Peloponnesians had risked sailing over to Ionia, daring to help those [i.e. the Mytileneans]. For they appeared to have effected the defection not on a basis of short-term planning.

This is the final link in the chain of situations resulting for Mytilene from its connection with Sparta. One understands *a posteriori* why Thucydides mentioned in the first place that the decisive (first) embassy reached the Peloponnese only ʻταλαιπώρωςʼ: without this embassy and its resultant (similarly hard-won: 25.1) promise of aid from Sparta, Mytilene would not have held out as long as it did—and presumably Athens' judgment would not have proven so harsh.

In connection with the speech of Teutiaplos, the passage quoted above (36.2) leads to the following conclusion: although success—even after the fall of Mytilene!—was almost within his grasp, *Alcidas accomplished the exact opposite of his mission* (the fact that the sentence passed against the Mytileneans is later not carried out in its harsher version is due to other factors that have nothing to do with Alcidas and his actions). To revisit the example of the *Heracles* (cf. n. 12): something which was intended to bring help in an emergency in the end contributes decisively to the *escalation of that emergency to a critical degree*.

If Thucydides really did see the significance of the series of events in this tragic component, then of course the speech of Teutiaplos—ignored in the factual realm—is the appropriate means of expressing it.

Even with the sentencing in Athens, the description has not reached its ultimate climax. On the very same day a trireme bearing the order of execution leaves for Lesbos: <u>κατὰ τάχος</u> κελεύοντες <u>διαχρήσασθαι Μυτιληναίους</u> (ʻunder orders to kill the Mytileneans as swiftly as possibleʼ, 36.3). The next day, conscience gets the better of the Athenians (36.4), and a new debate takes place. The extensive argument which ensues between Cleon and Diodotos (37–48) runs its course *while* the ship bearing the death sentence is crossing over to Lesbos. The longer the debate lasts, the slimmer become the chances of salvation for the Mytileneans. There can be no doubt that the historian is conscious of the dramatic element that these speeches (which point far beyond the subject of Lesbos) lend to the narrative (and indeed to the events of 427).

The end of the description confirms this impression. The Athenians vote—even now with a *slender* majority—to alter the sentence (49.1). At this point comes the *detailed description,* as we have observed elsewhere at literary climaxes in the narrative.[14] A second trireme departs 'εὐθύς' ('immediately') and 'κατὰ σπουδήν' ('in haste') to overtake the first one which has a head start of a day and a night. Certain Mytileneans who are present in Athens make promises to the crew and furnish special rations[15] (οἶνον καὶ ἄλφιτα, § 3). The crew rows in shifts (one half rows while the other sleeps), takes meals *while* rowing (i.e. οἴνῳ καὶ ἐλαίῳ ἄλφιτα πεφυραμένα, 'barley mixed with wine and oil', § 3: a curious detail, especially when mentioned twice in the same sentence). *By chance* (κατὰ τύχην, § 4) there is no headwind, and the first trireme's crew has not been in a hurry to discharge its unnatural (ἀλλόκοτον) duty. Thus the race for the lives of Mytilene's population is won by a hair's breadth: the Athenian general Paches has just read the first decision and is about to act upon it when the second trireme arrives. The climax of the narrative comes in a single sentence: παρὰ τοσοῦτον μὲν ἡ Μυτιλήνη ἦλθε κινδύνου ('by so small a margin did Mytilene escape the danger', § 4). The hyperbaton, distributed at the beginning and the end of the pronouncement, underscores the perspective essential to the entire course of events.[16]

After this climax, the historian's *interest in the presentation immediately declines.* Except for the (still high) number[17] of Mytileneans later executed in Athens, there are no further emphatic statements. The tone of the remaining narrative is that of a simple factual report ('But later they did not impose any tribute on the Lesbians, rather…'), ending with the usual neutral concluding formula: τὰ μὲν κατὰ Λέσβον οὕτως ἐγένετο ('Such were the events concerning Lesbos', 50.3).

This is the third time we have to state a discrepancy between the literary climax and the actual end of an event-complex.[18] This result confirms the methodological requirement set up in Chapter 2[19] for identifying the points of interest that guide the author in the choice and presentation of his material. It proved to be best not to resort to evidence lying outside the text so much as to look for the aspects that cause Thucydides to emphasize certain sections *within* his own work so that the applied observational categories point beyond the causal and chronological arrangement.

It is easy to see that not every event-complex meets the interest of the historian. On the other hand, the fact that certain sections do engage the author's interest leads the interpreter to the consideration that the significance seen and shaped by Thucydides must be *the more important for him* since this significance is in his eyes based on incontestably established *facts.*

In the most recent case it became clear—and the result in the other two cases was similar—that the episode as a whole is designed with a view to the final, extreme situation, which is of life-and-death importance for the population of Mytilene. The fact that the fatal outcome is averted literally at the last moment does not in the least diminish the historian's interest in the chain of events—and it is easy to see why. The final result is dependent upon such slight, uncontrollable factors, both in the human (only a slight majority for the alteration of the sentence; the extraordinary speed of the second ship, the tardiness of the first) and in the factual realm (there happened to be no headwind) that one's view of the whole is not affected. On the contrary, the improbable, but nevertheless factual rescue merely serves to confirm the haphazard quality of the entire complex as Thucydides presents it.

The 'randomness' of the whole event sequence is brought about in this case less by constellations of chance than by the limited perspectives of the actors. Already at the opening neither side feels itself in a position to act; each imagines itself impotent in the present situation and waits for the other to make a move. Both sides are quickly in favor of an armistice after the first engagement, each because of a misconceived notion of its opponent's might. The initiative oscillates. When Sparta promises immediate aid, Mytilene's position already begins to worsen; due to Athens' unexpected (and in reality merely apparent) strength, Sparta fails to keep its promise because it now considers the Mytilenean assessment of the situation to be wrong; just as the Mytileneans are ready to surrender, the promise of help arrives and gives them courage; when the relief fleet arrives, Mytilene has already fallen but *could* still be rescued.

Step by step the course of events shows from the very beginning how the people involved feel hampered in their freedom of action by the situation. By 'situation' I mean the constellation of circumstances which they each time subjectively *imagine* to be reality. Close investigation has shown that Thucydides is at pains at the numerous turning points to present, in addition to the facts, the picture that people make of those facts for themselves. It became apparent that each agent's picture of the situation, however inaccurate in its limited perspective, was decisive for the subsequent direction of events. It is from these one-sided assessments of the situation that the moods as well as the decisions of the actors arise.[20]

But this represents the consistent maintenance of a point of view which revealed itself already in Book 2. The discrepancy between projection and reality shifts with the progress of the war. The—subjectively—'free' activity of planning becomes with increasing frequency adaptation (or reaction) to what is perceived as an already pre-set reality. In other words, before the decision for war, pro-war advocates still subjectively believed they would be able to steer coming events or at least to launch operations, if not control them through to the very end, in accordance with their own will. Now, however, men find themselves at a point in a long chain of causes and effects where they can at most hope to make adjustments, but no longer expect to put their own overarching plans into action unimpaired. The historian emphasizes this at the beginning of the Mytilene sequence (ἀναγκασθέντες, 2.1 = 4.2; cf. 13.2). Certainly there will continue to be individual undertakings (e.g. Brasidas' campaign) in which an initiative is realized for the time being, but grand strategies such as those pronounced in Book 1 are no longer possible—except at the beginning of a *new* war, as in the case of the Sicilian expedition (cf. οὐ πολλῷ τινὶ ὑποδεέστερον πόλεμον ἀνηροῦντο ἢ τὸν πρὸς Πελοποννησίους, 'they were raising a war not much inferior to that against the Peloponnesians', 6.1.1). Here we find the whole gamut of projections, warnings and challenges played out anew until the actors once again find themselves in the unexpected experience of reality where the best of circumstances still allows of some adjustment—and at the end even this possibility ceases to exist.

What remains the same—and this is the contribution of Book 3—is evidently *the hopelessness of the final situation.*

This is made most evident in the description of the civil war on Corcyra (especially in 81). The bestiality of the ultimate situation, created by human beings for their fellows, is described so vividly as to require no interpretation.

But the significance of this description for the work of Thucydides must be pointed out, for, aside from its function in the context of the Corcyra sequence, it is intended *to be simultaneously representative* of numerous similar situations: οὕτως ὠμὴ <ἡ> στάσις προυχώρησε, καὶ ἔδοξε μᾶλλον, διότι ἐν τοῖς πρώτη ἐγένετο, ἐπεὶ ὕστερον γε καὶ πᾶν ὡς εἰπεῖν τὸ Ἑλληνικὸν ἐκινήθη... ('so savage the civil war developed, and *it seemed even more so because it was the very first*, because later even all of Greece, so to speak, was exposed to upheaval..., 82.1).

These words imply that the historian intends the description of affairs on Corcyra to be an indication of the upheavals of later civil wars. It is on Corcyra that the new kind of brutality appears for the first time in full force,[21] and *that is why* Thucydides gives his reader such a *detailed description.*

This characteristic is of no small significance for the author's pedagogically progressive technique (and, as Finley[22] has correctly argued against the Analysts, it is also an argument for the work's essential unity of composition). During the later discussion of the *long-standing* civil war in Rhegium (4.1.3), Thucydides feels no need to make special mention of the concomitant atrocities because they are familiar to the reader from the description of events on Corcyra. It is only when new phenomena make their appearance—e.g. the rabble-rousing at Athens in 415,[23] or in connection with the situation in 411 when the fear of a secret organization puts a damper on all inter-personal communication[24]—that the theme is taken up again.[25]

The quoted passage (3.82.1) may serve as an important justification for the method of the present work, which attempts to discover points of special interest to the ancient author through examination of those sections upon which the greatest detail has been lavished. In terms of narrative technique, the description of the civil war (the so-called 'pathology', 3.82 f.) as a unit has *precisely the same function* as the sentence παρὰ τοσοῦτον μὲν ἡ Μυτιλήνη ἦλθε κινδύνου ('by so small a margin did Mytilene escape the danger', 49.4) has in the Mytilene complex:[26] it follows *immediately* upon the literary climax (81) of the narrated events; what comes *after* (3.85) is a disinterestedly sober, summarizing, factual report.

In Chapters 82 f. the author for once draws the conclusion *himself* from the detailed description of events (81) by developing from the situation at hand those characteristics significant for the war as a whole, thus putting on record what is valid beyond the individual case—an effort he usually leaves to the attentiveness of his reader.

The structure which we have here recognized permits us, from a methodological perspective, to speak of the *exemplary* character of the highly detailed sections—of course not in the sense that the example in question would offer a repeatable *schema,* which, once recognized, could be evaluated in utilitarian terms (the subject matter alone argues against this). In this question, too, Chapter 82 can take us one step further. Here, against the background of the civil upheavals on Corcyra, the historian gives a rare indication of the direction in which he feels capable of discussing any sort of *repetition* in history (1.22.4):

καὶ ἐπέπεσε πολλὰ καὶ χαλεπὰ κατὰ στάσιν ταῖς πόλεσι, γιγνόμενα μὲν καὶ αἰεὶ ἐσόμενα, ἕως ἂν ἡ αὐτὴ φύσις ἀνθρώπων ᾖ, μᾶλλον δὲ καὶ ἡσυχαίτερα καὶ τοῖς εἴδεσι διηλλαγμένα... (82.2).

And many harsh events befell the cities by way of inner strife, events that *happen and will always happen as long as human nature is the same,* more intense and less turbulent, and *different in their forms of appearance…*

Nearly all interpreters have taken it for granted that this is a reference to the programmatic remarks of 1.22.4.[27] The significance of this pronouncement, made in the historian's own name, lies in the emphasis on the *inescapability* (αἰεὶ ἐσόμενα) of the cycle of violence in which human beings (not 'the Athenians' or 'the Dorians') pursue each other without finding a way out.[28]

This one sentence, placed as a sort of signpost just before the account of the so-called 'pathology', should be sufficient by itself to dispel both the optimistic picture of a historian who, through recognition of historical patterns, hopes to unlock a secure future,[29] and the picture of a patriotic historian who in accordance with his own life's experience seeks to justify the Athenian empire (rather than, say, subsequently describe a time of relative peace).

If any autobiographical traces are to be found in this work, we should rather ask whether the following comparison of people at peace with people at war[30] is not the product of a life that—according to 5.26—was for 27 years dedicated to the observation of the war on both sides, and for which as a result the state of war had become the rule and peace the exception.

The account of the so-called 'pathology' is to engage our attention here for two reasons. First, it allows methodological conclusions both about the structural elements of narrative passages and about the exemplary significance of detail in Thucydides. Second, it draws attention to the shift of accentuation in the events of Book 3 relative to those of Book 2: the darker side of the war as described in 1.23 becomes more and more prominent.

While Book 2, broadly speaking,[31] shows the increasing independence of the course of the war in relation to prewar projections, Book 3 presents an accumulation of the *results* of this independence.

We have already been able to conclude that the Mytilene-complex is composed in its entirety with a view to the final, decisive, life-and-death situation of the Mytileneans. The same kind of climax is present in the Corcyra narrative (70 ff.), where the coup perpetrated by the oligarchs leads eventually to their own destruction. Here, too, there is a *missed opportunity* similar to that seen by Teutiaplos. After the lost naval battle, the Corcyreans are fearful of an attack on their city by the Peloponnesian fleet. οἱ δ᾽ ἐπὶ μὲν τὴν πόλιν <u>οὐκ ἐτόλμησαν</u> πλεῦσαι <u>κρατοῦντες τῇ ναυμαχίᾳ</u> ('but they *did not dare* to sail against the city *in spite of having prevailed in the naval battle*', 79.2). Even the next day they sail οὐδὲν μᾶλλον ('none the more', 79.3) against the city, <u>καίπερ ἐν πολλῇ ταραχῇ καὶ φόβῳ ὄντας</u> καὶ Βρασίδου παραινοῦντος, ὡς λέγεται, Ἀλκίδᾳ, ἰσοψήφου δὲ οὐκ ὄντος ('*though they* [scil. the inhabitants] *were in great confusion and fear*, and *Brasidas* (it is said) *exhorted Alkidas,* – *but he did not have an equal vote.*') The Corcyrean *demos* even reaches *an understanding with the oligarchs,* so great is the fear of a Peloponnesian attack (80.1).

When upon learning of the approach of an Athenian fleet Alcidas finally takes to swift flight, the oligarchs are done for. The Corcyrean *demos* can begin its seven-day killing spree; the opportunity recognized by Brasidas, which would have meant salvation for the oligarchs, has been squandered.[32]

It is scarcely necessary to point out individual similarities also in the events at Plataea.

After the break-out[33] (favored by inclement weather) of perhaps half of those besieged in Plataea (3.20–24),[34] in which all had originally wished to participate (20.2), the time comes in the summer of 427 for those who have remained behind, when they no longer have the strength to continue their resistance, to surrender (52 ff.). Interpreters have long recognized that Thucydides wishes the Plataea-complex to be read in relation to the events around Mytilene (the two accounts are of course juxtaposed).[35]

Without forcing the issue, one can even discern a certain *parallelism*. Just as Mytilene was only holding out *because* Salaithos promised Spartan help, Athens had tried to persuade the Plataeans to hold out with a promise to help 'as much as possible' (2.73.3).[36] And just as the Spartan relief action failed miserably because of Alcidas' cowardice, the Athenians, in their rage over Mytilene's connection to Sparta, unhesitatingly kill Salaithos, *although* he offers, among other things, *to draw the Peloponnesians away from Plataea* (36.1: why should Thucydides mention this at all unless he himself saw in it a chance to save Plataea? The remark ἔτι γὰρ ἐπολιορκοῦντο, 'for they were still under siege', also points in this direction).[37]

Further, the concluding sentence hints that the end of the Plataeans reflected poorly on Athens: καὶ τὰ μὲν κατὰ Πλάταιαν ἔτει τρίτῳ καὶ ἐνενηκοστῷ ἐπειδὴ Ἀθηναίων ξύμμαχοι ἐγένοντο οὕτως ἐτελεύτησεν ('and the events concerning Plataea came to such an end, in the ninety-third year since they had become allies of the Athenians', 68.5).[38]

All the descriptions of Plataea, as we saw earlier,[39] are composed with a view to the deadly end which awaits its besieged inhabitants. This is true also of the speeches,[40] and the historian's sympathy with the fate of the condemned has always been felt.[41]

Likewise, in the (stylistic) emphasis on the final link in the chain of events, the description resembles the Mytilene-complex (the emphasis is perhaps even stronger in the latter sequence). A single long sentence which seems to have difficulty making its way forward (I count five connected participles and six subordinate clauses of various kinds) suddenly breaks off with the markedly curt statement: …ἀπέκτεινον καὶ ἐξαίρετον ἐποιήσαντο οὐδένα ('…they killed [scil. every one], and they excepted no one, 68.1).[42]

114

What follows is the familiar overview of the pertinent events (which, however, does not seem as streamlined as usual) with Sparta's opportunistic motives emphasized at the end. Complementary to this, the expanded closing formula refers back once again to the failure of Athens (68.2–5).

In terms of composition, two rings have closed. The reference to the actions of the two great powers takes up once again the tragic dilemma developed[43] at the beginning of the siege; the death of the defenders points back to the murder of the prisoners[44] which was given such prominence in an earlier passage.

The three event-complexes which the historian has singled out for more thorough presentation in his account of the year 427 bear surprisingly similar accents: all of them peak in the extreme situation. In none of the three is the literary high point identical to the end of the factual report, i.e. the chain of events is evidently only to a limited extent appropriate for expressing the significance meant by the historian. Further, none of the three places visited by the war is among the primary belligerents, but rather all are among those afflicted by the struggle of the two great powers. In Thucydides' view, their political insignificance does not detract from the historical significance of their fate. All three sequences also have a tragic omission in common—'tragic' insofar as the objectively existent, but squandered, opportunity no longer pertains to the possibility of success, as in earlier cases, but rather of mere survival. Moreover, the sequence of the three constitutes a sinister climax: for the Mytileneans (more precisely, only for the Mytilenean *demos*) the death sentence is set aside at the last minute; it is executed upon the Plataeans; and on Corcyra the situation ends in aimless, general slaughter that dispenses even with any appearance of 'legality' (81.4–5).

Accordingly, the writer appends to the last event his own judgment, informing it with a significance that points beyond the individual case. But this is not a significance which is valid merely for the remainder of the war, rather—one should recall the reference to the constancy of human nature— it is of such a kind as to be true of human behavior generally, thus pointing beyond the events recorded in this historical work into the future.

At the same time there is a feature overarching everything so far presented: the account of the revolution (3.82 f.) also takes up those characteristics of wartime mentioned in the preview of 1.23[45] and confirms them in the light of the facts observed in the meantime.

The three examples of Mytilene, Plataea and Corcyra may for now suffice as evidence for the significance attached to the *concrete situation*, in particular the situation of death, in the Thucydidean view of humanity. This dimension can only be presented in descriptive narration because it is characteristically beyond the realm of argumentation found in the speeches (which most of the time represents the active forces in events).

We have more than once pointed out that interpretations based almost exclusively on the picture presented in the speeches of the historical work can only partly grasp the reality intended by the historian. On the other hand, it would be impossible to doubt that the view of events presented in the speeches of the various actors is an integral part of understanding the historical process as a whole, especially since, as we have seen,[46] the impulses originating in the speeches have a decisive influence on actual events.

The historian himself, in the so-called 'pathology', analyses such subjective views (in particular their ethical component) and comes to the conclusion that the tenor of certain terms can dissolve, making room for a different tenor. 'Caution' can characterize an action which would otherwise be called 'cowardice'; 'courage' can become synonymous with 'irrational daring', etc. (3.82.4).

The cause of such changes, in Thucydides' view, is war itself, the βίαιος διδάσκαλος ('teacher of violence', 82.2) that teaches men to adapt their behavior to altered circumstances by taking away current material well-being (ὑφελὼν τὴν εὐπορίαν τοῦ καθ᾽ ἡμέραν, 82.2) to give free rein to the great impulses (αἴτιον ἀρχὴ ἡ διὰ πλεονεξίαν καὶ φιλοτιμίαν, 'the cause was thirst for power, motivated by greed and ambition', 82.8).[47]

If we ask, based on this analysis, where in Book 3 the actors attempt to achieve their goals by shifting the meaning of words, then of course what comes to mind—besides the speech of the Thebans—is the manipulation of the concept of justice with which Cleon argues for the death-sentence against the Mytileneans.[48] Here the ambivalence of ethical terms described at 3.82 f. is brought out in a practical example.

One cannot read the speech of Cleon without keeping in mind the speech of the Mytileneans at Olympia.[49] In this speech already the attitude behind such words as τὸ δίκαιον and ἀρετή is seen as the basis for a relationship between partners: ἐν γὰρ τῷ διαλλάσσοντι τῆς γνώμης καὶ αἱ διαφοραὶ τῶν ἔργων καθίστανται ('for in the difference of thought the differences of actions also manifest themselves', 10.1).

For the Mytileneans it became painfully clear that a stable alliance can only be founded on a balance of fear (11.2, cf. 82.7), and that the 'autonomy' supposedly guaranteed them by Athens itself was only a means for the more powerful partner to establish its own prestige in the eyes of the international public (11.3–4).

Cleon's speech confirms the ambivalence and devaluation of the δίκαιον by viewing it from the position of the stronger. Just as the Corinthians, having no advantage to offer, had clung to the δίκαιον in their first speech in Book 1;[50] and just as the Athenians had accused the Spartans of upholding the δίκαιον only out of consideration for their own immediate advantage (1.76.2);[51] so now Cleon tries to construct a δίκαιον that corresponds to what is ξυμφέρον for Athens (3.40.4; cf. 47.5). In order to accomplish this he must, of course, deny the true principles of Athenian power politics. If the ambassadors of Pericles' Athens had contemptuously dismissed the δίκαιος λόγος ('the argument of justice'), ὃν οὐδείς πω παρατυχὸν ἰσχύι τι κτήσασθαι προθείς τοῦ μὴ πλέον ἔχειν ἀπετράπετο ('to which so far no one, given the chance to acquire something *by force*, *has given priority* so that he was dissuaded from gaining his advantage', 1.76.2), Cleon now makes the application of precisely these Athenian principles into a reproach against the Mytileneans (ἰσχὺν ἀξιώσαντες τοῦ δικαίου προθεῖναι, 'who deemed it right to set force over justice', 3.39.3).[52] In other words, he defends the attitude for which the Athenian envoys had once upon a time reproached the Spartans as being insincere (...μέχρι οὗ τὰ ξυμφέροντα λογιζόμενοι τῷ δικαίῳ λόγῳ νῦν χρῆσθε, '...until you now, computing your advantage, make use of the argument of justice', 1.76.2).

This insincerity (a result of the desire to portray the Mytilenean revolt as a genuine breach of trust against the δίκαιον) is reflected in the rosy picture that Cleon paints of the situation of the Mytileneans in their alliance with Athens: αὐτόνομοί τε οἰκοῦντες καὶ τιμώμενοι ἐς τὰ πρῶτα ὑπὸ ἡμῶν ('living in autonomy and honored by us most highly', 3.39.2); he even speaks of εὐπραγία, their 'prosperity', which leads to ὕβρις ('insolence') and of ἡ παροῦσα εὐδαιμονία ('their present good fortune', § 4, cf. 3). Thus, in the chapter describing Athens' 'friendly' relations with Mytilene, no allusion to any dissatisfaction on the part of the ally is allowed (although Cleon had earlier—37.2—admitted that dissatisfaction existed generally among the allies), and the Periclean dilemma of Athens' 'tyranny' (ἣν λαβεῖν μὲν ἄδικον δοκεῖ εἶναι, ἀφεῖναι δὲ ἐπικίνδυνον, 'which to arrogate appears to be *unjust*, but to give up is dangerous', 2.63.2), as Saar has correctly pointed out,[53] is formulated with the greatest caution and in such a way as to avoid any use of the legal term δίκαιος (just): εἰ γὰρ οὗτοι ὀρθῶς ἀπέστησαν, ὑμεῖς ἂν οὐ χρεὼν ἄρχοιτε ('for if they defected *rightfully*, you would certainly rule *unrightfully*', 40.4). The speaker inadvertently (Thucydides' irony is, as usual, bitter) lets a reference to the true state of affairs slip out when he states that pity is out of place πρὸς τοὺς...ἐξ ἀνάγκης...καθεστῶτας αἰεὶ πολεμίους ('toward those...who *by necessity...are always enemies*', 40.3).[54]

This style of argument, it is true, is not unlike that of the Corinthians and Athenians in Book 1, but at this point in the work it acquires a more concrete significance. One must not forget that it is being used to accomplish the murder of the Mytileneans (and the enslavement of their wives and children), which our author has made the focal point of his entire account of the events at Mytilene.

Thucydides' horror at natures like the βιαιότατος (3.36.6)[55] Cleon finds regretful expression in the remark that during the war, 'the goodness of a simple mind, of which nobility is the chief component, was seen as ridiculous, and vanished' (3.83.1).

This sort of criticism need not be the result, as many have apparently taken it, of a personal nostalgia for the ethics of the past, which would have *caused* Thucydides to reject, in the area of ethics, the sophistic 'enlightenment' and its dismantling of traditional values. On the contrary, the critique proceeds from a first-hand experience of the consequences of a false 'enlightenment' optimism (the war in general and the sentence passed on Mytilene in particular are certainly among those consequences). Thus for him—and this is not the first time this has been found by us—*the results become the standard for evaluating the plans.* This method of 'observing from the end forwards' (as it might be called) is not oriented according to a table of old-fashioned values[56] but rather according to the norm of *correct understanding.* Just as Thucydides has again and again emerged during the course of our investigation as mastering (and practicing) the advances of contemporary logic and rhetoric, it is clear in the present case that the real object of the historian's criticism is Cleon's *error in thought* (naturally on account of its monstrous consequences; to limit one's view to the illogical combination of δίκαιον and ξυμφέρον is to overlook this point). The deterrent theory which Cleon here advocates (i.e. that the Mytilenean sentence will serve as an instructive precedent for the other allies, cf. παράδειγμα, 40.7) is shown to be absurd by his own words:[57] παράδειγμα δὲ αὐτοῖς οὔτε αἱ τῶν πέλας ξυμφοραὶ ἐγένοντο, ὅσοι ἀποστάντες ἤδη ἡμῶν ἐχειρώθησαν..., ('But they neither took example from the harsh experience of all those of their neighbors who upon defecting from us have already been put down...,' 39.3). In other words, the killing of the Mytileneans would not only be a violation of the true δίκαιον,[58] but also *pointless in terms of the purpose for which it was intended*! Viewed in this way as well, we can again understand why Thucydides emphasizes so vigorously the tragic moments in the events surrounding Mytilene.

Diodotos responds at the pertinent passage of his speech (45) by attacking Cleon's mistake, but first invalidates Cleon's pretentious claim to the δίκαιον of Athenian vengeance (44.1–4). For Diodotos, τὸ ξυμφέρον is the only thing which counts, and his own more realistic[59] way of looking at the situation turns what Cleon had termed the Mytileneans' ἀδικία and ἀδικεῖν into ἁμάρτημα and ἁμαρτάνειν (45.1, 3).[60] In refuting Cleon's specific case by a fundamental analysis of human behavior,[61] he for some time loses sight entirely of the concrete reason for the debate.

Scholars have long realized that it is the historian's own voice which speaks through this analysis.[62] It may serve as a touchstone for the correctness also of our own interpretation thus far.

It is important that Diodotos, although he at first speaks of the vain attempt of states to protect themselves from criminals by increasingly harsh punishments (45.1–3), subsequently leaves the judicial point of view aside completely. This is because in his opinion the principle of deterrence underlying the threat of punishment ignores certain fundamental elements of human nature. These elements are fundamental because they precede even any predication of man in terms of state or society. In this point Diodotos is very close to the account of the so-called 'pathology', where the functioning of the conventions which are necessary for any sort of community is seen almost as the exception ('peace'),[63] which, due to the μεταβολαὶ τῶν ξυντυχιῶν,[64] must all too soon give way again to the merely superficially restrained ὀργαί[65] (3.82.2).

I offer the following exegetical translation of the central sentence (45.4)[66] (threats of punishment are ineffectual), 'but

poverty	which, through	*distress of need,*	provides	the *courage to daring,*
power[67]	which, through	*insolence* and *presumption*	(provides)	the *desire for more*;
and, life's other situations	as each, through	men's *passion*	is controlled by	some *incurable stronger force,*[68]

—all these drive people to take risks'.

How much early Greek anthropology resounds through this passage need scarcely be pointed out. Gomme (*loc. cit.*) points correctly to Solon 1.33 ff.; perhaps an even closer relative to the second clause of the sentence is Solon 5.9: τίκτει γὰρ κόρος ὕβριν ('for satiety gives birth to insolence').

But it is precisely the similarities which clarify the differences. For Solon even Hubris in the end (as ἄτη) has a definite place in the world order of Zeus and Dike (1.11 ff., cf. 75 f.), and punishment remains unavoidable because it belongs to this same order (1.31). But in Thucydides' anthropology there is no indication that one must resort to a religiously grounded order (or an order grounded in metaphysics) in order to explain the phenomenon 'human being'. For the people that Diodotos has observed, laws (as well as penalties) are no more than hindrances that must be overcome on the path to attaining one's end (45.1).

If one at all wishes to grasp the reality of human behavior, the first step is to understand man outside ethical categories (and motivations) as a being for whom any means will serve for, and no restraint detain from, the achievement of a goal once conceived: ἁπλῶς τε ἀδύνατον καὶ πολλῆς εὐηθείας, ὅστις οἴεται τῆς ἀνθρωπείας φύσεως ὁρμωμένης προθύμως τι πρᾶξαι ἀποτροπήν τινα ἔχειν ἢ νόμων ἰσχύι ἢ ἄλλῳ τῷ δεινῷ ('it is simply *impossible* and a sign of great *naïveté*, whenever someone thinks, once human nature sets out eagerly to achieve some goal, *to possess a means of prevention in the strength of laws or some other intimidation*', § 7, cf. 1.76.2).

This ever-recurring stubbornness, which cannot be deterred from its plan even by the experience of others ('precedents'), is in all its irrationality the actual topic of discussion, and the sentence translated above (45.4) is devoted to its description.

It may serve as a confirmation of our interpretations so far, that Diodotos begins with the *situations* in which people find themselves, and that he considers the *emotions* arising from these situations as impulses to go beyond current circumstances towards a more desirable constellation, the prospect of which has an irresistibly powerful attraction—so powerful that people do not seek to avoid the risks (or perhaps do not face them).

Of course there is no schema implied here—Thucydides is not a systematic philosopher—into which one might force every psychological process related in the *History* (it has often enough been pointed out, sometimes disapprovingly, that the terms of 3.45.4 itself are not precisely parallel), but there is a sufficient number of similar processes to illustrate the point.[69]

What makes Diodotos' analysis so significant for our topic is in general the fact that he, too, sees man in the tension between the initiative and the result of his actions, and in particular that he expressly defines the starting position from which courses of action receive their initial impulses. This human position (or disposition) turns out to be anything but rational, since the combination of life circumstances and the wishful fantasy that transcends those circumstances is not due to a process of reflection. Indeed, wherever the reflective capacity is brought to bear it has an ancillary function. 'And hope and desire, the latter leading and the former following, the one devising the enterprise [the attempt] but the other prefiguring [suggesting] the availability of external circumstances, cause the greatest harm in all things…' (45.5).

It is clear: desire dictates the goal of the action and *only then* does hope of success command the intellect to look for reasons that also make the undertaking seem practicable in respect to supposedly objective facts.[70]

For this, too, there is ample evidence in the text. Within a smaller framework, Aristogeiton is a good example of someone driven to act by *emotion* (ἐρωτικῶς περιαλγήσας καὶ φοβηθεὶς, 6.54.3). It was for the sake of an erotic relationship (desire *par excellence*) that he devised the 'attempt' (ἐπιβουλεύει, § 3) in which he believed he could deal with the difficulties posed by his station as μέσος πολίτης ('a middle class citizen') with the '*hope*'[71] of spontaneous aid from his fellow citizens.

In a larger framework one thinks of the genesis of the Sicilian expedition (6.24.2–4). Here desire (ἔρως, ἐπιθυμία) and hope (εὐέλπιδες) put out of mind any thought of the danger (ἀσφάλεια νῦν δὴ καὶ πολλὴ ἔσεσθαι). The suggestibility of masses of people, outlined by Diodotos (3.45.6), also plays a role (6.24.2), as does the attractiveness of an unexpectedly (ἀδοκήτως, 3.45.6) favorable situation (παρὰ γνώμην, Nicias 6.11.5; cf. 26.2), also described by Diodotos. It is the speech of Alcibiades which lobbies for the 'availability of circumstances', laying an 'objective' foundation for hope with pseudo-rational arguments. This speech, from its insensitivity to justified warnings (from Nicias) to its dubious use of the εἰκός (6.17.4; 18.4), is similar to the final Corinthian speech of Book 1,[72] which likewise wishes to stimulate its audience to action.

These two factors then (i.e. the confirmation of Diodotos' analysis of human action by the concrete case of the Athenian decision in favor of the Sicilian expedition, and the fact that observation of this case suggests parallels to the speeches concerned with the beginning of the Peloponnesian War) offer insight into a structure found throughout the work. For further evidence we can look to the assembly which takes place in Syracuse, in response to the first news of the Athenian decision to go to Sicily, and which is characterized by the same categories of observation as the debate in Athens.

Scholars have often wondered about Thucydides' motive for including Hermocrates' long and, in the realm of action, ineffectual speech (6.33 f.). One answer has been that Thucydides wanted to record for posterity the simple strategy of meeting the Athenians on the open sea 'because of its boldness'.[73]

In reality, however, Thucydides saw this as an objective opportunity that was missed.[74] The cautionary tone of the entire speech, as well as the fact that it is ignored, puts it in a class with the speeches of Archidamus (1.80 ff.), Nicias (6.9 ff.), Teutiaplos (3.30) and with Lamachus' plan (6.49). It is similarly characteristic in that its potential effect (how much suffering would have been avoided in Sicily and especially Syracuse, had Hermocrates' advice been taken!) is thwarted by the blind, emotion-driven baiting of a party politician of Cleon's stripe (πιθανώτατος, 6.35.2 = 3.36.6).

But what elevates the speech to tragic heights and surrounds the statesman Hermocrates with the tragic irony of a Cassandra is not merely that his words contain the *truth* about Athens' hostile intentions or that his plan (to stop the Athenian force while still at sea or even before departure from Greece) offers the *only* chance for successful action. Rather, it is that the warner's knowledge is exposed not only to stubborn rejection from those who are threatened yet refuse to listen to reason, but even to ridicule (...ἐς γέλωτα ἔτρεπον τὸ πρᾶγμα, 35.1).

The speech of his opponent Athenagoras (6.36ff.) is also steeped in tragic irony, but this time with reference to Athens. His passionate perform-ance is thoroughly comparable to the prewar harangues of the Corinthians and Sthenelaidas. However, his insistence that the Athenians would never be party to such a senseless undertaking (as Hermocrates had outlined it) is *reasonable* (similarly his use of εἰκός, 36.3; cf. μοι δοκοῦσιν, 37.2). He uses the *same* arguments that Nicias put forward in his warning speech before the Athenian Assembly (6.9ff.).

But what good does it do to impute reason to an enemy when, like the Athenians, they have not based their decision to go to war on rational considerations?

Apparently Thucydides is using the person of Athenagoras indirectly to place in an ironic light the Athenian decision in favor of the Sicilian expedition.

Thus, Diodotos' remarks allow us to grasp three of the work's great speech complexes in a unified way. And since all three are concerned with the initiation of war (it is well known that Thucydides sees the Sicilian expedition as a war in itself, nearly as great a conflict as the Peloponnesian War, 6.1.1), it is here if anywhere that we should ask what Thucydides might mean by 'at one time similarly recurring circumstances' (1.22.4), i.e. by *repetition* in history.

To answer we need only take account of the parallels to be found in the three great debates at Sparta, Athens and Syracuse: justified warnings, argued on the basis of reason or objective truths (Archidamus, Nicias, Hermocrates), are thrown to the winds and forced to yield to unreason-able, untrue, even previously refuted, but in each case impassioned and haranguing, claims (Corinthians, Sthenelaidas, Alcibiades, Athenagoras), which advocate taking a dangerous risk. In Diodotos' words, αἱ δ᾽ ἄλλαι ξυντυχίαι ὀργῇ τῶν ἀνθρώπων ὡς ἑκάστη τις κατέχεται ὑπ᾽ ἀνηκέστου τινὸς κρείσσονος ἐξάγουσιν ἐς τοὺς κινδύνους ('life's other situations, as each – through men's *passion* – is controlled by some *incurable stronger force*, drive people *to take risks*', 3.45.4).

The *recurring* structure set forth here permits us to speak of a main thought unifying the multifarious developments and events which Thucydides presents, and preventing the disintegration of the work into isolated individual sequences.

At the same time, in terms of our comparative morphology of Thucydidean event-sequences, this structure authorizes us to compare the endpoints, too, and to see a relationship between the death march of the Athenians in Sicily and the unfortunate issue of the Mytilenean revolt.

If we originally set out to widen the scope of the present chapter by borrowing our interpretive categories from the speech of Diodotos, the attempt has been successful. Because this speech has validity beyond the case of the Mytileneans fighting for their freedom, it can justifiably be seen as one of the key passages of the work.

What is decisive for our thesis is that this expanded scope *is no longer bound to the political realm* (or, for that matter, to Athenian imperialism)—this must be emphatically asserted against de Romilly[75] and others; rather, it is inclusive not only of both parties (Corinthians and Athenians, Syracusans and Athenians) but of individuals (Aristogeiton and, as we will show later, Cleon).[76] There is a question which has come up again and again in the present study: beyond the political and (seemingly) rationalistic (positivistic) foreground of the work might there be a range of understanding which transcends this sphere? This question can now with good conscience be answered in the affirmative.

Thus the speech of Diodotos forms a genuine complement to the narrative of the year 427. Three series of events are described, all of which drive towards the extreme situation with increasing intensity, and at the end of the last one the author himself makes a statement which points beyond the concrete situation. Similarly, preceding the end of the first complex, Diodotos leaves behind the concrete occasion for the debate to consider the human causes of such events. Just as Thucydides himself (3.82), Diodotos has before his eyes the usual result of such initiatives.[77]

And just as the phenomenon of the human being eager to act without first reflecting reaches beyond party opposition in its significance, the fatal end of an event-complex has essentially the same weight, whether it involves the expeditionary force of mighty Athens or the last defenders of the politically insignificant Plataea.

Notes

[1] Cf. Gomme *ad* 16.1.
[2] See above, pp. 83 ff.

³ This corresponds almost verbatim to the 'hinge' passages 1.83.1, 92.7.

⁴ Cf. the time references at 2.86.5, 92.7 (above, pp. 86, 89).

⁵ πρὶν ἐκπύστους γενέσθαι, 30.1; cf. ἄφνω τε καὶ νυκτός, 3.

⁶ On the as yet not satisfactorily explained crux τὸ κενὸν (καινὸν, κοινὸν) τοῦ πολέμου (30.3), see besides the commentaries Bill 1937, 160 f.

⁷ The council of the Athenian generals at 6.47 ff. provides a parallel from outside the present context; three suggested strategies are under discussion:

(1) attack against peripherally situated Selinus, cautious reserve elsewhere (Nicias, 47);

(2) first canvassing for allies in Sicily, then attack on Syracuse and Selinus (Alcibiades, 48);

(3) immediate attack on Syracuse using the psychological effect of surprise; probability (εἰκός) of favorable circumstances; following a victory over Syracuse, the rest of Sicily will automatically come over to Athens (Lamachus, 49).

The following passages make it possible to conclude that Thucydides considers the—rejected—third suggestion the most promising:

(a) 6.50.1: Λάμαχος μὲν ταῦτα εἰπὼν ὅμως προσέθετο καὶ αὐτὸς τῇ Ἀλκιβιάδου γνώμῃ,

(b) 7.42.3: Demosthenes, having just arrived with the reinforcements from Athens, wants to attack Syracuse *immediately* in order to avoid 'what happened to Nicias'. In a parenthetical remark Thucydides explains that Nicias (after the recall of Alcibiades) had earned the contempt of the Syracusans, and moreover allowed them to secure help from the Peloponnese, by his failure to attack the city at once.

Lamachus' suggestion, so thoroughly described though remaining without consequence in the factual realm, becomes in Thucydides' eyes *ex eventu* a 'missed opportunity' that could have brought swift success and—viewed from the very end—could have saved the Athenian expeditionary force. (That such an opportunity is not likely to be granted twice is shown by the failure of Demosthenes—in the night battle on the heights of Syracuse—who essentially copies Lamachus' idea in connection with his own).

The parallel to Teutiaplos' suggestion, acceptance of which could have saved Mytilene, is obvious.

⁸ See above, pp. 53 ff., 59.

⁹ Finley (1947², 314 n. 42) does not take this into account.

¹⁰ A 'substitute action': ἐπειδὴ τοῦτον τὸν κίνδυνον φοβεῖται, 31.1; cf. above, p. 91 with note 34.

¹¹ It is similar in this point to the speech of Archidamus in Book 1 (see above, p. 54).

¹² Euripides' *Heracles* (734 ff.) may serve as an example: with the words μεταβολὰ κακῶν, the chorus sings of its joy about the arrival of the rescuing Heracles, who is at that very moment about to avert the impending destruction from his family by killing the usurper Lycus.

¹³ In the tragedy, the possibility of rescue exists only subjectively in the minds of the people affected; in Thucydides' narrative this possibility exists objectively, viewed from outside the situation. The decisive function of this speech for the

context as a whole makes it impossible for me to see it (as does Mathieu 1940, 242 f.) as a 'later' addition.

[14] Cf. above, pp. 66, 90.

[15] Cf. Gomme *ad* 49.3.

[16] Cf. the verbal echo in reference to a comparable situation in the fighting for Syracuse: παρὰ τοσοῦτον μὲν αἱ Συράκουσαι ἦλθον κινδύνου, 7.2.4.

[17] Cf. Gomme *ad* 50.1; Mathieu 1940, 248.

[18] Cf. above, pp. 6 f. (on 6.59.1 ff.) and p. 68 (on 2.6.3–4).

[19] See above, p. 28.

[20] On this topic, cf. p. 40 above.

[21] Cf. τοιαύταις ὀργαῖς ταῖς πρώταις, 85.1.

[22] Finley 1947[2], 159 f.; cf. Egermann 1942, 291 f.

[23] See above, Chapter 1.

[24] See especially 8.66.2–4, 92.11.

[25] A parallel instance of this technique (Finley 1947[2], *loc. cit.*, 1940, *passim*; Egermann, 1942, 292) is found in the detailed description of the first appearance of the plague (see above, p. 78), which is accompanied by the indication that it is valid for later occurrences (πρῶτόν τε ἦρξε…ἀνομίας τὸ νόσημα, 2.53.1; cf. ἐν τοῖς πρώτη, 3.82.1); the second appearance is mentioned only briefly insofar as it is necessary for that context (3.28). In a similar vein, see also Erbse's remarks (1953, 38 ff.).

[26] See above, p. 109.

[27] It should be pointed out that this passage—appropriately to the theme of civil war—takes into consideration only *one* side of the ἀνθρώπινον, namely, the suffering brought about by human beings, whereas in 1.22 (see above, p. 28) factors beyond human control are also meant.

[28] I have difficulty understanding how Müri (1947, 273 f.), in his otherwise excellent study, could have come to the conclusion that the *recognition* of such inevitability should become a 'useful' possession. Parry has argued correctly on this point (1981, 109).

[29] Cf. above p. 16 with note 32.

[30] 3.82.2b: this passage contains characteristics found in the comparison of Books 1 and 2.

[31] With the exception of the plague and the attack on Plataea (a sort of introductory paradigm of a complete sequence).

[32] On the Athenian attitude, see Gomme 1954, 146 ff.

[33] ἐγένετο δὲ καὶ ἡ διάφευξις αὐτοῖς μᾶλλον διὰ τοῦ χειμῶνος τὸ μέγεθος, 23.5.

[34] Winter 428/7.

[35] Cf. Gomme 1954, 123 f.; Diller 1962, 195.

[36] Cf. above p. 81.

[37] This *literary* purpose for the addition should prevent Analysts from using it as a 'superfluous' chronological indication (Mathieu 1940, 250).

[38] 68.5; cf. the expansion here compared to the normal concluding formula for Mytilene: τὰ μὲν κατὰ Λέσβον <…> οὕτως ἐγένετο.

[39] Above, pp. 70, 81.

[40] Cf. especially 3.53.3, 57.4, 59.3.

[41] Thucydides himself tells the reader which of the two speeches has right on its side: the word ὠφελίμους (68.4) picks up the expressions for advantage in the speech of the Plataeans (χρησίμῳ, τὸ ξυμφέρον, 56.3; ὠφέλιμοι, 56.4; κερδαλέως, 56.6; τὸ ξυμφέρον, τὸ...ὠφέλιμον, 56.7).

[42] Cf. the brevity of the statement at 2.6.3 (above, p. 68).

[43] See above, pp. 81 f.

[44] See above, p. 68.

[45] The κίνησις μεγίστη of 1.1.2 also reappears in the ἐκινήθη of 3.82.1, this time more specific in its connotation.

[46] Cf. Chapter 3.

[47] This amounts to a consistent continuation of the descriptions of human behavior as found in the so-called Plague Chapters (see above, pp. 77, 97 f.).

[48] Connections between Cleon's speech and 3.82 f. have often been pointed out, cf. Finley 1947[2], 187; Wassermann 1954, 46; Saar 1954, 80.

[49] For the interrelation of the Mytileneans' speech and Pericles' Funeral Oration see above, p. 51.

[50] See above, pp.38 f.

[51] See above, p. 48.

[52] Cleon's ἐν ᾧ γὰρ ᾠήθησαν περιέσεσθαι (39.3) corresponds to the Athenians' παρατυχόν... at 1.76.2; thus the thought of 1.76.2 is cited in its entirety.

[53] Saar 1954, 53 n. 2.

[54] The climax in the devaluation of the δίκαιον comes in the *deceitful* speech (labeled a 'Trugrede' by Strasburger 1958, 33) of Euphemos (6.82 ff.). The following may serve as a schema of that speech. 'I will prove that my intentions towards you are friendly by showing that my own ξυμφέρον is bound up with your wellbeing (no one really believes in other motives besides self-interest anyway).' It is precisely this demonstration of Athenian self-interest that is deliberately counterfeited (the reader has been aware since 6.6.1 that the Athenians intend to subdue *all* of Sicily). The δίκαιον–ξυμφέρον antithesis will no longer serve here: the only way left to outwit an opponent is to paint a false picture of one's own interests while hiding one's true motives. Through a kind of intellectual somersault the old alternative δίκαιον–ξυμφέρον becomes the new alternative: (counterfeited)ξυμφέρον–(true)ξυμφέρον.

[55] Considering the measures advocated by Cleon here, it is unlikely that Thucydides is applying this adjective in order to force on his reader his own personal dislike of the man (Woodhead 1960, 297).

[56] It scarcely needs to be stated that this does not preclude a strong ethical sense, which in any case is unmistakable in Thucydides' presentation of the material.

[57] On this point, see Saar 1954, 44.

[58] On the difference between Cleon's sentence and Diodotos' (the latter acquits the Mytilenean *demos*), cf. Bodin 1940, 50.

[59] 'The "realistic" argument against Kleon's theory', Gomme *ad* 45.1.

[60] Bodin translates the latter (probably going too far) as 'commettre des erreurs'

(1940, 41).

[61] See Bodin 1940, 43 f.

[62] Cf. Müri 1947, 251 f.; de Romilly 1951[2], 138; Saar 1954, 80; Wassermann 1956, 34 on the whole speech: 'mouthpiece of Thucydides' own position'.

[63] See above, p. 113.

[64] Cf. the significance of the ξυντυχίαι in Diodotos' speech 45.4.

[65] Cf. ὀργῇ, 45.4.

[66] The text as printed by Jones-Powell is entirely comprehensible. Even the change to τὸν ἄνθρωπον (Steup, *Anhang*) seems unnecessary. Gomme's interpretation (*ad loc.*) abandons the parallelism intended by the author.

[67] Gomme *ad loc.*

[68] ὡς ἑκάστη…κατέχεται is *variatio* for (αἱ δ᾽ ἄλλαι ξυντυχίαι ὀργῇ…) ἀνήκεστόν τι παρέχουσαι.

[69] For example, one thinks of the mood change of the Athenians resulting from the plague-altered situation. The constellation that points beyond the momentary circumstances and determines the action with an irresistible attraction is the vision of the end of the war (2.59.2). Clearer still is the behavior of the Corinthians (driven by the emotion of concern for Potidaea) in the conflict situation with Athens: the risk advocated (but not recognized as such) in the third Corinthian speech is the war itself.

[70] Thucydides says much the same thing himself at 4.108.4: '…they arrived at their judgments more through clouded desire than sure foresight—just as people generally entrust what they desire to thoughtless hope, but reject by means of rigorous [so Gomme—with the scholiast—*ad. loc.* against earlier interpreters] reasoning what they find disagreeable.'

[71] ἤλπιζον, 6.56.3, cf. above, p. 5.

[72] See above, pp. 55 f., 58. The role of 'mass-psychosis' in the genesis of the Sicilian expedition is overemphasized (at the expense of Thucydides' carefully worked-out differentiation of factors) by Topitsch (1946, 45 ff.). For Thucydides, Alcibiades must be judged according to the same criteria as the masses that follow him, even though in Topitsch's terminology he would have to be classified as an 'Einzelmensch'.

[73] Pohlenz 1919, 124.

[74] This aspect is treated in greater detail in Chapter 10 below.

[75] As long as one sees in the historian's work primarily only the story of Athenian imperialism, the Mytilene complex together with its speeches must remain an illustration of the problem κάθεξις τῆς ἀρχῆς, i.e. of a 'problème précis' of lesser 'historical' significance: 'Qui plus est, même limitée à la question précise du châtiment en cas de révolte, l'antilogie révèle plus de subtilité dialectique que d'insistence historique' ('What is more, itself limited to the precise question of punishment in the case of a rebellion, the antilogy reveals more dialectical subtlety than historical insistence.') (1951[2], 147). In what follows, de Romilly concludes, precisely because the debate goes beyond its concrete occasion and takes a position on certain contemporary issues as well (the danger of rhetoric, usefulness of punishment, etc.), that it is relatively unimportant to the 'late' Thucydides! As

a result, the anthropological material in the speech can only have meaning for her in the (evidently subordinate) dimension of 'entrainement psychologique' (1951², 268 ff., see esp. 274 f.). Müri's verdict is much more warranted when (1947, 273, cf. 269 f.) he ranks 3.45 among the 'ultimate' of the historian's statements, 'actually ontological in their intent'.

[76] See below, p. 147.

[77] Cf. ἐξάγουσιν ἐς τοὺς κινδύνους, 45.4; πλεῖστα βλάπτουσι, 5; ἐπὶ πλέον τι αὐτὸν ἐδόξασεν, 6.

RECURRING STRUCTURAL ELEMENTS
OF EVENT SEQUENCES
Books 3.94–114; 4.2–5.14

The previous chapter's analysis of the great event-complexes of 427 provides an indication of the general significance which Thucydides the writer is capable of deriving from an individual fact. The increasing emphasis placed on the final situation of each complex appears to indicate a mode of thinking which favors selecting the categories of historical observation based on the outcome of chains of events (though not, of course, in the 'naive' sense of early Greek religion which allows no one to be called happy before his death). A depiction so thoroughly tied as is Thucydides' to the ultimate facts of a series of events (which may all too often be aptly described as lamentable and irremediable) does not devote attention only to plans (to the extent that they form the polar opposite to results) and their various perspectives; rather it must also probe the structural elements of the event sequences taking place between the two poles.

At this point we will once again take up the theme of Chapter 5 by an analysis of two more event sequences. In doing so, due attention must be given to the categories newly evaluated in Chapter 6.

Twice already the historian has demonstrated his synoptic abilities by describing uncontrollably expanding conflicts. The internal discord in remote Epidamnus led by way of the intermediary stages Corinth/ Corcyra to the direct confrontation of the superpowers Sparta/Athens.[1] And the quarrel among the inhabitants of Amphilochian Argos, which soon embroiled the same superpowers, led to an unexpected test of the naval warfare concepts of both sides and in its final stage to the unexpected Peloponnesian advance in the direction of the Athenian harbor.[2]

The first sequence to be investigated here can be seen as parallel in its initial phases to the events emanating from Amphilochian Argos.[3]

In the summer of 426 the Athenian general Demosthenes, commanding a combined force of Athenians, Acarnanians, Zacynthians, Cephallenians and Corcyreans, conducts operations before the main city of the island of Leukas. His military situation is so favorable as to make success appear certain (3.94.1–2).

However, he allows himself to be persuaded (ἀναπείθεται, § 3) by Messenians from Naupactus, who point to the size of his assembled army (στρατιᾶς τοσαύτης ξυνειλεγμένης), to attack the Aetolians. They entice him with the prospect of extending Athenian influence also throughout τὸ ἄλλο Ἠπειρωτικόν; because of their opponents' *light* armament (σκευῇ ψιλῇ χρώμενον), military difficulties are forecast as negligible (3–4).

Demosthenes follows this advice not so much as a favor to the Messenians as out of personal ambition. He is thinking of advancing through Aetolia, Locris, Doris and Phocis all the way into Boeotia,[4] and ἄνευ τῆς τῶν Ἀθηναίων δυνάμεως (95.1) at that.

But already for the first stage—the conquest of Aetolia—the plan incurs deficiencies and is in need of certain corrections. The army, initially 'so large', shrinks with the loss of the Acarnanians (aggravated διὰ τῆς Λευκάδος τὴν οὐ περιτείχισιν, 'because of the non-circumvallation of Leukas', § 2) and the Corcyreans. Then the Ozolian Locrians, the only members of the force familiar with Aetolian tactics and terrain, fail to arrive (ἔδει αὐτοὺς πανστρατιᾷ ἀπαντῆσαι τοῖς Ἀθηναίοις, 'they *should* have met the Athenians with all their army', § 3). But because he meets with no resistance in his opening forays, Demosthenes is confirmed in his opinion, taken over from the Messenians, that the Aetolians are not to be taken seriously as military opponents (97.1). Thucydides criticizes his irresponsible recklessness both directly (τῇ τύχῃ ἐλπίσας, 'trusting the good fortune') and indirectly by describing the Aetolians' extensive and timely defense measures (96.3) *immediately before* reporting Demosthenes' expectations (97.1–2).[5]

Meanwhile, Demosthenes is induced to push deep into Aetolian territory without waiting for the Locrians: τοὺς Λοκροὺς οὐκ ἀναμείνας,[6] οὕς...ἔδει[7] προσβοηθῆσαι (ψιλῶν γὰρ ἀκοντιστῶν ἐνδεὴς ἦν μάλιστα) ('not waiting for the Locrians, who...*should* have arrived for help (for he was most in need of lightly armed spearthrowers)', 97.2). He achieves one last hollow victory with the conquest of Aigition, a town surrounded by mountains. From then on, however, he is vulnerable to retaliation from the neighboring heights, because his hoplite army is too sluggish to be effective against the quick charge and equally quick retreat of the *light-armed* (ψιλοί, 98.1) Aetolians. When his archers, not numerous to begin with, are finally exhausted and decimated and his Messenian guide killed, there is no longer even a chance for orderly withdrawal. The fleeing soldiers stumble into pathless ravines or fall in various other ways an easy prey to their *swift* pursuers (ἄνθρωποι ποδώκεις καὶ ψιλοί, 98.2). The Aetolians' *light* weaponry, which in the original plan had been calculated as a negligible factor,[8] develops into the chief reason for the defeat of the Athenians and their allies. Casualties are so high that the reporter lays aside his usual reserve (πᾶσά τε ἰδέα κατέστη τῆς φυγῆς καὶ τοῦ ὀλέθρου…, 'and every form of flight and destruction occurred…'), and there remains no hope of an invasion of Boeotia: the survivors 'with difficulty' manage to reach the starting point (ὅθενπερ καὶ ὡρμήθησαν, § 3). In the end there is only *regret for the senseless death* of the fallen: τοσοῦτοι μὲν τὸ πλῆθος καὶ ἡλικία ἡ αὐτὴ οὗτοι βέλτιστοι δὴ ἄνδρες…διεφθάρησαν ('so many in number and of the same young age these were killed…as the bravest men', § 4).

There is nothing more to say after this pronouncement. As usual, the narrative falls off after the compositional climax (98.5).

But Demosthenes' failure is only the first phase of a longer series of events, just as Knemos' defeat and the first naval engagement of 429 led to bringing about the real confrontation,[9] or as in 433 the battle of Sybota helped to draw Sparta into the conflict.[10]

For that same summer (426) the Aetolians manage to persuade (πείθουσιν, 100.1; cf. ἀναπείθεται 94.3 ~ πείθουσι 2.80.1) the Spartans (διὰ τὴν τῶν Ἀθηναίων ἐπαγωγήν, 'because of the introduction of the Athenians') to undertake a campaign against Naupactus.[11] The Peloponnesians launch their attack in the fall and, passing quickly through Locris, soon take an unfortified suburb of Naupactus. It is only with difficulty (χαλεπῶς διὰ τὴν ἐκ τῆς Λευκάδος ἀναχώρησιν, 102.3) that Demosthenes is able to persuade the Acarnanians to send a relief force to the threatened Athenian base (102.4). This foils the Peloponnesian intention; their general, Eurylochos, lets himself be talked into (πείθουσιν, § 6; cf. πεισθείς, § 7) a *substitute* plan for taking Amphilochian Argos. The psychological effect of failure has once again—as in 429[12]—diverted the momentum of events into a new area. The prospect of πᾶν τὸ Ἠπειρωτικόν ('all of the mainland', § 6) serves as bait, just as it had in the case of Demosthenes (τὸ ἄλλο Ἠπειρωτικόν, 'the rest of the mainland', 94.3), or the hope of taking Acarnania, Zacynthos and Cephallenia had in 429 (2.80.1). The local inhabitants' skill in manipulating the superpowers for their own purposes is stressed again and again (cf. 3.82.1b), and made into a continuous theme by the repetition of forms of πείθειν ('persuade'). It is in this πείθειν, which owes its success to the suggestion of a ξυμφέρον ('advantage'),[13] that we find the underlying 'hinges' in each of these series of events.

In the winter of 426/5 the Ambraciots march southward and take Olpae. The Acarnanians, in an attempt to block the Peloponnesian advance from the south, summon Demosthenes from Naupactus as well as an Athenian fleet from the Peloponnesian coast to help. At this the Ambraciots in

Olpae call up the entire Ambraciot army, fearing that the Acarnanian blockade might succeed in halting the Peloponnesian advance near Crenae (105.1–4).

However, Eurylochos and his troops manage to slip past the Acarnanians, and join forces with the Ambraciots in Olpae (106).

At this, on the opposite side of a ravine from the Peloponnesians and Ambraciots, the Acarnanians and their allies make camp under the command of Demosthenes, while the Athenian fleet drops anchor in the Gulf of Ambracia. The two armies lie encamped on opposite sides of the ravine for five days before the battle takes place (107.1–3; the reinforcements summoned from Ambracia—as the Athenian relief fleet in 429— have at that point not yet arrived).

Demosthenes and the Acarnanians win the all-day battle through a trick: by means of a surprise attack against the enemy's rear, devised before the fighting,[14] he destabilizes the numerically superior enemy force (108). Eurylochos himself falls, leaving the Peloponnesians in the situation brought about by his substitute plan: cut off on all sides.

The next day Demosthenes secretly grants a select group the opportunity to withdraw, his purpose being to isolate the Ambraciots and bring the Spartans, and indeed Peloponnesians in general, into disrepute for abandoning their allies (109).

At about the same time news arrives of the approach of the main Ambraciot force, which was sent for six days ago (105.4) and has as yet no knowledge of the battle. Immediately Demosthenes sends a portion of his army ahead to occupy strategically important positions and makes preparations to follow with the rest (110). His purpose is of course to prevent unification of the enemy forces.

At this moment (ἐν τούτῳ, 111.1)[15] the Peloponnesians specified in Demosthenes' agreement set out (some of them and many of the Ambraciots escaping with them are killed in the confusion), i.e. they free Demosthenes from the awkward position of having to fight on two fronts.

The ensuing battle on double-crested Mount Idomene (112) secures for Demosthenes a *reversal* of the situation into which he had blundered at Aigition. Evidently he has made use of his previous experience.

At dawn he attacks the unsuspecting Ambraciots, surprising their sentries with his (Doric-speaking) Messenians and quickly causing a massacre of the enemy. Familiarity with the terrain[16] provides him with exactly the same advantage that light-armed troops have over hoplites.[17] The situation of the fleeing Ambraciots is so similar to that of the defeated Athenians at Aigition that one formulation is even repeated verbatim (ἐσπίπτοντες ἔς τε χαράδρας...διεφθείροντο, 'and falling into the ravines...they were killed',

112.6 = 98.1; the phrase πᾶσα ἰδέα τῆς φυγῆς, 'every form of flight', from 98.3, one of Thucydides' strongest expressions, returns as well at 112.7). We may assume that the historian is counting on his reader to compare the descriptions of the two battles.

The most obvious conclusion of such a comparison would be that Demosthenes has made good his defeat at Aigition by achieving a corresponding success. This at least is the conclusion drawn by the general himself: his victory allows him to return to Athens (which he had not dared to do after his defeat: 98.5, cf. 114.1).

However, what matters to Thucydides is not the loss and restoration of Athens' or Demosthenes' military reputation—this is noted, as it were, in the margin. What is important is the idea of the *repetition* of *defeat*, viewed each time from the perspective of the sufferers. Just as he does after the description of the first battle, after the second (at Idomene) he abandons the restraint of the purely factual report, this time recounting (in dialogue form!) a conversation taking place the day after the battle (113).

A messenger[18] arrives from the Ambraciots who had fled along with the departing Peloponnesians to ask for the bodies of those killed during their flight. Since he knows nothing of the second battle, but his interlocutor takes him for an emissary from those Ambraciots who have just recently been defeated at Idomene, there at first arises some confusion. The gradual clarification of this misunderstanding (where the shields of the fallen Ambraciots serve as the first *gnōrismata*) eventually brings the messenger face to face with the fact of the more recent misfortune.

His reaction is the climax of the episode: ὁ δὲ κῆρυξ ὡς ἤκουσε καὶ ἔγνω…ἀνοιμώξας καὶ ἐκπλαγεὶς τῷ μεγέθει τῶν παρόντων κακῶν <u>ἀπῆλθεν εὐθὺς ἄπρακτος</u> καὶ <u>οὐκέτι ἀπῄτει</u> τοὺς νεκρούς ('But when the herald heard and realized…groaning and struck by the vastness of the present misfortune, *he left rightaway without having accomplished his task*, and *he no longer demanded* to have the bodies returned', § 5).

What is the meaning of this scene which falls outside the usual framework of the *History*?

We may first observe that Chapter 113 forms the literary climax of the entire section whose factual high points are the corresponding battles of Aigition and Idomene. This compositional feature is consonant with the technique we pointed out in the larger sequences of the year 427.[19] Immediately before the high point comes the stylistically enhanced report of the second battle (112); immediately afterwards, in sober narrative form, comes the overview of pertinent events, ending in the usual neutral closing formula (τὰ μὲν κατʼ Ἀμπρακίαν οὕτως ἐγένετο, 'So the events concerning Ambracia came to an end, 114.4). In other words, climax and section-end once again do not coincide.

This proves, on compositional grounds, that the messenger vignette contains the essential statement resulting from the sequence as a whole. Let us return to the question of its meaning.

We must keep in mind that the messenger had not come on some unspecified mission, but rather to facilitate the fulfillment of a *sacred* duty, namely, the burial of the dead. It is scarcely necessary to turn to *Antigone* for an illustration of the context. For Thucydides himself the decline of funeral customs during the plague (2.52.4)[20] is a symptom of the disintegration of the community's existential foundations. When the messenger abandons his mission (οὐκέτι ἀπῄτει) under the influence of the misfortune, essentially failing to carry out a sacred duty, this too is a symptom: the foundations of his own existence are so shaken that the most axiomatic conventions lose their grip on him.

Then there is the episode's formal construction: here a comparison with contemporary tragedy suggests itself (by its dialogue form alone) even more clearly than in the speech of Teutiaplos discussed above.[21] The step-by-step progression from misunderstanding towards the recognition (cf. ἔγνω, § 5) of the reality of the situation bears an unmistakable similarity to a *recognition* scene (I mention again the shields which function as *anagnōrismata*). For the individual stages of the recognition process from hearing (ἤκουσε) through to the act of fully understanding what has been heard (ἔγνω), we can compare (out of many possible examples) how Agave, under the circumspect guidance of Kadmos, comes to the full realization of what she has in her hands[22] (in her case the stages consist of 'beholding' and 'seeing with understanding'):

> Ag. ἔα, τί λεύσσω; τί φέρομαι τόδ᾽ ἐν χεροῖν;
> Κα. ἄθρησον αὐτὸ καὶ <u>σαφέστερον μάθε</u>.
> Ag. ὁρῶ <u>μέγιστον ἄλγος</u> ἡ τάλαιν᾽ ἐγώ.

> Ag. Alas, what do I see? What is this I am carrying in my hands?
> Ka. Look at it and understand more clearly.
> Ag. I, wretched one, see the greatest pain.

Why does Thucydides here resort to means normally used to signal a climax in tragedy?

His next sentence (113.6) gives the reason for the messenger's reaction: πάθος γὰρ τοῦτο μιᾷ πόλει Ἑλληνίδι ἐν ἴσαις ἡμέραις μέγιστον δὴ τῶν κατὰ τὸν πόλεμον τόνδε ἐγένετο ('*For* this calamity certainly was the greatest among those during this war for a single Greek city in as many days'). Thucydides goes on to say that the reported number of slain is so incredibly high that he prefers not to mention it.

If this objective attestation of the calamity is intended to 'give the reason for' (i.e. in this case, 'make comprehensible') the messenger's behavior, then evidently the episode—appended to the account as it is with the purpose of describing that behavior—must have the function of giving the *reader* an impression of the calamity by viewing the horror of it through the eyes of an *individual* experiencing and being overwhelmed by it. In other words, the disaster is so immeasurable that it can only be made comprehensible (or communicable) by a limited representation of it.

This excess of misfortune, then, is the goal towards which events have been developing; and it is what enables the reader to recognize the chain of cause and effect in all its gruesome logic. A brief recapitulation of the points emphasized by our author may help to illustrate this. (It should be stressed that the sequence restated was in this case neither interrupted by chance nor can be taken in the sense of an exactly predictable and repeatable necessity. Each impetus of the events is determined only by the desires of the actors as they occur abruptly at what we called the 'hinges' in the course of events.)

The beginning lies with Demosthenes allowing himself to be persuaded to give up a promising position on the island of Leukas—for the prospect of a larger success. Because he, hoping for success, irresponsibly fails to take the necessary precautions, his desire for victory in the real world turns into the deplorable and pointless death of young soldiers (first climax). The simple fact of this (unsuccessful![23]) attempt draws the Peloponnesians into the area bent on retaliation. Failure to achieve this retaliation produces in the Spartan commander Eurylochos the psychological disposition to score a compensatory success if possible. The Ambraciots, who till now have been uninvolved, see in this constellation the opportunity to settle an old score. However, the first action undertaken by the combined Ambraciots and Peloponnesians is a failure, and the Ambraciots' new allies, themselves in a hopeless situation, seek safety in a withdrawal that savors of betrayal. The Ambraciots, now entirely on their own, surprisingly suffer the worst defeat inflicted on any people during the whole war (second climax).

It is here if anywhere that we can speak of 'tragic' historiography—*not*, however, in the sense of the rhetoricizing historiography of later centuries which made use of stereotypes borrowed from tragedy to create tension psychologically. It would be out of place to speak of *topoi* in reference to such statements in Thucydides.[24]

Here lies an essential point for understanding our author:[25] for Thucydides, the 'meaning' of a series of events is never something fixed in advance (in the sense that 'material' is selected according to how well it exemplifies a preformulated theory—or pathos),[26] rather the sense of each series of events grows out of that series and is *inseparably* joined to it. Even in the case of the messenger, who is speechless in the abrupt realization of the calamity and who leaves without accomplishing his mission, there must be no doubt about the historicity of the event. On the contrary, it is only because the tragic outcome *is part and parcel of the facts themselves* that Thucydides takes advantage of the opportunity to rely on forms of expression borrowed from tragedy. This circumstance permits us to speak of a *symbolism of the facts* in Thucydides.

It is worthwhile to ask why it is so important to the historian to enhance the immanent tragic quality of this series of events. It should be clear that this is the continuation of a perspective ascertained in the previous chapter: the characteristic feature of the final situation in a given event sequence, i.e. that there is no way out, remains the focus of observation.

But the Ambraciots' explicit πάθος (113.6), which involves the reader by being expressed in terms of one individual, probably goes deeper still.

As evidence that this perspective is not mere chance, we can point to the familiar misfortune (ξυμφορά) of Mykalessos. This occurrence, though far removed from the sphere of the great political events, is thought worthy to be singled out for emphatic treatment.

A horde of Thracians, returning home from Athens, falls upon the unsuspecting village of Mykalessos and slaughters every living thing in it: men, women, children (including the pupils of the largest school in the place—they have just assembled in the school building), even the draught animals: καὶ <u>ξυμφορὰ</u> τῇ πόλει <u>πάσῃ οὐδεμιᾶς ἥσσων</u> μᾶλλον ἑτέρας <u>ἀδόκητός</u> τε ἐπέπεσεν αὕτη καὶ <u>δεινή</u>, 'And, as calamities go, this one befell *the whole city smaller than none*, more *unexpected* than any other one and *terrible*'—this statement forms the climax of the description (7.29.5). The calamity is so great that Thucydides takes it up again in his usual concluding formula, expanded for precisely this occasion: τὰ μὲν κατὰ τὴν Μυκαλησσὸν πάθει χρησαμένην οὐδενὸς ὡς ἐπὶ μεγέθει τῶν κατὰ τὸν πόλεμον ἧσσον ὀλοφύρασθαι ἀξίῳ τοιαῦτα ξυνέβη ('Such did the events concerning Mykalessos come to pass: in relation to its small size the city experienced a calamity less worthy of lament than none during the war', 30.3).

Both judgments (7.29 and 30, cf. also 3.113), in that they stress relative size, demonstrate that the historian's essential statements are determined by proportionality, not by absolute quantity. The recurrence[27] of judgments that place a qualitatively high value on people and events which, in terms of the enormity of the war itself, would seem insignificant permits us to ascribe also to the climaxes of Ambracia and Mykalessos fundamental significance for the work as a whole.

Where is the significance in these last cases?

The mention, which they have in common, of pathos refers back to the παθήματα that, next to its length, were the most conspicuous general characteristic of the war (1.23).[28] That is, *in the suffering* at Ambracia and Mykalessos, *we grasp the war as Thucydides himself saw it.* When this suffering is further characterized as ἄξιον ὀλοφύρασθαι ('worthy to lament over'), it draws the observer in (author as well as reader)—and demands *sympathy.*

In the face of the experience of human suffering, then, this most distant of all historians, who never moralizes and never makes generalizing ethical pronouncements (how often has this ἐποχή been mislabeled as power-political amorality!), who at the most inserts a 'prudently' or 'foolishly' (and then usually in view of the bitterest consequences)—it is here, then, that he dispenses with the impenetrable distance he normally maintains between himself and his work (and his reader).

Grene[29] believes that Thucydides lays aside his usual reserve when events might have turned out otherwise,[30] i.e. where, as at Mykalessos, not the 'necessity' of the greater events of the war generates misfortune, but rather where contingency (Grene uses the word 'chance') is an appropriate observational category:

> …the peculiar ironies of chance inspired him with a kind of horror…the disproportion between the people and their fate awakened a human pity which is *nonetheless explicable* according to his own *theory of history* and its development.

Grene may be taken as representative of a large group of interpreters who ascribe to Thucydides a theory of history whose backbone they find in the concept—ultimately borrowed from *our* history of philosophy—of '*anankē*'.[31] Against this background, any of the author's statements that seem too personal can easily be 'justified': they only apply to accidental occurrences that have nothing to do with the inexorable progress of history.

But such interpretations are basically a (probably unconscious) way of avoiding the challenge of letting even the historian's seemingly 'subjective' statements stand at full value. The reference to 1.23 by itself prevents relegating the category of suffering to the work's periphery. In addition, as we have already pointed out, Mykalessos and Ambracia are by no means exceptional in terms of the work as a whole (I would remind the reader of the conclusion of the attack on Plataea, the Corcyrean civil war, and also the end of the Sicilian expedition).

Grene is certainly correct in detecting horror on the part of the author in a passage such as 7.30.3—but not merely at the irony of an accident (one thinks of the Ambraciot messenger, of the pointless death of the young soldiers at Aigition), rather at the *senselessness* of the πάθος, which is a *general* characteristic of the war.

Perhaps this feature does not fit very well into the system of a 'theory of history', but it forms—just as its opposite, the optimistic plan—a perpetually recurring, and therefore constitutive, category in the statements which this historian makes about the place of human beings in history. We would scarcely be wrong in seeing the personal experience of war in the genesis of such a concept. The objection that Goethe was the first to put personal experience into a literary framework is pointless.[32] Leaving aside for the moment the questionable validity of literary historical moulds, this objection may be appropriate in the case of long-established genres that rely upon a more or less fixed tradition (and collection of *topoi*). But Thucydides comes at a beginning, and (rejecting the methods of his 'predecessors') makes his own rules for his own presentation (1.22)—just as he also chooses for himself the categories with which to grasp (and, for that matter, constitute) the object of his inquiry.

The perspectives gained so far may prove their potential in the second sequence to be analysed in this chapter, namely, the action around Pylos and Sphakteria (4.2 ff.). The historical significance of this segment is quite on a par with the developments in Book 1 that lead to the war, inasmuch as the developments of Book 4 go in the opposite direction: from war to the possibility of peace.

Commensurate with its political theme, this complex has long been subjected to special questioning. To what extent is there an (unjust) *antagonism* on the part of (the aristocratic or exiled) Thucydides towards the demagogue Cleon?[33] Did the *Periclean* Thucydides see in the Athenian policy of expansion a departure from the—in his view the *only* valid—defensive program of Pericles?[34] To what extent did the *Athenian* Thucydides consider the rejection of Sparta's offer of peace to have been a missed opportunity for his native city?[35]

Within this network of problems, taken over in nearly all its variations from the nineteenth century, is lodged one further dilemma. The Pylos affair was the starting point for Cornford's 'Mythistoricus' thesis because he saw in it the first appearance of a *new principle*,[36] chance ('Fortune')[37] as a personified agent in history. '...the occupation of Pylos was THE MOST CASUAL THING IN THE WORLD.'[38] We have already shown[39] to what extent his (certainly exaggerated) thesis stood in the way of later, especially positivist interpreters.

Opinions have since been divided on this question. Did Thucydides intend to represent the chance-determined nature of events around Pylos and Sphakteria as decisive,[40] or to assign it a secondary significance?[41]

If we subject this much-explored passage to yet another scrutiny, it is without any systematic notions about τύχη in the historical thought of our author or speculation about party politics.

In the spring of 425 Demosthenes, after his return from Naupactus no longer occupying the office of *strategos*, asks for and receives permission to employ at his own discretion an Athenian fleet (bound for Corcyra and Sicily) 'around the Peloponnese' (4.2.4).

While under way, the admirals receive word that the fleet is urgently needed at Corcyra. As a result they reject the private citizen's bidding to land at Pylos (an understandable response in view of the insignificance of this barren and uninhabited coastal place). But a chance storm forces the fleet to put in at Pylos (and Thucydides is explicit about the accidental nature of the storm):[42] ἀντιλεγόντων δὲ <u>κατὰ τύχην</u> χειμὼν ἐπιγενόμενος κατήνεγκε τὰς ναῦς ἐς τὴν Πύλον (3.2).[43]

Demosthenes, pointing to the naturally strong location of the place, the fact of its being uninhabited and the availability of building material (stones and timber, 3.2; notice the kicking in of *detail* normally found at points of special interest to Thucydides), demands that the admirals fortify it immediately: this had been his original purpose in coming along. There is an exchange of words with the admirals: there are plenty of uninhabited headlands in the Peloponnese if he wants to waste the city's money by seizing (them)...[44] Suddenly the reader understands why Demosthenes has not revealed his intention at home, but rather waited until arriving at Pylos itself: he would never have obtained permission for this 'questionable' undertaking...[45]

Now we learn his plan: he wants to create a base from which his Messenians (from Naupactus now but originally from this area) can raid Spartan territory. He expects once again to make use of their Doric Greek, which had earlier[46] proved such an asset.

Nevertheless the admirals refuse. Even an appeal to the taxiarchs[47] and then the crews is of no avail. The chance which at first had seemed so favorable for Demosthenes brings him no success—until the crews themselves, out of *boredom* brought on by the inability to sail,[48] hit upon the idea (ὁρμὴ ἐνέπεσε) of building the fortification after all, and enthusiastically (παντὶ...τρόπῳ ἠπείγοντο, 4.3) at that. In the absence of iron stonemason tools the soldiers select serviceable stones by hand and fit them together. Invention also supplies a substitute for hods: the soldiers clasp their hands behind their backs and, bowing forward, carry the clay in the space thus created (§ 2—such zeal!).

Why does Thucydides offer such details? Doubtless to illustrate the extent to which the realization of the plan depends upon factors beyond

Demosthenes' control. The work proceeds (for six days!) undisturbed because the Spartans *happen* (ἔτυχον, 5.1)[49] to be observing a festival that keeps them at home (additional factors are their unconcern because of the insignificance of the place and the absence of the main army in Attica).

However, the main force under King Agis takes the news of the fortification of a headland on their coast much more seriously (νομίζοντες...οἰκεῖον σφίσι τὸ περὶ τὴν Πύλον, 6.1). Their considerably more vigorous reaction leads to the *first metabole* of the situation: in an attempt to remove the thorn from their side, the Spartiates themselves march for Pylos *immediately* (εὐθὺς ἐβοήθουν, 8.1) upon their return from Attica; they also send word both around the Peloponnese for troops to come to Pylos as fast as possible (ὡς τάχιστα) and to their sixty ships which are at Corcyra (8.1 f.). On the enemy's side, too, then, the development runs counter to Demosthenes' expectation.

Demosthenes, left behind at Pylos with a small force, thus finds himself in a difficult position. Spartan hopes of easily taking the place (ἐλπίζοντες ῥᾳδίως αἱρήσειν οἰκοδόμημα διὰ ταχέων εἰργασμένον καὶ ἀνθρώπων ὀλίγων ἐνόντων, § 4; cf. ἄνευ τε ναυμαχίας καὶ κινδύνου...κατὰ τὸ εἰκός, § 8) appear justified. This is especially true since Spartiates occupy the island (Sphakteria) situated in front of the only natural harbor on the coast and both entrances (north and south) are to be blockaded[50] to prevent the Athenian fleet, recalled[51] by Demosthenes, from finding any base (§§ 4–8).

For Demosthenes—aside from the fact that his plan elicits such an energetic response—it comes as a particular surprise that the enemy *also* intends attacking *from the sea*. He had not reckoned with this possibility (9.3) and so had more strongly fortified only the side of the place facing inland. In addition, the fact that the surrounding country is far and wide uninhabited (a feature Demosthenes originally regarded as an advantage: ἔρημον αὐτό τε καὶ ἐπὶ πολὺ τῆς χώρας, 3.2) plays out, in view of the impending enemy assault, as a disadvantage in that he is unable at least to obtain weapons for the crews of the few ships left to him: οὐ γὰρ ἦν ὅπλα ἐν χωρίῳ ἐρήμῳ πορίσασθαι, 9.1. *Once again*, however, chance (ἔτυχον)[52] comes to his aid: Messenian pirates appear just in time to provide him with the most necessary (though shoddy) weapons as well as 40 hoplites.

The defenders' only hope lies in the *offensive*. They must attack the Spartans while they are still trying to gain a foothold somewhere on the rough coastline; once the Spartans are on land, Pylos can on the sea side no longer be held. With this in mind, Demosthenes *leaves* the fort with 60 hand-picked hoplites and a few archers and takes up a position right on the beach. His address to these troops reflects just how desperate a situation his plan has led him into: he expressly *forbids* his soldiers to think rationally about the urgency of the present situation (ἀνάγκη, ἀνάγκην, 10.1); rather he urges them to adopt an attitude of *thoughtless optimism* (ἀπερισκέπτως εὔελπις), i.e. blind impetuosity: ὅσα γὰρ ἐς ἀνάγκην ἀφῖκται ὥσπερ τάδε, λογισμὸν ἥκιστα ἐνδεχόμενα κινδύνου τοῦ ταχίστου προσδεῖται ('for, whenever matters have come down to necessity like these, *they least allow of calculation* but require facing the danger as quickly as possible'(10.1).[53] The inversion of the situation seems complete.

However, the ensuing battle (4.11 f.) justifies Demosthenes' measures. Because the ships are forced by the narrowness of the landing area to put in a few at a time, he is able to prevent the soldiers from disembarking. For almost two full days he stands his ground against their attempts (in which the Spartans under Brasidas' leadership heedlessly allow their ships to be wrecked on the beach). What is grotesque about the situation is that the Spartans (landlubbers that they are) are attacking their own land from the sea, and the Athenians, who place all their pride in their naval power, are on land resisting an attack from the sea. (ἐς τοῦτό τε περιέστη ἡ τύχη…, 12.3). At last the Spartans decide to bring up siege machinery and to approach from the landward side.

It is in this situation (ἐν τούτῳ δέ, 13.2) that the recalled Athenian fleet arrives, but in the absence of an available base (the Spartiate occupation of the island has thus proven effective) it is forced to withdraw to the more distant island of Prote.

Despite the warning thus provided, the Spartans for some reason (ἔτυχον, 4) do *not* carry out the blockade of the two passages (an integral part of their plan: 8.7). As a result, the next day the Athenians, prepared for battle and recognizing (γνόντες, 14.1) this opportunity, sail into the inner harbor and succeed in surprising and neutralizing the enemy fleet. The Spartans, περιαλγοῦντες τῷ πάθει, ὅτιπερ αὐτῶν οἱ ἄνδρες ἀπελαμβάνοντο ἐν τῇ νήσῳ ('greatly pained about the calamity, because their men were cut off on the island', § 2), plunging into the water and desperately attempting to prevent the Athenians from towing off their ships, are nonetheless unable to forestall an Athenian victory.[54] Even the arrival around this time of the allies summoned from the Peloponnese (8.2) does not alter the situation (§ 5).

The Spartan reaction illustrates how completely this *second metabole* has reversed the situation: the appropriate officials are sent ὡς ἐπὶ ξυμφορᾷ μεγάλῃ ('under the impression of a great calamity') from Sparta down to the base camp to make a decision based on their on-the-spot impression of the situation (i.e. without consulting the government at home). But their decision is as follows: a (local) armistice with Athens (with guarantees of provisions for the men who have been cut off on the island), during which an embassy should be sent to Athens for *peace negotiations* (4.15–16).

This is the second reversal not foreseen in Demosthenes' plan. Indeed, its consequences are so significant that they attain dimensions *unimaginable* in terms of the original plan. The caprice of occurrences has ridden rough-shod over the man and his plan. This is made clear by the decisive factors highlighted in Thucydides' analysis: serendipitous weather, bored soldiers, a coincidental festival in Sparta, unexpected reaction in King Agis' camp, lucky timing on the part of the arriving Messenian pirates, grotesque battle situations, harbor entrances that happen not to be blocked—the 'randomness'[55] of the sequence of events is only too obvious.

The chain of occurrences, beginning at insignificant Pylos (as unimportant as Epidamnus had once been), leads to the same situation as the impulse that began at Epidamnus in Book 1: to the *decision between war and peace.* The question arises how people will respond to this unhoped-for situation after several years' experience of war.

The speech of the Spartan emissaries at Athens (4.17–20) refers repeatedly in the relevant section (17.4–18.5) to the part played by chance in creating the present situation.[56] Taken as a whole, this passage is one long *warning* to Athens not to be seduced by its present good fortune. In its allusions to the unpredictability of chance, the speech is the polar opposite of the optimistic final prewar speech of the Corinthians:[57] ...οὐκ εἰκὸς ὑμᾶς διὰ τὴν παροῦσαν νῦν ῥώμην πόλεως...καὶ <u>τὸ τῆς τύχης</u> οἴεσθαι <u>αἰεὶ</u> μεθ' ὑμῶν ἔσεσθαι ('...it is not reasonable that you, because of your city's present strength..., believe that *the element of chance* will also be always on your side', 18.3). The Spartans continue, pointing out that war does not abide by human wishes: its direction is in the hands of the τύχαι (how much more positively the Corinthians viewed—at 1.122.1—war's unpredictability!); the Athenians ought not to let it come about that, if they should at some time later suffer some setback (as could easily happen), even their present success be attributed to chance (as opposed to strength and capability) (4.18.5).

The last words constitute an unmistakable *vaticinium ex eventu,* one, however, which applies not only to the future but to the chance-dependent nature of the present success. In so doing, it contributes considerably to the reader's appreciation of the unexpected *situation of decision-making.* This aspect is brought out again after the offer of peace and alliance (4.19): 'Reconciliation is fitting now more than ever for us on both sides, before some irreparable harm[58] (ἀνήκεστον) occurs between us and takes hold of us...' (20.1). In the latter case, however, there would remain only 'eternal enmity'. <u>ἔτι δ' ὄντων ἀκρίτων</u>...διαλλαγῶμεν, καὶ αὐτοί τε ἀντὶ πολέμου εἰρήνην ἑλώμεθα καὶ τοῖς ἄλλοις Ἕλλησιν ἀνάπαυσιν κακῶν ποιήσωμεν ('*as long as matters are still undecided*…let us come to a reconciliation, and let us both ourselves choose peace instead of war and provide the other Greeks with a rest from their sufferings', § 2). The remaining Greeks could offer no hindrance since they do not have the means to oppose the combined superpowers Sparta and Athens.[59]

This speech has an unambiguous function: an event sequence, whose development was beyond all human control, in the end confronts the actors for a single moment with a situation of *free choice* (cf. ἑλώμεθα, 20.2) such as has not been possible since the decision for war in Sparta: ἀντὶ πολέμου εἰρήνην ('peace instead of war').

We saw earlier[60] how Thucydides in the prewar section of his history enhanced with speeches those places where the actors determined a still open future development by means of their attitudes and decisions. Among these, the cautionary speech of Archidamus (warning because of his *experience* of previous wars) proved to be the *last opportunity* for peace. The same may be said of the speech of the Spartan emissaries in the year 425.

'But people who have experienced very many reversals (μεταβολαί) in both directions are least likely to put their faith in favorable turns of events—a piece of knowledge which your city (and we) should probably own by experience (δι' ἐμπειρίαν)' (17.5). What 'experience' could be meant here if not the experience of this very war? The reader may think of the losses caused by the unforeseeable plague or the picture of the war sketched in the first half of the present chapter.

'For you can deal[61] with your present good luck…without suffering just what happens to people who, while being unfamiliar with such a situation, meet with some good fortune: αἰεὶ γὰρ τοῦ πλέονος ἐλπίδι ὀρέγονται…' (17.4).

But just as the Corinthians and Sthenelaidas had once thrown Archidamus' (in Thucydides' opinion, well-founded) caution to the winds, here *once again*—this time on the Athenian side—the irrational forces carry the day; and that, even though once again the voice of reason grounded in experience has been enabled to have its say:

οἱ δὲ τὰς μὲν σπονδάς, ἔχοντες τοὺς ἄνδρας ἐν τῇ νήσῳ, ἤδη σφίσιν ἐνόμιζον ἑτοίμους εἶναι, ὁπόταν βούλωνται ποιεῖσθαι πρὸς αὐτούς, τοῦ δὲ πλέονος ὠρέγοντο. μάλιστα δὲ αὐτοὺς ἐνῆγε Κλέων… (21.2).

But they (i.e the Athenians), since holding the men on the island, believed that *the treaty would be available* to them whenever they would feel inclined to conclude it with them (i.e. the Spartans), *yet they wanted more*. And Cleon especially pushed them…

143

Already Cornford saw that Cleon here displays behavior which he himself has condemned in the Mytilenean debate (3.39.4).[62] Topitsch[63] also adduces 3.39.4 and recognizes a correspondence to 4.17.4:

εἴωθε δὲ τῶν πόλεων αἷς ἂν μάλιστα καὶ δι᾽ ἐλαχίστου ἀπροσδόκητος εὐπρα-γία ἔλθῃ, ἐς ὕβριν τρέπειν· τὰ δὲ πολλὰ...κακοπραγίαν ὡς εἰπεῖν ῥᾷον ἀπωθοῦνται (scil. οἱ ἄνθρωποι) ἢ εὐδαιμονίαν διασῴζονται (3.39.4).

But unexpected success usually leads those states to insolence which it visits to the highest degree and in the shortest time; and most often...they [scil. human beings] so to speak more easily shake off a failure than preserve a situation of good fortune.

This is how a bit of truth, contained in a demagogue's harangue, turns out to be true of its speaker.[64]

This is a striking example, given in terms of a single individual, of the impossibility of getting human nature under control (even *self* control) by rational considerations. Even the calamity of an ongoing war—a leading category for this historian—is not capable of setting reflection before action.[65] Diodotos' analysis proves itself yet again: every situation has an ἀνήκεστον ('element of "incurable"', 3.45.4) hidden within it like a thorn that irresistibly pricks people to reach beyond the situation they have currently attained—even when they have been warned that they will by their very reaching bring about an ἀνήκεστον (4.20.1) which will cause them to lose their existing attainments. The dilemma of the irrational, uncontrollable, and irresistible impulse on the one hand and the irreversible result on the other is one of the most important 'repeti-tions' that Thucydides knows. One might call this a 'lesson', but only if one keeps in mind that the author of this realization could find no one who had 'learned' the lesson, either at the outbreak of the war or at the possibility of ending it in 425—or at the decision in favor of a new war against Sicily in 416.

Can we really suppose that the historian expected future generations of humanity to be more docile, as so many of his interpreters have believed? Or that he intended to provide any maxims at all (particularly within a narrow, exclusively political framework) like some proto-Machiavelli?[66]

It seems to me that the doubts[67] which arose during our systematic retrospective have now definitely been confirmed. In the events around Pylos, *chance* creates a favorable situation—this situation is blindly gambled away by the *people* to whom it ought to appeal. Neither the course of events nor the behavior of human nature displays here the faintest appearance of a *predictable* (calculable) 'constant'. What remains *constant*—as we said earlier[68]— is the *unpredictability* of the factors (whose various types cannot be considered singly, isolated from the entirety of the events, and without consideration of the combined effects of the other factors).[69]

For whose eyes would Thucydides have attempted to make history transparent and predictable? Surely not (in the opinion of many interpreters) for *Spartan* politicians! The neuralgic point in the secondary literature on Thucydides lies where, behind Thucydides the 'rationalist', there suddenly pops up the partisan writer; next the 'Athenian' historian comes along to confuse the issue further: how could Thucydides disapprove of Cleon's behavior (when, after all, peace in the year 425 offered Athens no 'real advantages'!), how could the 'Periclean' and admirer of Themistocles speak in favor of an Athenian–Spartan double hegemony (the policy of a Kimon!)? And how could the *chance* element in the events of 425 be of importance for Thucydides, when in the long run they contribute nothing to the *outcome* of the war (= the fall of Athens)?

It is a truism that the way a question is asked to a certain extent prejudices the answer. If the fall of Athens were the historian's main theme, the chain of occurrences at Pylos would (perhaps) be relatively unimportant.

However, it is expressly the course of the *war itself* (1.1.1) from the perspective of conditions recurring for the *people* concerned (1.22.4) that constitutes the theme. Consequently, the rejection of peace in 425 is a decisive situation both for the theme (the war) and the thesis (repetition) and is on a par with the decision to go to war in 431.

The importance that the Spartan peace proposal held for Thucydides can be illustrated also from another direction. In the previous chapter and in the first half of the present chapter we have attempted to show how he judges the war—true to the characteristics given at 1.23—primarily in terms of its effects on the people involved. Must not the mere thought of an 'ἀνάπαυσις κακῶν', brought about by chance (and occurring under the aegis of both the superpowers whose consent made the outbreak of war possible in the first place), take on the quality of a unique and irretrievable opportunity for Greece[70] (even in the eyes of a 'late' Thucydides who had lived through the whole war)?

Far be it from us to pin the label 'pacifist' on Thucydides, especially since this designation—just as the picture of the objective historian—has likewise been reduced in the secondary literature to the stamp of a partisan position. Just as, thanks to Schwartz, Thucydides was seen with a contemporary slant as the representative of Athenian power politics, he later automatically became an opponent of the 'party' designated by Pericles as ἀπράγμονες, 'unpolitical', (2.63), a group which in turn was enrolled in the ranks of unpatriotic 'pacifists'.[71]

It is our task to secure for this historian—without in the least seeking to minimize his political reflections—the position of the impartial observer to which he personally and justifiably lays claim. If he himself thinks in categories that point beyond the political realm, then his interpreter must respect this fact.[72]

We return to the narrative. The Athenian refusal comes as a surprise to the Spartans (since they expected that the Athenians would be just as grateful for an offer of peace now as they would have been earlier: 21.1; cf. 2.59.2), while the Athenians imagine that the Spartan offer will remain on the table indefinitely (since Athens has a kind of security deposit on Sphakteria).[73] As a result, the Spartan emissaries are confronted with treatment and demands that—even though ὑπὸ τῆς ξυμφορᾶς ('under the influence of the calamity') they are ready to compromise—make continued negotiation impossible (22.3). With this, the armistice at Pylos has run out (4.23).

And now comes the *third* (once again unforeseen: παρὰ λόγον, 26.4) *metabole,* which justifies the warnings delivered by the Spartan emissaries in Athens.[74] The blockade of the island continues with no prospect of capturing the Spartiates. On the contrary, the men on the island are constantly receiving provisions by one means or another despite the Athenian blockade. Yet each day that the siege drags on takes its toll on the Athenian fleet (which has no harbor and is depending on long supply lines; 4.26). The originally high spirits of the Athenian forces plummet: ἀθυμίαν τε πλείστην ὁ χρόνος παρεῖχε παρὰ λόγον ἐπιγιγνόμενος, οὓς ᾤοντο ἡμερῶν ὀλίγων ἐκπολιορκήσειν... ('and greatest *despondency* was caused them by the fact that, *against their calculation*, time went on, since they were holding the belief that they would force them to capitulate within a few days…', § 4).

In Athens the news of the difficult position of the troops (ὅτι ταλαιπωρεῖται, 27.1) raises intense concern because continuing the blockade into the winter is, for technical reasons, unthinkable. πάντων τε ἐφοβοῦντο μάλιστα τοὺς Λακεδαιμονίους, ὅτι ἔχοντάς τι ἰσχυρὸν αὐτοὺς ἐνόμιζον οὐκέτι σφίσιν ἐπικηρυκεύεσθαι ('Most of all they were afraid because they thought that the Spartans were no longer making any peace offers to them for the reason that they were holding something positive in their hands', 27.2): openness to peace has disappeared as quickly on the Spartan side as it once had on the Athenian side (21.2). Again human beings find themselves at the point where they must suffer the consequences of their foolish decisions: καὶ μετεμέλοντο τὰς σπονδὰς οὐ δεξάμενοι ('and they regretted not having accepted the treaty', 27.2).

There follows the famous account of the assembly in which the continuation of the undertaking is entrusted to Cleon, who rashly promises to bring the Spartiates alive to Athens in twenty days or kill them on the spot (27.3–28). The fact that he chooses Demosthenes as his fellow *strategos* (29.1, cf. 2), and asks only for *light* armed troops (but no more Athenian hoplites) shows that he is already familiar with Demosthenes' plan of attack and its requirements.[75]

Demosthenes had decided on this expedient when he could no longer stay in control of the increasingly difficult situation: οἱ γὰρ στρατιῶται κακοπαθοῦντες τοῦ χωρίου τῇ ἀπορίᾳ καὶ μᾶλλον πολιορκούμενοι ἢ πολιορκοῦντες ὥρμηντο διακινδυνεῦσαι ('for the soldiers, *suffering* under the difficult conditions of the place and *being besieged rather than besieging*, *were set on* making the desperate attempt', 29.2).

Exactly as when the Spartans had attacked his fort, counterattack is once again the only opportunity left him. But there is also the additional factor that the general is now under pressure from his soldiers: earlier the execution of his plan had depended upon the whim of the ships' crews, this time the soldiers' mood forces him to attack (ὁρμὴ ἐνέπεσε...ἐκτειχίσαι, 'the *impulse* to fortify...befell them', 4.1; cf. ὥρμηντο διακινδυνεῦσαι, '*they were set on* making the desperate attempt', 29.2).

And *again* (lucky general that he is) *chance* comes to his aid: an unintentionally (ἄκοντος, 30.2) set fire on Sphakteria is spread by the addition of wind (πνεύματος ἐπιγενομένου)[76] and without being noticed (ἔλαθε) burns down most of the forest. The state of affairs on Sphakteria thus becomes visible, and the Spartiates lose the advantage of better orientation (a factor which since Aigition has held terror for Demosthenes)[77]: ἀπὸ δὲ τοῦ Αἰτωλικοῦ πάθους, ὃ διὰ τὴν ὕλην (cf. ὕλην, 3.98.2) μέρος τι ἐγένετο, οὐχ ἥκιστα αὐτὸν ταῦτα εἰσῄει ('This consideration entered his mind not least resulting from the Aetolian calamity, which happened partly because of the forest', cf. forest at 3.98.2, 30.1).

Demosthenes' plan (29.3–4; 32.3–4)—as well as its execution (32.1–2, 33.1 ff.)—goes strictly according to the schema distilled from his defeat at Aigition and his victory at Idomene. The basic concept, which has twice proven sound, is that light-armed troops have the advantage over hoplites; while there are 800 (31.1) of the latter, the Athenians have 800 *each* of archers and peltasts (32.2; besides auxiliaries). The first attack is against the advance guard post and takes place πρὸ τῆς ἕω ('before sunrise', 31.1; cf. ἅμα ὄρθρῳ, 3.112.3); the enemy is killed while still ἐν ταῖς εὐναῖς ('in their beds', 32.1 = 3.112.3); if the Ambraciots had once taken the approaching Athenian force for friends (3.112.3–4), then the Spartans now believe the *few* (31.1) ships that land at first to be blockade ships making a routine pass (32.1). Demosthenes uses his hoplites *only as bait:* once both hoplite forces are arrayed against each other and the Spartiates advance as in a normal battle, the Athenian hoplites *do not move*. The approaching Spartan force marches directly into the range of the light troops who are stationed behind and to the sides, and grows increasingly vulnerable to them: the ψιλοί ('lightly armed')[78] dominate the scene. Plan (φεύγοντές τε γὰρ ἐκράτουν, 'for in fleeing they [scil. the lightly armed] held the advantage', 32.4) and execution (see esp. 33.2) correspond precisely to the experiences of Aigition (ὅτε μὲν ἐπίοι τὸ τῶν Ἀθηναίων στρατόπεδον, ὑπεχώρουν, ἀναχωροῦσι δὲ ἐπέκειντο, 'whenever the Athenians' army attacked, they withdrew, but attacked them when they gave ground', 3.97.3) and Idomene (ψιλῶν πρὸς ὁπλίτας, 'lightly armed against hoplites', 3.112.6).

No wonder, then, that the *new tactic* terrifies the Spartans—as it had once terrified the Athenians and their allies— (...ἔκπληξίς τε ἐνέπεσεν ἀνθρώποις ἀήθεσι τοιαύτης μάχης, 34.2) and forces them to withdraw with heavy losses to the other, more inaccessible end of the island, where there is an old fort.

Here of course they are less vulnerable to attack, and their position only becomes untenable when a group of Messenian light troops on a circuitous route manages to climb to a high position in their rear. But in contrast to their ancestors at Thermopylae (36.3: Thucydides points out the similarity of the two situations in which contemporary Spartan military renown was respectively won and lost) they now withdraw before the superior force. When events develop to the point where Cleon and Demosthenes fear that all their potential prisoners will be killed, they demand surrender. After some negotiations the Spartans comply with the demand (37–8).

The climax of the battle description is reached in the comparison with Thermopylae (36.3) and the style, as usual, descends noticeably thereafter (37–39). In the post-climactic portion of the account three things are emphasized. The Spartans on the mainland encourage those on the island to make their decision in accordance with the code of honor (38.3); Cleon has fulfilled his 'insane' promise (39.3); and Thucydides relates, creating a fresh climax in its own right (40), the impression that the Spartan defeat makes in Greece: παρὰ γνώμην τε δὴ μάλιστα τῶν κατὰ τὸν πόλεμον τοῦτο τοῖς Ἕλλησιν ἐγένετο: no one in Greece would have believed that Spartans 'οὔτε λιμῷ οὔτ' ἀνάγκῃ οὐδεμιᾷ' ('neither by hunger nor by any necessity') could ever be induced to lay down their weapons. An individual voice (indirectly reported conversation between an Athenian and one of the prisoners, 40.2) must—as after Idomene, but less pointedly—be adduced to explain this fact: the light troops' hail of missiles made no distinction between the brave man and the coward.[79]

After the larger significance of the battle's result has been duly considered, Thucydides delivers his final remarks on Pylos (41). These refer to the success of the *original* Pylos plan which now (after so many unexpected consequences) begins to have its effect: Messenian raids press the Spartans hard, especially since the Helots begin to defect in large numbers.

Both the capture of the Spartiates and the fear of a Helot uprising force the Spartans once again, while attempting to maintain their dignity (καίπερ οὐ βουλόμενοι ἔνδηλοι εἶναι), to seek negotiations in Athens. The Athenians are thus in the *same favorable situation*[80] as after the blockading of the island, and which they had gambled away to their own later chagrin: the *fourth metabole* is complete. And how do they react this time? Are human beings capable of learning in areas of fundamental importance, if not from the warnings of others, at least from their own experience (as one might say that Demosthenes has done in the field of tactics)?—οἱ δὲ μειζόνων τε ὠρέγοντο (cf. 21.2) καὶ πολλάκις φοιτώντων αὐτοὺς ἀπράκτους ἀπέπεμπον ('but they *desired more* and sent them away, though they *came many times, without having achieved their objective*', 41.4).

This closes the account of the events around Pylos and Sphakteria; but Thucydides, as has often been realized,[81] retains the vocabulary that characterizes the antagonists' attitudes: the series overconfidence-reversal-remorse continues. Let us now briefly bring to a close our observations on this continuation.

Next year (424), after Cythera (4.54) is also taken by the Athenians, Spartan morale sinks to an all-time low. Nearly all the defeats Sparta suffers have had an unpredictable quality—the quality that the Corinthians had once relied on in their projections before the Peloponnesian League (cf. πρὸς τὸ παρατυγχάνον, 'in reaction to whatever chance may bring', 1.122.1):[82] 1. γεγενημένου μὲν τοῦ ἐν τῇ νήσῳ πάθους ἀνελπίστου καὶ μεγάλου... ('since the calamity on the island had occurred, *unexpected* and grave...') 2. Πύλου δὲ ἐχομένης καὶ Κυθήρων... ('since Pylos was being held [scil. by the enemy] and also Cythera...') 3. πανταχόθεν...περιεστῶτος πολέμου ταχέος καὶ ἀπροφυλάκτου... ('since on all sides...a *swift* and *unpredictable* war was surrounding them...') 4. ξυνεστῶτες...ναυτικῷ ἀγῶνι, καὶ τούτῳ πρὸς Ἀθηναίους ('being involved...in a naval contest, and this one against the Athenians') (contrast the Corinthians, at 1.121.4: μιᾷ τε νίκῃ ναυμαχίας κατὰ τὸ εἰκὸς ἁλίσκονται 'they are likely to be conquered by one single victory in a naval battle'!); 5. καὶ ἅμα τὰ τῆς τύχης πολλὰ καὶ ἐν ὀλίγῳ ξυμβάντα παρὰ λόγον... ('and since at the same time *the effects of chance* occurred with frequency and in a short time *against their calculation*'); and finally the fear, μή ποτε αὖθις ξυμφορά τις αὐτοῖς περιτύχῃ οἵα καὶ ἐν τῇ νήσῳ ('lest at some time again some calamity might happen to them like the one on the island') and μὴ σφίσι νεώτερόν τι γένηται τῶν περὶ τὴν κατάστασιν ('lest some rebellion might happen to them in matters concerning their constitution', 4.55.1–3). The mood is quite different in Athens. The generals—who had originally been sent out to *put an end* to the Sicilian war (3.115.4)—are *punished* for agreeing to the Gelan peace accord, ὡς ἐξὸν αὐτοῖς τὰ ἐν Σικελίᾳ καταστρέψασθαι (!) δώροις πεισθέντες ἀποχωρήσειαν ('on the accusation that they, although it was possible for them to gain the mastery over affairs in Sicily(!), had left upon accepting bribes', 65.3).[83]

In characterizing the Athenian attitude (65.4) the historian uses allusions to the speech of the Spartan emissaries:[84] οὕτω <u>τῇ παρούσῃ εὐτυχίᾳ</u> (cf. εὐτυχίαν τὴν παροῦσαν, 17.4) χρώμενοι ἠξίουν σφίσι μηδὲν ἐναντιοῦσθαι...αἰτία δ' ἦν <u>ἡ παρὰ λόγον</u> τῶν πλεόνων <u>εὐπραγία</u>, 'Thus, drawing on *their present good fortune* (cf. 'your present good fortune',17.4), they expected that nothing would place itself in their way... But the cause was their *unexpected success* in the majority of their undertakings, which provided for them the strength of their expectation' (in sense = 17.4; 17.4 itself takes up the 'unexpected success' ἀπροσδόκητος εὐπραγία, 3.39.4) αὐτοῖς ὑποτιθεῖσα ἰσχὺν τῆς <u>ἐλπίδος</u> (cf. ...τοῦ πλέονος...ὀρέγονται διὰ τὸ...ἀδοκήτως εὐτυχῆσαι, 'they yearn for more because of being lucky...unexpectedly' 4.17.4). We have already noted, in connection with the Spartan peace proposal, how close this is to the terminology of Diodotos' speech.

This mood description comes at a compositionally important place, namely, the zenith of Athenian success (εὐπραγία). The Athenian setback in Megara (4.66 ff.) follows immediately and simultaneously forms the first (70.1 ff.) in Brasidas' string of victories. Spartan <u>κακοπραγία</u> ('misfortune', 79.3) leads to a *counter*attack (cf. <u>ἀποτρέψειν</u>, 'divert [them, scil. the Athenians]', εἰ <u>ἀντιπαραλυποῖεν</u> 'if they harmed them *in turn*', 80.1) against the Athenian territories on the Thracian coast.

Parallel to Brasidas' successes run the Athenian preparations for a pincer movement against Boeotia (77; 89 ff.), in which Demosthenes' old plan (which had failed so miserably at Aigition) is resurrected. But a ridiculous mistake in the time calculation (γενομένης διαμαρτίας τῶν ἡμερῶν, 89.1) spoils the *synchronized* departures on which the plan is based and leads to the Athenian debacle at Delium (96). The loss of Amphipolis finally (103 ff.) generates serious fears (μέγα δέος, 108.1) in Athens for the Thracian territories. Sparta, on the other hand, cannot really enjoy its victories in the north-east because the men of Sphakteria are still Athenian prisoners (117.1; cf. 5.14.3; 15.1). Thus it comes to the armistice of the spring of 423 (4.117 ff.), which in the following year, after the deaths of Brasidas and Cleon, passes into the Peace of Nicias.

In his description of both sides' inclination to make peace (5.14), Thucydides once again resorts to the categories of his Pylos narrative. The Athenian losses at Amphipolis and Delium thus gain the significance of a *fifth metabole* in this connected series of events: ...καὶ οὐκ ἔχοντες τὴν ἐλπίδα τῆς ῥώμης πιστὴν ἔτι, ᾗπερ οὐ προσεδέχοντο πρότερον τὰς σπονδάς, δοκοῦντες τῇ παρούσῃ εὐτυχίᾳ ('...and, no longer holding the firm *trust* in their strength by which they *earlier* kept rejecting the peace treaty in the belief, caused by their present *good fortune*' (catchword! cf. εὖ φερόμενοι, 'as long as they were successful', 15.2) καθυπέρτεροι γενήσεσθαι ('that they would <continue to> have the upper hand', 14.1). And with the added fears of more allied revolts, their reaction is finally *exactly the same* as before: μετεμέλοντό ('they felt remorse', = 4.27.2) τε ὅτι μετὰ τὰ ἐν Πύλῳ[85] καλῶς παρασχὸν οὐ ξυνέβησαν ('because *after the events at Pylos* they had not acceded to an agreement though they well could', 5.14.2).

Five reversals of the fortunes of war; two instances of confidence based on favorable situations; two instances of regret over the behavior resulting from that confidence, with the second case exactly mimicking the first each time; and in the end a situation even less favorable than that *before* the first (chance-given) success: ...γιγνόμενα...καὶ αἰεὶ ἐσόμενα, ἕως ἂν ἡ αὐτὴ φύσις ἀνθρώπων ᾖ ('...occurring...and always to occur as long as human nature is the same', 3.82.2).

And on the Spartan side? οἱ δ' αὖ Λακεδαιμόνιοι παρὰ γνώμην μὲν ἀποβαίνοντος σφίσι τοῦ πολέμου, ἐν ᾧ ᾤοντο ὀλίγων ἐτῶν καθαιρήσειν τὴν τῶν Ἀθηναίων δύναμιν, 'but the Spartans, on the other hand, since *the war developed against their judgement* – the war in which they believed they would *destroy the Athenians' power within a few years...*' (this was the hope expressed in the final speech of the Corinthians) ...περιπεσόντες δὲ τῇ ἐν τῇ νήσῳ ξυμφορᾷ, οἵα οὔπω ἐγεγένητο τῇ Σπάρτῃ, '...since they had experienced the calamity on the island – a calamity *such as had not happened to Sparta before*' (etc.: Pylos and Cythera as a thorn in the side, continuous fear of revolution, imminent conflict with Argos, 5.14.3). Who would not think of the cautionary prewar speech of King Archidamus?

In our first chapter, in connection with the events of 415, we attempted in a preliminary way to sketch the historian's attitude as that of a detached observer who regretfully discerns the inevitability of occurrences which to rational hindsight seem to have been avoidable.[86] Both aspects, the attitude of—often grieving—regret as well as the fact of the irrationality of human behavior, reappear in the account of the Archidamian War as fundamental categories encompassing *both* belligerents, with the result that our earlier assumption stands confirmed.

In order to ascertain Thucydides' view of the place of man in the historical process we at first used as an heuristic principle the antithesis of plan and outcome. This principle, which has proven effective in the investigation of individual event sequences, now seems justified with regard to the broad outlines of the Archidamian War as well. The historian's answer to the optimistic forecasts of the Corinthians and Sthenelaidas (but to some extent also of the confident Athenian emissaries) in Book 1 is, in political terms, the peace *based on the status quo* of 431;[87] but seen in terms of the ἀνθρώπινον ('the human condition') it is the *high price of the* παθήματα ('suffering', 1.23.1) for a 'peace' that proves to be no more than an intermission. The fact that a similar (or even a better) peace was possible years earlier already (after Pylos), but that this opportunity was blindly gambled away twice (and without the responsible side's having anything to show for it) is perhaps—aside from the decision to go to war in 431—the most tragic *discovery* made in the process.

We close our investigation of the structural elements of Thucydidean event sequences with the consideration of the series Aigition–Idomene and Pylos–Sphakteria.

It may seem apposite to point out the majority of typical categories encountered along the way in a single, outstanding complex, the Sicilian Expedition. But it might have been difficult convincingly to exemplify in Books 6–7 our thesis of the non-partisan historian who looks beyond politics. The prejudice that Thucydides is writing of Athens' tragedy has always sought justification in just these two Books. So we shall build their analysis on the broad basis of our preceding investigations.

But this much may already be said. According to our understanding, the literary completeness of Books 6–7 is not so much a result of the fact that in Sicily the historian's native city suffered a decisive defeat—a fact which of course is undeniable. Rather, it arises from the fact that this is a *war within the war*,[88] which contains those characteristics 'writ large'—of planning and warning through to the bitter end—that also distinguish the entire Peloponnesian War (which is more difficult to view as a whole because of its sheer magnitude).

Thus if one wanted to maintain that Thucydides' understanding of history is tragic, it would be necessary in my opinion to qualify the assertion as follows. Thucydides writes not merely the tragedy of Athens, but in a much broader sense the *tragedy of humanity itself*: of human beings who make themselves and others into the victims of their vast plans. With no knowledge of the limited perspective which frames their intellectual capabilities, they blindly place their trust in the supposed availability of factors whose effects are beyond their reach (and control).

This kind of tragedy of course speaks so often and with such clarity (σαφὲς) in the history of the Peloponnesian War, that for the historian of this war the criteria gleaned from insight into the past do not lose their validity even for the events of a—in terms of the human condition—comparable future (1.24.4).

Notes

[1] See above, p. 37.

[2] See above, p. 83.

[3] Cf. above, p. 83.

[4] This is the first outline of a concept that will eventually lead to Athens' defeat at Delium (see below, p. 150).

[5] There is at this point no hint of the later positive evaluation of Demosthenes (Treu 1956, 424 ff.).

[6] His behavior corresponds precisely to that of Knemos (2.80.8): οὐ περιμείνας τὸ ἀπὸ Κορίνθου ναυτικόν, see above, p. 84.

[7] Emphatic repetition of 95.3! Cf. further, above, pp. 85, 89.

[8] ψιλός is the guiding term in the military analysis here: 94.4, cf. μεγάλη ὠφελία, 95.3; 97.2; 98.1; 98.2.

[9] Cf. above, p. 85.

[10] Cf. above, p. 40.

[11] As the Ambraciots had earlier persuaded them (2.80.1): ἐλπίδα δ᾽ εἶναι καὶ Ναύπακτον λαβεῖν.

[12] Cf. above, p. 93, also note 34.

[13] See above, p. 83.

[14] Cf. de Romilly 1956a, 128 f.

[15] The simultaneity of these events indicates a 'hinge' or link in the series, as previously at 2.86.1 (above, p. 86).

[16] The ἐμπείρων-ἀπείρων word play at § 6 is the same as in the description of the fighting at Plataea (2.4.2, above, p. 67).

[17] Cf. ψιλῶν πρὸς ὁπλίτας, § 6; above, p.131 n.8.

[18] One is reminded of the significance of the messengers sent to and fro in the Plataea-complex (2.6, above, p. 68), and of the dialogue between Archidamus and the Plataeans (2.71 f.; above, p. 81).

[19] See above, p. 115.

[20] See also pp. 78 f. above.

[21] See p. 106.

[22] Euripides, *Bacchae* 1280–2.

[23] One thinks of Alcidas' similarly unsuccessful mission and its consequences for Mytilene (above, p. 107).

[24] 'Echte Tragik gibt es in echter Geschichtsdarstellung nur, wofern sie dem Historiker…nicht mehr erlaubt ist' ('In genuine historiography, there is genuine tragicality only if it is…no longer permitted to the historian.') (Reinhardt 1960, 212).

[25] And for misunderstanding him: Katicic (1957, 181) correctly emphasizes that

Thucydides has so often been carped at by his critics (Katicic names Dionysius of Halicarnassus, von Wilamowitz and Schwartz) because they want to measure him against an inapplicable standard, namely, the stylistic ideal developed in, and in force since, the fourth century. Where this sort of criticism has led can be read in the work of C. Meyer (1955, 1 ff.): historical documents cited by Thucydides are dismissed as spurious (or as not belonging to the final revision) because they do not correspond to the stylistic usages of Thucydides' successors. Remember that Jacoby (in Zahn 1934, n. 5) believed that for purposes of interpretation even in the *speeches* considerations of rhetoric should take second place.

[26] Cf. Grene (1950, 74): '…the implications spring from the story, not the story from a theory.'

[27] On the valuation of events seemingly marginal to the greater conflict see above, pp. 72, 115. Reinhardt, too, sees in the events at Mykalessos not a marginal occurrence, but rather a 'symptom of the war'; the 'point' of the final sentence is, according to Reinhardt, 'Menschenschicksal unter dem Gesetz des Krieges' ('human fate under the law of war') (1960, 207 f.).

[28] See above, p. 29. The accompanying dative, each time referring to the sufferers, indicates that the meaning of the word is the same in all three cases (on παθήματα, cf. also 4.48.3); see further Immerwahr (1960, 279; 284).

[29] Grene 1950, 75 ff.; he adduces the account of Mykalessos among others.

[30] 'A piece of history that might have been different' (Grene 1950, 78). My italics in passage cited in the main text above.

[31] The actual use of the words ἀνάγκη and ἀναγκάζειν in this historical work leaves no room for such a hypostasis.

[32] Cf. the controversy between Schadewaldt (1929, 6) and Kapp (1930, 81).

[33] See Woodhead 1960, 311.

[34] Ed. Meyer (1899, 342).

[35] On this see Herter 1954, 332 ff.

[36] Cornford 1907, 81; cf. above p. 14.

[37] Cornford 1907, 89.

[38] Cornford 1907, 88.

[39] See above, p. 13.

[40] So Luschnat 1942, 34; de Romilly 1951[2], 151.

[41] So Gomme, vol. III, 488 f. and *passim*; Neu 1948, 99.

[42] One is reminded of the significance of the weather at Crete in 429 (2.85.6, above, p. 86).

[43] V. Wilamowitz' aperçu (1921, 310), that the storm was invented by the admirals for their official report and that Thucydides was taken in by it, is as unfounded as his thesis (sufficiently refuted by Gomme 1923, 36 ff.) that Thucydides had available only Athenian sources for the entire segment. I reiterate that we are interested here *only* in how the events looked to Thucydides *himself*; it is an implicit assumption of our interpretation that the report is subjectively honest.

[44] Steup understands the text correctly (*ad loc.*).

[45] This is the simplest (and a sufficient) explanation for the relatively late revelation of the plan. Thucydides himself occasionally discloses long-standing

facts at the point when they become effective; cf. 6.46.

[46] 3.112.4; ironically, the Doric dialect will later contribute decisively to Demosthenes' greatest defeat: 7.44.6.

[47] On the difficulties of the rank hierarchy, cf. in addition to the commentaries v. Wilamowitz 1921, 309 n. 1.

[48] ὑπὸ ἀπλοίας (4.1), whether one transposes it or not, should be taken with σχολάζουσιν.

[49] Gomme (vol. III, 488) rejects the notion of chance in the case of the festival: '…the most that is meant is that Demosthenes had not timed the arrival at Pylos in order to coincide with it.' But this is by itself a sufficient reason for seeing the festival as a chance element relative to Demosthenes' plan.

[50] For the topography see esp. Burrows 1898 (with photographs), 1908. Nearly all interpreters agree that it would have been quite impossible to block the southern passage (Thucydides makes it too narrow). But aside from the impossibility of proving such hypotheses (due to alteration of the coastline by the current), there remains the fact that Thucydides, when constructing his account, believed it to be not only possible but intended by the Spartans (8.6f.; 13.4). A more recent investigation (Strassler 1988) tries to solve the topographical problems by locating the harbor Thucydides describes in the "cove" on the mainland facing the north shore of Sphakteria. Cf. above, p. 139, note 43.

[51] Luschnat (1942, 33) correctly sees the success of the recall (ὑπεκπέμπει φθάσας, 8.3) as an accidental circumstance.

[52] 'Chance' here refers not to the arrival generally, but to arrival *in the nick of time* (so Stahl correctly, cited by Gomme *ad loc.*).

[53] That here the 'perspective of the Athenian spirit of enterprise (thought to be positively valued by Thucydides)' (Luschnat 1942, 37) plays a role seems to me as far-fetched as the assertion (35) that Thucydides wants to absolve Demosthenes from the 'responsibility' for the desperate situation as it has developed. Both views belong to an interpretation that sees Thucydides as an Athenian first and an historian second. (Luschnat's own considerations suggest that 'thoughtlessly hopeful' makes more sense as a characterization of Demosthenes—cf. 3.97.2 τῇ τύχῃ ἐλπίσας, Luschnat 1942, 36—than as some sort of 'Völkercharakteristik'.)

[54] Thucydides even considers their predicament similar to the hopeless situation of the Athenians during the final battle in the Syracusan harbor, cf. his reference at 7.71.7; here, too, he highlights the grotesqueness of the situation (14.3).

[55] See above, p. 110.

[56] For details see de Romilly 1951[2], 151.

[57] 1.120ff.; see above, pp. 55f.

[58] This alludes to a possible (disgraceful or deadly) defeat of the Spartans cut off on Sphakteria, cf. 2.

[59] ὑποδεέστερον ὄν, 4; Gomme (vol. III, 459) overlooks the fact that the Greeks would have to honor (τιμήσει) the peace because of the military *superiority* of the superpowers.

[60] Above, pp. 57f.

[61] καλῶς θέσθαι: luck is seen here (appropriately to the cautionary character

of the speech) as something negative that must be neutralized if one wants to avoid its harmful consequences. On the use of τίθεσθαι (+ adv.) in this sense, cf. Classen-Steup *ad* 1.25.1.

[62] 'Thucydides puts into Cleon's mouth the very moral which his own career is to illustrate' (150). Cornford (1907) speaks of 'tragic irony'.

[63] Topitsch 1946, 93, cf. 94; in his view Thucydides makes Cleon (in Book 3) 'pronounce judgment on his own and Athens' later conduct and characterize it as hybris' (translated from the German).

[64] On the 'pedagogical' effect, see above, pp. 111 f. with note 22.

[65] Another example of this kind of behavior is found in the Corcyrean civil war: it does not cease until there is no one left alive to continue it (4.48.5).

[66] Thanks to Reinhardt's (1960) research, we can say with certainty that there is a (decisive) distinction to be drawn between Thucydides and Machiavelli, *pace* Nestle (1948b, 361) *et. al.*

[67] Above, p. 14.

[68] Above, pp. 97 f.

[69] Accordingly it would seem impermissible to ask what latitude Thucydides has left for, say, 'τύχη' or 'ἀνθρωπεία φύσις' or 'the statesman', because such questions place the objects of investigation as definable entities into a larger, firmly preset context. This easily produces judgments such as the following: Thucydides was the first to 'build' *tyche* 'into an historical system' (Schmid 1948, 31); and the war is declawed and made into a *Demonstrationsobjekt* for historical method ('Das Wechselspiel dieser Kräfte läßt am besten ein großer Krieg erkennen' ['The interplay of these forces is best recognized in a great war.'], 40; 'He used the war, so to speak, as a *field of experiment* to which the general laws of human response could be applied and by which the presumption of their truth could be established', Finley, 1947[2], 294 [my italics]; according to Howald (1944, 81), history is for Thucydides 'eine Art Experiment' for his problem of power.)

[70] Cf. παθήματα…τῇ Ἑλλάδι, μῆκος…μέγα, 1.23.

[71] So Nestle (1948c, 374 ff., first published in 1925), clearly in Schwartz' train; similar in concept are Corsen 1915, 332; Ehrenberg 1947; de Romilly 1951[2], 123. Nestle (1948d, 385; also Eberhardt 1954, 308) wants in the final analysis to see Thucydidean polemics directed against *Socrates*,—so that it will be known that (in accordance with the stereotypical pair of opposites thought-action) Thucydides comes down squarely on the side of the politicians.

[72] One must remember that Reinhardt found in Thucydides three (increasingly broad) varieties of 'the not expressly expressed'. Of the third, and most sweeping, he says, 'I can think of no better designation than 'the human [das Menschliche]', with very nearly the same connotations given that word by the tragedians'. The meaning of this 'human' arises 'from its oppositeness to the war itself' (1960, 207).

[73] Once again each side's assumption about its opponent's attitude is erroneous (νομίζοντες 21.1 ~ ἐνόμιζον 21.2); cf. above pp. 1–13 (Aristogeiton–Hippias), p. 66 (Thebans–Plataeans), p. 104 (Mytilenians–Athenians).

[74] As in the case of the (fruitless) suggestions of Archidamus, Teutiaplos and Nicias, the subsequent narrative makes reference to the warnings. For citations

see de Romilly 1951², 151 f.

⁷⁵ So Gomme, correctly, against others *ad* 4.28.4; the confirmation comes at 30.4 (cf. Ed. Meyer 1899, 340); Cleon sends word that he is coming with the army ἣν ᾐτήσατο. The subject of the relative clause is (with Steup, against Grote and, recently, Hornblower *ad* 4.30.4) Cleon. τε…καὶ at 30.4 distinguishes the participles προπέμψας and ἔχων, i.e. "Cleon arrives at Pylos (a) after sending ahead word that he would be there, and (b) in possession of the army he had asked for [scil. in the assembly, 28.4]." It would be more than casual, if the sub-clause were to provide *new* information about *Demosthenes* so far unknown to the reader.

⁷⁶ *Loc. cit.*; cf. κατὰ τύχην χειμὼν ἐπιγενόμενος, 4.3.1.

⁷⁷ The antithesis …τοὺς ἐλάσσους, ἐμπείρους δὲ τῆς χώρας, κρείσσους ἐνόμιζε τῶν πλεόνων ἀπείρων (29.4) should be understood as repetition from the battle descriptions of Aigition (ὧν οὐκ ἦσαν ἔμπειροι, 3.98.1) and Idomene (ἐμπείρων-ἀπείρων, 3.112.6, cf. above p. 132, note 16). Another example of how Thucydides consciously highlights the structural elements of his event sequences and cross-references them. Cf. also what follows.

⁷⁸ 32.4; 33.1, 2 (2x); 34.1; 35.2; 36.1; cf. above, p. 131, note 8.

⁷⁹ Thucydides in his own account seems to pay attention to the (less than honorable) technique used by the Athenian side (cf. 34.2–3, where the unequal situation is described from the point of view of the Spartans' own lines); cf. Euripides' *Heracles* 151–64, 188–203.

⁸⁰ Of course it is questionable whether, in addition to peace, any sort of *friendship* with Sparta would still be possible, since the loss of Spartan honor might well represent an ἀνήκεστον. Cf. 20.1.

⁸¹ For details, cf. de Romilly 1951², 152.

⁸² See above, pp. 55 f.

⁸³ Cf. Westlake 1960, 399 ff.

⁸⁴ So de Romilly 1951² correctly, *loc. cit.*

⁸⁵ Cf. 15.2 ἤρξαντο (scil. οἱ Λακεδαιμόνιοι) …εὐθὺς μετὰ τὴν ἅλωσιν αὐτῶν πράσσειν, 'they (scil. the Spartans) began…to negotiate immediately after their capture' (to be compared with 4.41.3: καὶ πολλάκις φοιτώντων αὐτοὺς ἀπράκτους ἀπέπεμπον, 'and though they came many times they (scil. the Athenians) kept sending them away unsuccessful'). When de Romilly (1951², 153) states that Thucydides "criticizes" (blames) the Athenians for regretting the first (i.e. not the second) missed opportunity, she is, by basing her observations on a purely political perspective, missing the significance of the cycle (which she herself stresses, 150 *et al.*) confidence-regret-confidence-regret. A reader who has traced the narrative can only understand that Thucydides here alludes to the *second* group of Spartan attempts at negotiation, those which initiate the second cycle (the same objection is true of Herter 1954, 336 n. 56).

⁸⁶ See above, p. 10.

⁸⁷ The literary process of course runs in the opposite direction: the forecasts of Book 1 have been drafted with a view to later factual developments.

⁸⁸ οὐ πολλῷ τινι ὑποδεέστερον πόλεμον ἀνηροῦντο ἢ τὸν πρὸς Πελοποννησίους, 'they were raising a war not much inferior to the one against the Peloponnesians', 6.1.1; see above, p. 121.

BEHAVIOR IN THE EXTREME SITUATION
Book 5.84–113

In the previous chapter we investigated two event sequences whose respective momenta (seen from the perspective of the historian's presentation) carried them forward in different ways. The first led without delay to the destruction of the flower of a small nation, while the second at first unexpectedly placed victory within reach of one side (and peace within reach of both) and thus seemed to offer a favorable end. Nevertheless, man, when chance offered him a choice, made such poor use of the reprieve that the outcome of the apparently 'favorable' course of events appears to the observer scarcely less hopeless than the first, which arrived at its conclusion without a pause.

The situation of man facing a choice or decision (which in addition will decisively influence his own future), touches upon a complex of problems we have brushed against repeatedly since the decision to go to war presented in Book 1. A specific problem (it belongs closely with our inquiry about the place of the human being in the historical process) arises once again, and with utmost urgency, for the councillors of Melos, when an Athens poised to attack asks them to choose between immediate political dependency and certain destruction. In deciding to interpret the so-called Melian Dialogue (5.84–113) predominantly from the point of view of its Melian participants, we must be clear from the outset that this perspective can encompass only *one* position among the several to be found in this many-layered conversation. But we are justified in doing so because the impulse for the entire discussion comes from the Melian reactions to the unequivocal Athenian demand.

The aspect under which the Melian Dialogue has till now usually been interpreted is the antinomy of might vs. right, in which the latter is assigned to the Melians, the former to the Athenians. This point of view, which generally advocates a simple black-and-white characterization, can be varied in a number of shades. The application of a *moral* standard produces the basic concept of ἄδικος λόγος ('the unjust argument') *contra* δίκαιος λόγος ('the just argument'),[1] which can be explicated as the conflict between enlightened human calculation and traditional religious faith[2] or, more generally, as the incompatibility of realistic and idealistic attitudes.[3]

In the latter case, the question of what is *politically* the proper behavior comes into play. The result is that the Athenians come off as clever (because they are successful) and the Melians as foolish (because they are not equal to the situation).[4] If the interpreter in addition emphasizes the political 'lessons' the historian is supposed to have wanted to teach, his reader learns that we are dealing with 'a false religious faith, if one imagines one can get one's head through the wall and may call upon the divinity for it'.[5]

But if one understands the political aspect as arising from *historical* pairs of opposites in the author's lifetime, then the conflict can be between two political ideals (or institutions), namely, empire vs. polis,[6] or—in the field of the much misused 'Völkerpsychologie'—'the innate characteristics of moral strength on the Dorian side' against 'the artificial monetary power of the Athenians'.[7] Finally, it has been found ironic that the Athenians treat the oligarchs, who are their Melian interlocutors, in accordance with the same principle that oligarchic Sparta applies to its Helots.[8]

When the search is on for Thucydides' *personal* (contemporary political) stance, the interpretative possibilities become myriad and labyrinthine.

Schwartz, who discovered here the Athenian Machiavelli,[9] had a relatively simple position since he saw Thucydides as thoroughly (up to the 'anti-moral paradox', *anti-moralischen Paradoxie*)[10] pro-Athenian and anti-Spartan.

Problems regularly arise when one has the *Athenian* Thucydides in the Melian Dialogue taking the side of the pitiable Melians. In order to avoid a resultant general condemnation of Athens on the part of the historian, one has explained Athenian conduct on Melos as an exaggerated form of Athenian imperialism that is no longer comparable to the ideal conditions obtaining under Pericles. For this purpose, expressions of even tenor by Athenians under Pericles (1.76) and at the time of the conquest of Melos are interpreted differently. What was intended in 431 as a 'defense' against accusations, is said to be used in 416 to justify an attack.[11]

There is also the possibility of admitting negative criticism of Athens but then (by appealing to the *general* human desire for power) neutralizing this criticism:[12] the rule that might makes right excuses the stronger party, rather than condemning it.

The commonest interpretation is the one which sees in the outcome of the Sicilian Expedition a corrective to Athens' overbearing treatment of Melos.[13] Occasionally someone seizes the opportunity to expose a kind of objective connection between the two events and—by some more or less mythic flight of the imagination[14]—to point out an immanent justice in

Thucydides' view of history (whose influence I would have difficulty finding compatible with the rest of the categories in the work). Of course interpreters are not always conscious of the fact that they may not be providing an argument in favour of any morality of history at all, but rather formulating a Macchiavellian rule of conduct for the benefit of politicians.[15]

This sort of reading would imply that the historian's presentation is not disinterested. Rather, it makes him—after the fact—search for certain pieces of advice that, had they been followed in time, would have spared his native city the loss of its empire. This is a fundamentally different point of view from that which sees in the Athenians of the Melian Dialogue the general blindness and limited perspective also of the (temporarily) powerful.

Against the thesis that Thucydides rejects the excessive misuse of power, one now and then encounters the opinion that he abstains altogether from seeing the right of the stronger as a norm (but rather contents himself with the presentation of phenomena drawn from historical experience).[16] The latter reading can easily be taken to mean (though this is not logically cogent) that the historian, because he did not share the might-makes-right view, must *therefore* have been interested in the 'problem of correctives', i.e. the 'question of political ethics'.[17] And with this, we have returned to the notion of the historian as physician to society.[18]

We will not survey all the possible (or even the already exploited) combinations,[19] nor abstract from the Melian Dialogue any new 'teachings' or 'laws of power'.

Our question is rather what *happens in* the Melian Dialogue, *within* the movement of the conversation. In other words, what interests us is the situation itself and the participants' response to it.

If the thought that might comes before right (or συμφέρον, 'expediency', before δίκαιον, 'justice') does not appear in the foreground of our discussion, there are two reasons. First, this thought in any case constitutes for our author the most general assumption (but by no means the goal) of historical investigation.[20] Second, in the Melian Dialogue itself (5.89) the Athenians, when dictating the limits of the discussion, establish from the very beginning the right of the stronger as an inviolable perimeter within which the exchange is to take place.

The only chance, then, the Melians have of broadening the basis for discussion is to accept the principle of the right of the stronger but to question whether the present case fulfills the conditions for its application. This is why they point out that Athens may not *always* be in the stronger position and consequently would do well to let the κοινὸν ἀγαθόν ('the common weal') stand intact (90).

161

But already in this temporal extension of the present situation (far beyond the impending destruction of Melos!) there is a failure to observe the given circumstances about which the Athenian negotiators had warned them. Melian 'speculation'[21] about the unequal starting positions of the negotiating partners and its effects on the course of the discussion (86) was disallowed from the beginning: the *only* purpose of the conversation is to consult about the interests of the city ἐκ τῶν παρόντων καὶ ὧν ὁρᾶτε (one could scarcely outline the situation more concretely) περὶ σωτηρίας ('about your survival on the basis of the present situation and of what you have before your eyes', 87).

Accordingly, the Athenian answer (to 5.90) directs the conversation back to the previously set topic of concrete σωτηρία (91.2)—after explaining that in the event of a defeat one superpower has much less to fear from another superpower than from subjects who have successfully rebelled (91.1); what is now important is that the Melians yield to the συμφέρον of those who are clearly the stronger. Athens is even interested in the 'salvation' of the Melians since an intact Melos would be a far more useful subject than a ruined Melos (91.2; cf. 93). A variation of the antithesis between Cleon (3.39.8) and Diodotos (46.3) is discernible in these remarks.

Once the power principle's essential validity for the present case has been established (91), the only course open to the Melians is to discuss *how* to bring about the greatest possible συμφέρον for the stronger, i.e. in concrete terms: surely a well-wishing, neutral Melos (φίλους μὲν εἶναι…ξυμμάχους δὲ μηδετέρων, 94) would be more useful to Athens than a Melos forced into the naval alliance, especially considering the psychological effects that Athenian action against Melos will have on those who have so far remained neutral (98). In the point-by-point refutation of the casuistry of the Melian objections, the author paints an impressive picture of the consistency and logic of Athenian thinking on the subject of power and of the perfection that Athens displays in the practice of dominance.

But for the Melians the refutation also of this last point (99) means being reduced to the position of receiving an ultimatum.[22] The course of the conversation so far, by gradually hemming the Melians in, has shown that the Athenian stance permits of no modification. The right of the stronger has proven irrefutable, its application to the Melian–Athenian relationship has been shown to be applicable, and the συμφέρον of the more powerful party has been clearly defined (it requires submission). The negotiations have now reached the point at which a clear decision is required about a clearly delineated situation.

But the decision is not made because the Melians are still not prepared to accept the alternatives before them as reality. *Instead, the conversation turns to unreality.*

The shift takes place in Chapter 100 and is also signaled formally. If the Melian councillors have so far gleaned information about the inflexibility of the Athenian position (Chapters 92, 94, 96 and 98 are formulated as questions addressed to the Athenians), they now begin to develop their own 'concepts', formulated as statements. The Athenian negotiators answer in similar fashion with the result that one thesis answers another: they are talking at cross-purposes.

The Melians' first thrust is to the effect that—given that the Athenians would risk everything to maintain their hegemony, and their subjects would risk everything to gain their freedom—it would be shameful and cowardly for the Melians as a free people to give up their independence without a fight (100).

The riposte: 'No, at least if you consider rationally (sober-mindedly); for this is for you not a struggle for honor from a position of equality…but rather the discussion (council) concerns your very *lives,* lest you oppose an opponent who is much stronger than you' (101).

The admonition to σωφρόνως βουλεύεσθαι ('to consider rationally'), and the categorical denial that any motive such as honor could constitute an acceptable viewpoint under the circumstances, serve as yet another attempt to lead the Melians back to considering only the concrete situation. The issue is life and death, not a chivalrous joust between equals. The catchword σωτηρία, pronounced here for the third time by the Athenians (cf. 87; 91.2), makes clear the function of their statement.

For the stronger, then, honor (and shame) is no more than a fiction. Can Thucydides have thought so himself? Can he really have chosen the side of the amoral 'realists' against the 'idealists' (if anywhere, this pair of opposites is explicit in Chapters 100–1)? In view of the Melians' final answer (112.2), some have felt that the 'aristocratic historian' could not have remained unmoved by the 'proud notice' served to the stronger by 'this courageous people'.[23]

The argument is earnest and impressive. Nevertheless, it does not impress in the sense of binding Thucydides to a code of honor whose limitations (and political affiliations) he does not otherwise acknowledge.[24] One need not be an oligarch to recognize heroism in the face of a more powerful enemy or to feel the horror of the Melians' fate.

Nor is it the *people* who give the courageous answer. Thucydides has clearly emphasized that the people were not even asked (ὅπως δὴ μὴ…οἱ πολλοὶ ἐπαγωγὰ καὶ ἀνέλεγκτα…ἀκούσαντες ἡμῶν ἀπατηθῶσιν, 85),[25] with the result that—in an 'idealistic' interpretation—the Melian oligarchs come dangerously close to the spirit of the 'idealist' Max Piccolomini (in Schiller's *Wallenstein* drama), who unscrupulously takes his

300 Pappenheimers to death with himself (for in the end—contrary to the treatment of Mytilene—*all* the Melians are executed, aristocrats and commoners alike). The above-mentioned argument (along with its variations) does carry some weight inasmuch as it suggests that our author, by not acknowledging the heroic motive of honor, may think in 'value-free' terms or even 'does not personally believe in ethical values'.

This reproach is, however, unfounded. We have often enough been able to demonstrate from the material we have submitted to our reader[26] how Thucydides, despite his living in a time of crumbling value systems, makes his judgments 'from the end forward'. It could be in the present case as well (even aside from the responsibility which the oligarchic speakers bear for *all* the inhabitants of Melos) that, standing outside the perspectives of his dialogue figures and in full view of the terrible fate of the Melians, he believes that he has to set aside the traditional view of honor—and we would scarcely have the right to condemn his judgment.

Yet it seems *altogether questionable* whether the theme of heroic downfall is at the heart of the Melian Dialogue, since the possibility of risking everything for freedom later turns out to be merely one *among others*. If the first Melian assertion (100) had allowed an heroic interpretation, it is a completely different picture that appears after the renewed Athenian reference to σωτηρία ('survival'): the Melians no longer speak of destruction but of *possible success*.

The shift toward unreality is thus complete. Once it is clear that they can expect no concessions from their superior enemy (99), they begin to survey their own objectively hopeless situation for supposed advantages.

The first of these 'positive' points is as follows. *Sometimes* (ἔστιν ὅτε) the fortunes of war (τὰς τύχας), as far as we know, take the weaker side (102)—again the reader thinks of the last prewar speech of the Corinthians.[27] 'And immediate surrender is a hopeless choice for us, but in connection with action there is still hope that we may stand upright' (102).

An intellectual somersault has taken place. Chance, i.e. that which is by definition incalculable, becomes the guarantee of wish fulfillment. The meanings of the words seem to get turned upside down: the only thing that could save the Melians from death according to objective observation of their situation becomes from their perspective a case of hopelessness, an ἀνέλπιστον, whereas a course of action that is *a priori* without prospects is seen as the only ἐλπίς ('hope'). Wishful thinking has once again, as we have observed on many previous occasions, closed off the view of reality.

It is in vain that the Athenians object to this on the basis of a salient characteristic of hope: only those who control vast resources can afford to rely on it. But in a life-or-death situation, 'one recognizes it [hope] when one has fallen, and at the same time it leaves one no bastion inside which still to guard oneself against it, now that it is known for what it is' (103.1).

The Athenian speech is almost imploring in tone and, as Steup correctly points out, it does not lack a certain poetic coloring.

> Weak as you are and dependent upon one tipping of the scales, do not choose to experience that nor to become like the majority of people who (though they could still be saved by human means), as soon as the visible sources of their hopes leave them in their plight, turn to the invisible ones, prophecy and oracles and all the other things of the same kind that, in league with hopes, lead to destruction (§ 2).[28]

Are the Athenian negotiators likely to utter such an urgent warning with so deep an understanding of the Melians' situation—the Athenian negotiators whose only intention is the brutal pursuit of their empire's συμφέρον ('advantage')? That the speakers are the same as before is indicated by the fourth use of the catchword σωτηρία 'survival', this time intensified to ἀνθρωπείως ἔτι σώζεσθαι ('to be saved still in human manner').

At the same time, other catchwords show that the author himself is simultaneously speaking: the reader is already familiar with the ἐλπίδες ('hopes'), especially the ἀφανεῖς ('invisible ones'), from Diodotos' analysis.[29] Hope and desire do the most damage (πλεῖστα βλάπτουσιν, cf. λυμαίνεται, 5.103.2) καὶ ὄντα ἀφανῆ κρείσσω ἐστὶ τῶν ὁρωμένων δεινῶν ('and *being invisible*, they are stronger than the dangers *that can be seen*', 3.45.5).

This reference to the speech of Diodotos generalizes the significance of the Melians' situation, or rather (not to speak in the abstract) their situation in this way acquires symbolic force.

The intensity of the Melian Dialogue even exceeds that of Diodotos' speech. The latter had given a general analysis of human nature with specific reference to the invincible drive to reach beyond a given, unwelcome situation at the cost of one's own suffering. Here the *process itself* is depicted step by step with a directness the reader cannot escape (an effect achieved not least by the choice of the dialogue form).

But what distinguishes the Melians' situation from previously investigated situations of decision[30] is the fact that it no longer develops out of an originally free planning of some action still to be undertaken (and which will eventually fail). Rather, the end is already here (in the shape of a present and overwhelmingly powerful enemy) at the time of the conversation. The structural elements of *plan* and *outcome* that lie temporally distant from one another in other event sequences are in the Melian Dialogue compacted *into a single* highly dramatic moment. This feature reveals the

Melian Dialogue as the final stage in a previously noted compositional (and factual) climax.[31]

The dramatic concentration of plan and result constitutes a second intensification of themes found earlier in Diodotos' speech. It is true that he, too, had seen in the struggle for freedom (or in the drive to have power over others) one of the strongest of human motives, and this applies as well to the Melians. But the general starting points which he considered (dependency, poverty, power position, etc.) were construed so as to create an opportunity for human πλεονεξία for the moment to translate its initiative into a planned *undertaking*. But this sort of initiative (cf. μετὰ τοῦ δρωμένου, 'in connection with strong action', 5.102) is *de facto* no longer available to the Melians. By rejecting the Athenian ultimatum they can at most opt for a (longer or shorter) siege of their town, and this is too severe a limitation of the freedom of action to be called initiative.

With this, their search for ostensible advantages takes on an almost utopian character. *Diodotos' psychological starting point,* from which human action receives its impulses, *remains valid even in the extreme situation* when action in the proper sense is no longer possible. The fact that the intellect is assigned only an ancillary function (it projects the availability of external circumstances)[32] also remains in force. *Even in the face of his own destruction, man refuses to recognize the reality of the situation.* Instead, he flees into unreality, or better: into a world of fantasy produced by his own wishes.

This attitude would perhaps be comprehensible if there were really no way out of the situation (or if the available solution were *consciously* rejected). But this is not the case. While the Athenians point to the possibility of ἀνθρωπείως ἔτι σῴζεσθαι ('to be saved still in human manner'), the Melians look for their σωτηρία ('survival') in the humanly improbable:

> It is true that we, too, consider it difficult (as you may well believe!) to fight against your strength and against fortune if it won't be impartial. Nevertheless, we trust (cf. πιστεύσαντες, 113 end) that we shall fare no worse by the fortune that comes from the gods because we are fighting as god-fearing men against an unjust opponent...' (we will compensate for our own lack of power through our alliance with Sparta) '...and (thus) our confidence is not at all so unfounded' (or 'illogical') (104).

So: blind flight from reality, even though salvation is still objectively possible, and *although* this possibility has been *pronounced in the form of a warning.*

What are we dealing with here, folly (in the sense of stupidity) or a tragic failure to recognize the reality of the situation?

Some scholars have actually assumed that Thucydides found the Melian attitude incomprehensible or downright absurd:[33] α γνώμης ἁμάρτημα, then, a mistake in thinking brings about destruction. In that case, the Melians' behavior would amount to no more than an intellectual (and in a repetition of similar circumstances, soluble) problem, their destruction would be the result of a miscalculation (as perhaps their Athenian dialogue partners might see it).

That such simple rationalism (or 'realism') does not do the historian's thinking justice can be demonstrated by the example of an individual who finds himself in a situation just as hopeless as that of the Melians: Nicias. He gives his final speech (probably the most 'human' in this work) at the moment when the last defeat in the harbor of Syracuse has eliminated all hope of returning home and the once so hopeful army is setting out on its death march through Sicily.

Just as the Melians do, Nicias pins his hopes on the improbable: καὶ ἐκ τῶν παρόντων...ἐλπίδα χρὴ ἔχειν (ἤδη τινὲς καὶ ἐκ δεινοτέρων ἢ τοιῶνδε ἐσώθησαν), 'even on the basis of *the present situation*...one must have *hope* (some were saved already *even from a more dreadful situation* than this one)' 7.77.1. In regard to the enormous reversal of his own fortune he says, ἀνθ᾽ ὧν ἡ μὲν ἐλπὶς ὅμως θρασεῖα τοῦ μέλλοντος..., 'therefore my *hope* for the future is nevertheless *confident*...', (§ 3), and of the general calamity: τάχα δὲ ἂν καὶ λωφήσειαν (scil. αἱ ξυμφοραί): ἱκανὰ γὰρ τοῖς τε πολεμίοις ηὐτύχηται, καὶ εἴ τῳ θεῶν ἐπίφθονοι ἐστρατεύσαμεν, ἀποχρώντως ἤδη τετιμωρήμεθα, 'perhaps they (scil. our misfortunes) might also come to an end: for the enemy has encountered *enough* good luck, and if we went to war looked upon with jealousy by one of the gods, we have by now been punished *enough*' (§ 3). καὶ ἡμᾶς εἰκὸς νῦν τά τε ἀπὸ τοῦ θεοῦ ἐλπίζειν ἠπιώτερα ἕξειν (οἴκτου γὰρ ἀπ᾽ αὐτῶν ἀξιώτεροι ἤδη ἐσμὲν ἢ φθόνου)..., 'and it is *apposite* for us now to expect that what we receive from the divinity will be more gentle (*for* by now we deserve their pity rather than their jealousy)...' (§ 4). 'What still wants subjectively to be grounds for hope comes out objectively as an expression of despair.'[34]

This is the same behavior that the Melians display. And how does Thucydides judge this highly superstitious man (ἦν γάρ τι καὶ ἄγαν θειασμῷ τε καὶ τῷ τοιούτῳ προσκείμενος, 'for he was given somewhat too much to superstition and what goes with it', 7.50.4), whose belief in an omen had once prevented the rescue of the expeditionary forces at a time when it was still objectively feasible? '...he least of all among the Greeks of my time deserved to suffer such misfortune,—because of all his striving for virtue, which clung to law and tradition' (7.86.5).

Respect for a life that clung to traditional (and in the historian's eyes decayed and outdated) ethical-religious ideas,[35] but not a word of rationalistic criticism in the Necrologue—in contrast to the Athenians of the Melian Dialogue, who to the very end (5.113) represent the Melian behavior as folly.

We can only compare Nicias and the Melians in terms of their behavior in the extreme situation, since the characterizing thought in Nicias' Necrologue, his dedication to virtue (ἀρετή), is abandoned by the Melians themselves (from 5.102 on). In the Melian Dialogue we have a view of humanity, not in terms of its values, but rather primarily in terms of its (in)capacity to grasp the reality of a given situation.

In what follows the Melians' religious faith is refuted by the assertion that the right of the stronger is universal and probably valid even among the gods (105.1–2), and the Athenians can only smile at the naïveté of the Melians' trust in Sparta: …μακαρίσαντες ὑμῶν τὸ ἀπειρόκακον οὐ ζηλοῦμεν τὸ ἄφρον ('while pronouncing you happy for your lack of negative experience, we do not envy your foolishness', § 3). Sparta, too, finds what is pleasant good, and what is useful just—there are many examples of this (…πολλὰ ἄν τις ἔχων εἰπεῖν…, § 4). This may bring to the reader's mind Alcidas' betrayal at Mytilene, the death sentence pronounced at Plataea to please the Thebans, or the cities that paid so dearly for their accession to Brasidas so that Sparta could win back its prisoners. καίτοι οὐ πρὸς τῆς ὑμετέρας νῦν ἀλόγου σωτηρίας ἡ τοιαύτη διάνοια 'and indeed such an attitude does not speak in favour of your – under the present circumstances – *irrational preservation*' (§ 4)—a line of reasoning with which the reader of the work must agree in respect to its practical applicability.

Just as Athens' position had proven inflexible at the beginning of the conversation, so now Sparta's probable position is shown through corresponding casuistry to be *a priori* as unambiguous as the Athenian. Desire for the good will of the other Greeks (106), or feelings of Doric kinship (108) are not ξυμφέροντα ('advantages') for which Sparta would commit forces in the Cyclades (109). And the (unlikely) event of a Spartan retaliatory expedition on land (against Attica or any of the Athenian allies, 110) would not in the least delay the siege of Melos, as experience teaches (111.1).

With this, all the Melians' attempts to break free of reality have been confounded.

ἐνθυμούμεθα δὲ ὅτι φήσαντες περὶ <u>σωτηρίας</u> βουλεύσειν οὐδὲν ἐν τοσούτῳ λόγῳ εἰρήκατε ᾧ <u>ἄνθρωποι</u> ἂν πιστεύσαντες νομίσειαν σωθήσεσθαι, ἀλλ᾽ ὑμῶν τὰ μὲν <u>ἰσχυρότατα ἐλπιζόμενα μέλλεται</u>, τὰ δ᾽ ὑπάρχοντα βραχέα πρὸς τὰ <u>ἤδη ἀντιτεταγμένα</u> περιγίγνεσθαι (111.2). πολλήν τε <u>ἀλογίαν</u> (cf. 104 end; 105.4 end)…παρέχετε, εἰ μὴ…ἄλλο τι τῶνδε σωφρονέστερον γνώσεσθε (111.2).

But we consider that you, though saying you would take counsel (or: advise, scil. your city, cf. 87) about your *preservation*, have in *so long a conversation* said nothing in which *humans* might put their trust so as to believe they *will be saved*, but on the one hand *your strongest points, being objects of hope, are still to become reality* while on the other hand what is available is insufficient (for you) to survive against *what has been drawn up* against you *already*. And therefore you show great lack of reason…, if you…are not going to come to a different decision still – one that is more sound-minded than these arguments.

All of chapter 111 (which makes up the longest continuous statement in the dialogue) must be understood as an appeal to the Melians, after all their arguments have been refuted, to open their eyes at last and not run voluntarily into destruction (cf. ξυμφοραῖς ἀνηκέστοις[36] ἑκόντας περιπεσεῖν, 'to fall with your eyes open into an irremediable calamity', § 3), since they still have the freedom to choose: δοθείσης αἱρέσεως πολέμου πέρι καὶ ἀσφαλείας (§ 4).[37]

But as in all previously examined situations, the warning goes unheeded (or is not understood), and the Melians, too, respond with the same long-refuted arguments (112.3: the only new point is the reference to their 700-year history of independence, as if a stable past could guarantee them a secure future).

…τὰ μὲν μέλλοντα τῶν ὁρωμένων σαφέστερα κρίνετε, τὰ δὲ ἀφανῆ τῷ βούλεσθαι ὡς γιγνόμενα ἤδη θεᾶσθε, καὶ Λακεδαιμονίοις (cf. 104b, 106 ff.) καὶ τύχῃ (cf. 102a, 104a, 105) καὶ ἐλπίσι (cf. 102b–103) πλεῖστον δὴ παραβεβλημένοι καὶ πιστεύσαντες πλεῖστον καὶ σφαλήσεσθε (113).

…*what is going to come* you deem to be *more clear* than what is before your eyes, but *what is invisible* you view by wishful thinking *as already taking place*; and having risked most on, and placed your trust in, the Spartans (cf. 104b, 106 ff.) and chance (cf. 102a, 104a, 105) and hopes (cf. 102b, 103), you will also fall furthest (113).

These are the Athenians' final words and, as the reader of the work knows, they are wrong only to the extent that they see the Melians' attitude as *unique* (μόνοι…ὡς ἡμῖν δοκεῖτε, 113). But for the dialogue's composer the 'result' of this resultless discussion is so paradigmatic that he has devoted to its genesis one of the climaxes (if not *the* climax) of his work.

In the light of our own investigation, it is doubtful that the Athenians should be regarded as the 'main character' of the dialogue,[38] and they should certainly not be so regarded merely because they represent the author's native city. Just as the Athenians behave as exemplary power-holders, so the Melians behave in a manner typical of people who are threatened. Nor is Thucydides out to brand the parties (the 'bad' or 'clever' Athenians and the 'foolish' or 'brave' Melians). The point is not to defend or attack the attitudes represented on either side but to *present* them as historically significant discoveries, that is, in the final analysis, as constitutive elements of the general human way of existence.

Does this mean we should forego asking any question about the historian's own attitude? Certainly not, but much depends on the level upon which the question is raised.

At the end of our investigation, there is at least *one* view of our author that we can dispense with, namely, that Thucydides' problem was 'to justify his admiration for what was so justly hated'.[39] We are at the same time freed from the necessity of excusing Thucydides for his supposed might-before-right way of thinking, or of having to demonstrate the undesirability (or irrelevance) of such an excuse. For we have been careful from the beginning not to identify the right of the stronger, as recognized by the historian, with his own personal views.[40]

We began with the dialogue's *structure* advancing step by step (or, it turned out, of walking in a circle)[41] and we found evidence that the author had taken a position somewhere outside the perimeter encompassing the two opposing parties. It seemed—to retain the image—that the Athenians were at the perimeter (the position of the more powerful) looking inward at the Melians, and that the Melians were looking outward towards the perimeter, which they were unable to recognize as their real and binding limitation.

The behavior of the Melians leads back to the question raised in our introductory chapter:[42] how does man in the historian's hindsight define himself in his actions? The answer: as 'foolish' is too simple in view of the Melian Dialogue, for it is a judgment from the perspective of the side that 'knows better' because it happens to be successful at the moment.

The historian's answer would seem to take into account the tragic aspect of Nicias' last speech as a parallel to the Melians' situation and, spoken with insight and regret, run something like this: 'incapable of grasping himself within the limitations of his own current situation'.

Notes

[1] For example, Nestle 1948b, 352 f.

[2] Nestle 1948b, 352 f.; 1934, 159 he differentiates between the 'naive-amateurish' (*naiv-laienhafter*) and 'political-natural' (*politisch-natürlicher*) *Weltanschauung*.

[3] Herter 1954, 317; cf. Deininger 1939, 81 f.

[4] Ferrara 1956, 340; cf. Parry 1981, 194 f.; Méautis 1935, *passim*; sometimes, however, the Melians are seen as empiricists and not at all unintelligent (Topitsch

1946, 102) and the Athenians are seen as—in the long run—making short-sighted use of correct theoretical knowledge.

[5] Nestle 1934, 160 ('ein falscher religiöser Glaube, wenn man meint, mit dem Kopf durch die Wand zu können und dafür die Gottheit in Anspruch nehmen zu dürfen').

[6] Wassermann 1947, 25.

[7] Schmid 1948, 111 ('die gewachsenen Eigenschaften sittlicher Kraft' vs the 'künstliche Geldmacht der Athener').

[8] Mackay 1953, 570 ff.

[9] Schwartz 1929², 141.

[10] See above, p. 20.

[11] Topitsch 1946, 12; Umfahrer 1946, 120; Braun 1953, 236; on the views of 431 (1.76) see above, pp. 47 ff.

[12] De Romilly 1951², 258, cf. 280.

[13] So already Jebb 1907: 'The simple juxtaposition of insolence and ruin is more effective than comment' (436). A sub-variety of this interpretation sees in Athens' attack on the Dorian Melos an unnecessary provocation directed at Sparta and consequently an endangering of the Peace of Nicias which Athens can ill afford (occasionally the end of the war itself is adduced in this connection beyond the Sicilian Expedition, cf. 5.90–1); cf. Herter 1954, 321 ff.

[14] 'Following the "guilt" of the Melian tragedy comes the "atonement" of the Sicilian Expedition', Scharf 1954, 510 with n. 17 (translated from the German); cf. Herter 1954, 330 ('Nemesis').

[15] One can also call it 'dietetics of power' (*Diätetik der Macht*, Vogt 1950, 9; Treu 1953/4, 271) or 'historicobiological realism' (geschichtsbiologischer Realismus): 'One can overdo the power principle. Then it turns on the one who applies it' (translated from the German), Eberhardt 1954, 332.

[16] Deininger 1939, 106 ff., cf. 113.

[17] Braun 1953, 239 (*Problem des Korrektivs; Frage der politischen Ethik*).

[18] See above, p. 15.

[19] The question of whether Thucydides manipulated historical facts to produce a situation convenient to the scope of his inquiry need not be addressed here. The last such attack against the historian's credibility (Treu 1953/4) has been adequately refuted by Eberhardt's (1959) response. Raubitschek's (1963) attempt to support Treu's thesis is unconvincing. The remark on which he has based his first assertion (that the word ἀδικούμενοι at 5.89 indicates a previous injury to Athens on the part of the Melians, p. 79) is intended (as the Athenian speakers themselves say in the same sentence) as merely theoretical (and not founded in fact): λόγων μῆκος ἄπιστον = 'a long speech that would not be credible anyway'. The argument to the effect that the participation of Athenian allies in the action against Melos suggests that the Athenian measures are somehow justified (so also Andrewes 1960, 2) lacks any factual basis. One need only compare 1.99.2; 3.11.4. Cf. further Kierdorf 1962.

[20] Cf. above, pp. 47 ff. That for Thucydides human nature is to the highest degree defined by the desire for power and πλεονεξία can nowadays be cited as

the *communis opinio.*

[21] ὑπονοίας τῶν μελλόντων λογιούμενοι, 87.

[22] That is, the position they have been in from the beginning without accepting it, cf. Deininger 1939, 25.

[23] Herter 1954, 323 (translated from the German).

[24] Many attempts to label Thucydides as an aristocrat are unpersuasive because they explain his aversion to blind mass reactions and suggestions as an oligarch's contempt for the *demos* (or *ochlos*). For his impartiality in constitutional matters, see above, pp. 4 with n. 2; 22 f.

[25] One may remember how successful Brasidas was on the other side with his speech (inclusive of ἐπαγωγά, 4.88.1) before the people of Akanthos: 4.84 ff.

[26] Cf. especially above, p. 118.

[27] 1.122.1; cf. above, p. 56.

[28] ὃ ὑμεῖς ἀσθενεῖς τε καὶ ἐπὶ ῥοπῆς μιᾶς ὄντες μὴ βούλεσθε παθεῖν μηδὲ ὁμοιωθῆναι τοῖς πολλοῖς, οἷς παρὸν ἀνθρωπείως ἔτι σῴζεσθαι, ἐπειδὰν πιεζομένους αὐτοὺς ἐπιλίπωσιν αἱ φανεραὶ ἐλπίδες, ἐπὶ τὰς ἀφανεῖς καθίστανται μαντικήν τε καὶ χρησμοὺς καὶ ὅσα τοιαῦτα μετ᾽ ἐλπίδων λυμαίνεται, 5.103.2.

[29] See above, pp. 118 ff.

[30] See above, pp. 59 ff. (summary of decision to go to war); pp. 121 ff. (decision on the Sicilian Expedition); pp. 142 ff. (Spartan warning after Pylos).

[31] On this, see above, pp. 121 f.

[32] See above, p. 120 with n. 70 on 4.108.4.

[33] Méautis 1935, 275; M. (he, too, sees Ch. 5.103 as central for the work as a whole) imagines on the part of Thucydides a *hate* of hope, oracles and irrational behavior, because, beneath the *impassibilité* of his thought, there lurks 'une âme violente, passionnée' (a result of his Thracian blood)—thus the historian is attacking a temperament related to his own.

[34] 'Was subjectiv noch Grund zur Hoffnung sein will, erscheint objektiv als Ausdruck der Verzweiflung', Reinhardt 1960, 212 n. 18 (on 7.77).

[35] Cf. Abbott 1925, 83 f.

[36] Cf. ἀνήκεστον 4.20.1 (above, p. 144).

[37] Cf. ἑλώμεθα 4.20.2. Above, pp. 142 f.

[38] 'Their partner in the dialogue recedes very much into the background', Scharf 1954, 510 (translated from the German).—Of course I do not mean to dispute the greater political significance of the Athenian side.

[39] Andrewes 1960, 6. Andrewes sees—along with many others—in the Melian Dialogue the historian's personal 'dilemma': 'He both admired the Athenian empire, and thought it immoral according to those standards by which the doings of private citizens are called δίκαια or ἄδικα'; cf. *op. cit.,* p. 1.

[40] See above, p. 21.

[41] Cf. Ludwig 1952, 142.

[42] Above, p. 10.

9

SPEECHES vs. COURSE OF EVENTS
IN BOOKS 6 AND 7:
Attitudes – perceptions – responses[1]

The title and contents of this chapter derive from the ever-present tension in the *History* between planning and outcome, and from the historian's manifest interest in the reactions of those involved. Scholarly judgments concerning the relationship of speeches and narrative in Thucydides have changed a great deal. It seems scarcely exaggerated to say that there was a time when interpreters felt that the course of events as told by Thucydides contains not more than the 'naked facts', while only the speeches, more or less mouthpieces of the author, can supposedly tell us of the meaning of history, which otherwise would remain mute. That such a concept is as simple as it is false, our preceding analyses have sufficiently shown. It disregarded—to single out only one aspect—e.g. the fact that Thucydides often presents pairs of two contradicting speeches (which then cannot both express his opinion, but may both *not* express his opinion), sometimes even up to four speeches, on the same problem with as many different viewpoints. Our second chapter has highlighted how earlier philology, unable to deal with such a situation, reduced and simplified Thucydidean complexity by breaking up the composition into 'layers', presumed to have been written at different times and to be mutually exclusive.

Meanwhile, we have learned to be cautious in claiming any single speech for the author's opinion unless our claim is corroborated by a passage, mostly of the narrative, in which Thucydides expressly speaks in his own name. We do not any longer, as was once done, see Thucydides as a partisan of Athens' imperial policy (we have learned to hear the voice of Athens' subjects, too, in the *History),* nor do we, as was also once done, simply declare that Pericles' speeches give us the historian's own views and convictions; rather we would carefully separate, e.g., Pericles' admirable logistical planning from his failure to distrust the general instability, physical as well as emotional, of human nature. And it is only in more recent time that one has begun to realize that the apparent homogeneity of style in Thucydides' speeches, which on the surface makes them seem all alike, admits of differences of characters: Alcibiades, for example, uses a more paratactic and comparatively simple way of speech, while his opponent Nicias employs hypotactic constructions to such a degree of complication that he has few rivals in the whole *History*.[2]

All this, needless to say but not needless to stress, cannot mean a change on Thucydides' part of the author-reader relationship; for his text has stayed unaltered for more than two thousand years. The change is with us: we face a process of learning on our, the interpreters' side, a process which allows us to rediscover and appreciate increasingly the richness of aspects and dimensions which Thucydides consciously incorporated into his speeches. Giving up positions which were held in our discipline at an earlier time therefore in this case does not mean impoverishment, but goes together with a broadening of our understanding.

It may, to turn from speeches to narrative, have been a bitter lesson for historians to learn that their discipline would never be able to achieve that sort of 'objectivity' which scientific disciplines at one time allegedly possessed. But we have to be aware that mere narration of any set of historical facts already implies a subjective element (because presentation includes judgment, evaluation, selection, arrangement, in short: interpretation)—to recognize, I say, the inherent subjective character of any historical narration at the same time allows us, in this area too, to rediscover and appreciate more fully the care and the categories which Thucydides applied in selecting and presenting events.

Even more: by abandoning any simple mouthpiece-of-the-author theory about the speeches, and, instead, respecting their dramatic setting (i.e. the limited viewpoint of the speakers), we allow the author to be wiser again and less shortsighted than the speakers he depicts. In fact, we allow him to correct his speakers by his own presentation of the events. This evaluation of the relationship between speeches and course of events is nearly the reversal of the one outlined at the beginning of this chapter: not elucidation of events by speeches, but, to put it pointedly, elucidation of speeches by the ensuing (or preceding) narrative of events now seems the appropriate method of reading Thucydides.

The effect is far-reaching. For example, Thucydides has often been praised for his allegedly scientific attitude towards history, mainly because his speakers occasionally use a seemingly scientific, especially medical, approach when analysing situations and making prognoses on future developments. If, however, it now turns out that not the speech, but the following narrative may contain Thucydides' last word on a prognostic method or on a speaker's way of handling such a method, then Thucydides no longer appears to be a representative, but a critic of that scientific attitude towards history. He becomes for us a historian not only of the history of a war, but specifically of the underlying *intellectual attitudes* of the parties involved in that war, himself being detached from and not necessarily adhering to such reflections or theories and their applications as he records. (A similar distancing is found in his report on the deplorable intellectual license which, by way of misnomer, increasingly undercuts inherited moral standards, 3.82 f.)

If it has not always been seen that only the combination of speeches and course of events gives us Thucydides' full judgment on inherent intellectual attitudes, it is, I must repeat, *our* fault for having overlooked this complex relationship, not his: *we* had to undergo a process of learning in order to be able to appreciate Thucydides' high level of art and consciousness. (The same is true—I should like to say in parenthesis—about emotional utterances in speeches and their effects during the future course of events. For the sake of avoiding unnecessary complication, I will treat them too under the heading of intellectual attitudes.)

If indeed it is Thucydides' intention to be, at his highest level, a historian also of the *intellectual* history of the Peloponnesian War, then we are of course interested to learn in which terms he chooses to conceive of intellectual aspects in the course of events, and also, which judgments he would like to suggest as his own and final ones to his readers. A procedure which our introductory argument recommends would allow us to evaluate and elucidate this question in three steps of increasingly broad scope:

1. The first step is to compare a speaker's reflections on past, present or future developments with the foregoing or following narrative. Here we are on relatively firm ground and can often definitely show what Thucydides' judgment is of a speaker's intellect—as well as of those who follow and those who reject his arguments; on occasion, the setting of a speech may even reveal that the audience understands the speaker in a way other than, or even opposite to, what he himself wishes to be his message.

2. The difficulties would lie with the second step: if, on the first level, following Thucydides' leads, we trace single strands of action that consist of speech (or speeches) plus events related to the speech, then we have, for the matter of clarity, dissected the much more complicated and complex body of Thucydides' work, which consists of *many* such strands and their *interplay* in action and reaction.[3] Now, on the second level, this interplay would become the object of study. The preceding chapters suggest that the result one can expect from analysing such a complex texture should by no means be a simple or even reapplicable technical formula of 'how to handle history', but a description of the successive moods and reflections

of human beings who face the contingencies of war. However, addressing such complexity amounts to a separate enquiry, which will be offered in the following chapter. I have chosen to survey Books 6 and 7 here for a large-scale demonstration because their main content, the so-called Sicilian Expedition, offers the advantage of a limited action of relative unity rounded out and formed into a whole by the author himself.

3. The third step would ideally consist in a comparison between war and war as described by our author. If he does not offer us the description of at least two full-scale wars, we should try to compare as large units as he himself is prepared to compose to confirm the assertion of his program (1.22.4) that he found features in history that are inevitably recurrent according to the condition of man. One of these large-scale units is the Sicilian Expedition as described in Books 6 and 7. To compare it to the other large-scale unit the historian offers us, viz. the whole Peloponnesian War, clearly exceeds the limits set by the work's unfinished condition. Thus, we shall have to confine our treatment of step three to a short outline at the end.

I have drawn out the general part of this chapter to indicate its character of a survey rather than the detailed investigation typical of the earlier chapters. Let us now turn to the first step, the comparison of the speakers' reflections on historical developments and the actual course of events itself. For this purpose, I have chosen the speeches of Alcibiades and Nicias at the beginning of Book 6. A few introductory remarks as to the situation may be helpful: in Sicily, two cities, Selinus and Segesta, are at war with one another. Selinus has been successful in calling Syracuse to her help, and the Segestans now, for their part, turn to Athens for support, using two key arguments: (a) if Syracuse is allowed to help Selinus, and, further, is not punished for having depopulated the city of Leontini, she may soon turn her growing power even against Athens' empire in central Greece; (b) the Segestans offer 'money sufficient for the war'. It is a classic case of escalation, not dissimilar to that over Epidamnus in Book 1, which led to the outbreak of the Peloponnesian War, then, however, in two steps: first, Corcyra–Corinth, then Athens–Sparta. In 416, the Athenians, who do not like to interfere unless openly invited, are not at all unhappy about the Segestans' request for help because they would like to conquer Sicily anyway. But they are at least cautious enough to send an embassy to Segesta with orders to check whether the money they have been offered is really there (6.6). Next spring the envoys come back with sixty talents of uncoined silver as a month's pay for sixty Athenian ships and a report 'both attractive and untrue' (6.8.2). The Athenians vote to send out the sixty ships, and five days later they hold another assembly on the subject of the expedition's further equipment. Nicias, chosen commander against his will, is concerned about his city and takes the opportunity to ask for reconsideration. Alcibiades, the second commander of the expeditionary force, opposes Nicias, largely, as Thucydides tells us in his own name (6.15), for personal reasons: he hopes to gain personal prestige and to avoid bankruptcy by military victories in Sicily. Nicias, when asked to give his estimate of the equipment necessary, gives another speech and again tries to make the Athenians change their minds, this time by confronting them with his enormously high demands for war material.

These three speeches of the second assembly (6.8.1–24) supply us with ample material of the kind I have in mind. And the reader quickly realizes that Thucydides himself favors the views of Nicias, whom the Athenians did *not* follow. Nicias, like Thucydides himself in Chapter 15, speaks of Alcibiades' personal motivation of prestige and wealth (12.2). Of the money allegedly waiting for them in Sicily, Nicias says: 'the money…which is spoken of as available over there, you better believe to be available above all in speech' (22). This utterance directly echoes Thucydides' own words about the report: 'both attractive and untrue, and especially about the money that it was available', etc. (8.2). There are direct contradictions between Alcibiades and Nicias. Alcibiades: 'The [Sicilian] cities are populous with mixed crowds, who easily accept departures of citizens as well as new arrivals' (17.2). Nicias, on the other side: 'For we…are about to attack cities that are great and not subject to each other nor in need of change' (20.2). Nicias even makes a prediction on their probable behavior (using the technical term εἰκότως, 'probably'). Again Alcibiades: 'And it is not likely that such a mob listens to planning with one mind or turns to action in a coordinated fashion' (17.4). He, too, ventures a prediction here on their probable (εἰκός) behavior. Nicias, however, expressly considering the possibility 'if the cities, frightened, take a united stand' (21.1), will, two years from now, turn out to be right when, in a letter from Sicily, he tells the Athenians, 'all of Sicily is taking a united stand' (7.15.1), thus bitterly disproving Alcibiades from the later course of events. Even more ghostly in the light of later events appears Alcibiades' haughty assertion, 'But the safety of staying, if there is some progress, and of departing our ships will guarantee; for we shall be masters of the sea over all the Sicilians together' (6.18.5). Nicias, however, in that same letter from Sicily will have to write: 'but now our ships, at sea for so long a time already, are rotten, and our crews reduced…' (7.12.3).

There can be no doubt, I believe: only the *combination* of speech and course of events can give us the full impact of Thucydides' judgment—or of his condemnation.

What I have done so far has been to compare two or three passages in each case. But I would like in one case at least to follow up more fully the development from speech to result, so that I can show more clearly Thucydides' method of presentation. Of Nicias' concerns I have mentioned so far Alcibiades' irresponsibility, the expedition's lack of money, a combined defense action of the Sicilian cities, the inner (and democratic!) stability of the main cities. I now come to some very solid worries, which will later turn out to be of decisive importance: besides money, Nicias several times mentions the difficulty of supplies and supply lines for a foreign army in Sicily, and, above all and over and over again, the danger that will come from the Syracusan cavalry: here he actually talks in terms of *defense* (ἀμυνούμεθα ἱππικόν, 6.21.1; ὅπως πρὸς τὸ ἐκείνων ἱππικὸν ἀντέχωσι, 22.1), and not at all in terms of conquest! He demands archers and slingers against the enemies' horse and contemplates the difficulty of supplying horses for his own army in Sicily. Later, in the catalogue of the Athenian force, as it crosses from Corcyra to Southern Italy, Thucydides lists the thousands of men and the vast supplies that sail. At the end he mentions the smallest number of all: 'and one horse transport carrying thirty horse-men' (6.43). Author's irony by 'no-comment' method? Before the first full-sized battle in Sicily, Thucydides lists among the dispositions on the side of the Syracusans: 'the cavalry they arranged on the right, being no fewer than twelve hundred' (6.67.2). The Athenians have, it is true, received some horses from Segesta in the meantime (6.62.3), so that the relation is not quite like twelve hundred to thirty, i.e. forty to one. But indeed, no comment could be more sobering than the naked numbers.

A similarly unwelcome justification of Nicias' speech by ensuing experience deals with *money*: before the expeditionary force leaves Corcyra for Italy and Sicily (and before Thucydides gives that summarizing catalogue of their strength which I mentioned above), the commanders send three ships ahead to gather information (6.42.2). When the bulk of the expeditionary force has arrived in Italy, the Athenians, before even considering action in Sicily, 'waited for the ships they had sent ahead to come back from Segesta, because they wanted to know whether the money which the emissaries had spoken of at Athens really existed' (6.44.4)—a clear reference to Thucydides' own remark (6.8.2) on the 'report both attractive and untrue'. When the three ships come and bring the news that there is only a ridiculously small sum at Segesta, Thucydides remarks, 'And for Nicias the news from Segesta came expected, but for the other two generals [scil. Alcibiades and Lamachus] even rather absurd' (46.2). Nicias did 'expect' the bad news: an indisputable justification of his statement in 6.22 that the money was available at most in speech. And by thus honoring Nicias,

Thucydides implicitly exposes Alcibiades (and those who voted for his plan). The immense Athenian force, instead of capturing Syracuse, now moves along the northern coast of Sicily to Segesta to fetch that small sum of money (30 talents in all) and on the way captures Hykkara, in order to sell the inhabitants as slaves (6.62). Cash amount: 120 talents. War begins to show its true face.

I return from money to the question of horses. The summer is gone, and so is the element of surprise. In the winter of 415 to 414, the Athenians are constantly insulted by the Syracusan horsemen, who ride up to their camp at Catana and ask whether the Athenians have come to live with them (i.e. the Syracusans) in a foreign land or to resettle the Leontines in their own (6.63.3). The Athenian generals *have* to react, and do react, by luring the Syracusans and their horse away from Syracuse to the north, and by sailing themselves at nighttime (at nighttime!) around to capture a place (the Olympieion) for a camp south of Syracuse (65). The Syracusans, coming back home, accept a battle and are defeated except—in accordance with Nicias' warning before fighting starts (68.3)—for their cavalry, which restrains the Athenians from completing their victory by pursuing the Syracusan troops (70.3). The day after the battle the Athenians even leave the scene and sail back to Catana:

> For it was winter, and it seemed not yet possible to wage the war on the spot, until they had sent for additional horsemen from Athens and gathered (horsemen) from their local allies, lest they be so utterly inferior in cavalry battles—and until simultaneously they collected money locally and money came from the Athenians…and until they prepared the other supplies and corn and whatever else they needed, in order that towards spring they might attack Syracuse (71.2).

And again (74.2): 'And they sent a trireme off to Athens for *money* and horsemen to be there with the spring.' *Money, horse, supplies:* what a sad triumph for Nicias to find the analysis he gave at Athens so thoroughly justified by the later course of events, even to the point which he had hoped to avoid, viz. that he would have to ask for reinforcements. But it becomes worse still before spring. Not only do the Syracusans build new fortifications to their city, but they even march to Catana with all their forces and 'set fire to the Athenians' tents and camp' (75.2), while the Athenians themselves had left their camp and retired into winter quarters at Naxos. Clearly, the Syracusan attack on the Athenian camp indicates a change in the power situation in Sicily: the large Athenian force, superior in the beginning of the summer, is now reduced to a power equal to that of Syracuse, and this change is largely due to the Athenians' lack of money and horses.

The change from the initial superiority of Athens and the initial inferiority of Syracuse to the equality and balance of power between the two indicates a new phase of the Sicilian War. Thucydides marks this moment of indecision, when the pendulum might swing to either side, by an assembly in Camarina (75–88) and a pair of speeches by the Syracusan politician Hermocrates and the Athenian envoy Euphemos: both speakers want to upset the equilibrium by winning over Camarina as an ally, and both, lacking at present the power of forcing Camarina, have recourse to skillful argumentation. Both lie, of course, according to their respective expediency. But both may also tell the truth, where the truth seems useful to their intentions. The meeting at Camarina clearly is part of the intellectual history of the Sicilian war and it is in keeping with what Thucydides tells his reader at 3.82 f. about the progressive moral corruption the war brought on. Being another twist of the interweaving strands of action, the new power balance played out at Camarina would fall under the kind of complexity we reserved for the following chapter.

I will end for now my observations on Nicias' speeches and the ensuing facts with just a few remarks. It is well known how devastating the effect of the Syracusan cavalry is in the later stages of the war, when the encircled Athenian soldiers cannot even go and get water without being attacked by the horsemen, or in the final stage when they try to get away from Syracuse by marching on land, and we also know the decisive role the lack of supplies plays for the Athenians all the time. The horsemen arriving from Athens in the spring of 414 upon Nicias' request are no more than 250, and they come 'without the horses' (6.94.4). The highest number Thucydides ever gives for the Athenian cavalry is 650 in all (6.98.1), as compared with 1200 Syracusan horses, as we noted earlier. No wonder, therefore, that the relief is not of any durable effect, so as to alter decisively any of the other factors involved.

In the introduction of this chapter, I said I would give special attention to showing how Thucydides writes a sort of intellectual (and emotional) history of the parties involved in the Sicilian War. Facts, whether they come expected (as for Nicias the financial plight in Sicily) or unexpected (as the same plight for Nicias' colleagues), are reflected in human minds, often as if in a sort of mirror, and often also distorted. We can, without being dogmatic, distinguish three sections of the Sicilian War:

(a) The initial stage when both sides are still at the peak of their strength or are even still increasing it. Correspondingly both sides have great (not to say: wild) hopes for victory.

(b) The middle period, repeatedly marked by a certain balance of power (for example, when both sides woo Camarina), but by no means stable:

changes may occur, e.g. according to the arrival of reinforcements on either side, like that of the Athenian general Demosthenes and his fresh troops in the summer of 413 (7.42), or of the Spartan general Gylippus at Syracuse (7.2). The corresponding feeling usually is that things have gone out of control and that one must, instead of pursuing the initial program of victory, adapt one's actions to the facts of the day.

(c) The final stage, when the dice are really cast and, as the outcome shows, decisive changes no longer occur. This would be after Nicias' decision to comply with the soothsayers and delay the final departure from Sicily for twenty-seven days (7.50.4), or, at the latest, after the final naval victory of the Syracusans in their Great Harbor (7.52–4).

As this survey shows, there tends to be a correspondence between the state of affairs and the state of mind of the parties involved. What I wish to bring out into the open now is Thucydides' technique of making large parts of the material he presents—facts stated (as we met them in the earlier section of this chapter), events recorded, speeches held—serve the idea of describing attitudes, perceptions, reactions, in short: the workings of the human mind.

I start out with a very factual, even dry, passage: the 'digression', as it is sometimes called, at the beginning of Book 6 (6.2–5) on Sicily, its geographical size, its vast population, cities, history of settlements and colonization, and so on: an impressive and often admired document of Thucydidean research. But we understand only part of Thucydides' intentions if we do not regard the setting of the alleged digression: in the sentence immediately before it he introduces to us the Athenians' intention of conquering all of Sicily, adding: 'the majority of them being ignorant of the size of the island and the large number of its inhabitants, Hellenes and barbarians, and of the fact that they were undertaking a war not much inferior to that against the Peloponnesians. For…', etc. With 'for' he introduces the digression, logically speaking: in the chapters on Sicily he justifies and elaborates on the predicate 'ignorant', which he used for 'the majority of the Athenians' (Nicias, of course, excepted).

Characterizing ignorance by supplying the facts not known seems to be his method, and not here only. He uses the same device elsewhere: as Chapter 1 has shown, the so-called digression, *Exkurs,* on the alleged tyrant-killers Harmodios and Aristogeiton (6.54–9) likewise serves to correct wrong beliefs and explain historical ignorance, led by which the whole city of Athens was driven into a state of unjustified frenzy. Similarly, the *Pentecontaetia* (1.89–118) serves to make plausible Sparta's fear of Athens' rising power. Both these digressions, too, are introduced by γάρ ('for'). This is also true of the catalogue of all the troops involved in the last battle before Syracuse (7.57–9): certainly a set of facts worth recording for later generations. But also, it is designed to prove (the introductory γάρ serves this purpose) that the Syracusans' present hopes for everlasting fame are well reasoned, if one considers the size and variety of the armies participating (τοσοίδε γὰρ, κτλ., 57.1). Even more: at the same time, Thucydides throughout the catalogue expressly lists the participants' motives for helping one side or the other, thereby finding further confirmation of his thesis of 3.82, that the violent schoolmaster War teaches men's minds new concepts. The motives for taking sides before Syracuse are not the traditional ones of right and kinship, by no means, but advantage or force throughout. On this level, a catalogue, apart from being by no means a digression, also becomes a summarizing contribution to the intellectual history of the war.

I return to the beginning of Book 6. The Athenians' ignorance about Sicily is grotesque. Thucydides, when writing, of course knew from autopsy about Syracuse's key position in the Mediterranean and the potential of Sicilian cities. (Even today, the archaeological sites of Siracusa or of Agrigento rival the size of ancient Athens.) The Athenians could know too, if they listened to Herodotus, who (in an important passage in Book 7) credits Gelo of Syracuse with the power to defeat even Xerxes. But Thucydides has to end his report by stressing again the unknown size:

> So many peoples of Greeks and non-Greeks inhabited Sicily, and against it being so great the Athenians were set to campaign, striving on the truest account to become masters over all of it, but at the same time wishing under a decent-sounding label to help their relatives and the newly added allies (6.6.1, referring to 6.1.1).

The setting proves it: ignorance (combined with desire for conquest) is the keynote for understanding the following process of decision-making at Athens (Chapters 8–24). Only a few are excepted from that ignorance, among them, of course, Nicias, who (to quote Thucydides' own words) 'thought that the state was not well advised, but by a short and decent-sounding pretext was going after all of Sicily, a vast undertaking' (8.4). Nicias' thoughts here participate in the same wording in which Thucydides expressed his own judgment at the beginning of Book 6. We may say that Thucydides himself felt puzzled by the Athenians' refusal to follow Nicias. The atmosphere at the time of the decision, however, is not one of sound judgment, but of heat and of calumny: Nicias himself, before speaking against the general enthusiasm, feels the embarrassing compulsion to prove his own honesty first (9.2) and to implore his own contemporaries to display courage: 'I…in turn call upon the older men…not to be ashamed, fearing to appear cowardly if one votes not to go to war…' (he even speaks of 'the ill

desire for what lies in distant lands', δυσέρωτας εἶναι τῶν ἀπόντων, 13.1).
In short, Nicias very much uses the same language which the Athenians
use in the Melian Dialogue when they warn the Melians, while Alcibiades'
speech has much in common with the irrational desires and hopes of the
Melians. We may say that facts and true information do not count, but if
we say so our statement implies a new fact: when the unfounded view, that
of Alcibiades (I need not repeat again his main arguments, but note that
he does not even mention cavalry), prevails, then the *unreal* becomes *real,*
because people are going to act out their hopes and desires, and the *real,*
like the facts Nicias warns his audience about, becomes, at least for some
time, *unreal,* because it is flatly disregarded. (The great surprise, however,
is that the irrational desires might even have been realized successfully:
in 6.47–50 Thucydides makes it quite clear that an attack on Syracuse
immediately upon the Athenians' arrival in Sicily would have had a very
real chance of victory because the Syracusans were then panic-stricken and
inadequately prepared. Of course it was a chance, no more. Demosthenes,
when bringing the reinforcements for Nicias in 413, tries to correct his
predecessors by taking just this chance of surprise. (He is defeated, although
for other reasons, as the following chapter will show.)

I return to Athens: we may say that the speech of Alcibiades (like the
speeches of other, unnamed, men) creates new facts, a new course of events,
so overwhelmingly, that existent facts are reinterpreted by his followers.
Nicias' large-scale demands for equipment, designed to have a deterring
effect, are now taken as supporting Alcibiades' view, namely as a guarantee
for safe return, or, psychologically speaking, as silencing any doubts that
might still exist unpronounced in the Athenians' hearts (24.1: this chapter
alludes five times to the idea of safety). From now on, Thucydides will
continuously characterize the Athenians' moods through the language of
irrational hope and ignorance as they derive from Alcibiades' arguments;
but slowly, step by step, he will reintroduce the facts of Nicias' speech and
confront the Athenians with them, and each time he will list the Athenians'
surprised reaction. In other words, running parallel with the increasing
justification of Nicias which I outlined in the earlier part of this chapter,
we see a process on the side of the blind Athenians of waking up again from
mad dream to reality. I pick a few passages for confirmation, beginning
with stage (a), the initial period of the war.

(i) 6.24: The initial mood at the time of decision-making: Nicias' second
speech makes the Athenians 'much more eager'. (In passing, I would like
to remark that Nicias himself from here on is very much a figure like
Cassandra, meeting his fate open-eyed: he knows it, we the onlookers
know it, but those with him do not know: three levels of information, and

another proof of how intensively Thucydides may speak through devices which he took from tragedy.) The Athenians 'fell in love' (ἔρως, § 3, recalling Nicias' δυσέρωτας εἶναι, cf. 13.1) with the enterprise on different levels: the older, the younger, the common soldiery, each having special motives. But 'if perhaps someone did not like it, he kept quiet—from fear he might, by voting against it, appear to be of ill will toward the city' (24.4)—in spite of Nicias' appeal to show courage. (Let me just point out a parallel: the open vote plays an important part in Sparta's decision of 432 to begin the Peloponnesian War [1.83.2]. Then, too, the warning of the wise and moderate—ξυνετὸς καὶ σώφρων—, as Thucydides describes King Archidamus' reputation, was useless.)

(ii) 6.31–2: The departure of the expeditionary force from Athens. This scene of splendor doomed to be destroyed has often been admired. The moment of saying goodbye to kindred, sons, friends (all listed) is a very short glance at the truth:

> at the present moment, when they were now at the point of leaving each other, the fearful aspects overcame them more than at the time (scil., in the assembly) when they voted to sail. Nevertheless, by the present strength, because of the huge quantity of all the things they saw, they regained courage through the visual impression (31.1: the eyes are closed again quickly).

And the accompanying foreigners appreciate the spectacle. Now follows a 'digression' (introduced by γάρ, of course) giving the reason of the Athenians' confidence as well as of the onlookers' fascination: the catalogue of the departing force. However, it is not, as one has sometimes thought, that Thucydides himself endorses their strength without qualification. He describes much more the money value, the outside appearance, the impression on other Greek cities, even the emotional side: prayers together—not singly—singing of the hymn, sailing out in column, racing to Aegina. But when he compares it to Hagnon's and Pericles' (short-term and more modestly equipped) expedition, he mentions, also, *their* three hundred horse; he does not mention any contingents for the present expedition at 31: but at 43, he lists 'a single horse-carrier, with thirty riders' (see also 37.1). To the attentive reader the realities of Sicily as outlined in Nicias' speeches are present throughout, unmasking mistaken perceptions and illusions. When the enterprise is viewed in Greece under the aspect of 'the greatest hope (expectation) for the future in relation to the existing resources' (31.6), the reader is prepared to be sceptical.

(iii) 6.46, a passage we know already, but not in this dimension: Upon arrival in Sicily the Athenians learn that the money offered them by Segesta does not exist. Except for Nicias, the generals are surprised (they find the facts fairly incomprehensible, ἀλογώτερα), and—first encounter with reality!—are 'right away disheartened' (46.2). And it is only now that Thucydides tells us by what means the Athenian embassy to Segesta had been tricked into believing in the money's existence. To tell the fact of deceit to the reader at the same time as he tells of the Athenians' discovery of it helps explain the disappointment, and is another example of the same technique of using facts to characterize human moods and attitudes. 'And the ones who had been tricked...received a lot of blame from the soldiers' (46.5).

So much from stage (a), the initial period. I leave out here section (b), the middle period of undecided, but often changing, warfare (on which the following chapter will throw some light), and proceed to give three examples picked from what I would call the final period (c).

(i) 7.55. The situation: Demosthenes and the reinforcements he brought from Athens have not only failed when trying a surprise attack on Syracuse, but the whole Athenian navy, attacked by the Syracusan coalition, has lost a decisive battle. The text: 'The Athenians were in every kind of despair, and their surprise about the unexpected [naval defeat] (ὁ παράλογος) was great; but much greater still was their regret (μετάμελος) of [having undertaken] the campaign' (55.1). Here we have the reverse mood from that of 6.24, which led to the decision to go to war. Ἔρως then is now answered by regret (μετάμελος; the same happened twice after the chance victory of Pylos ten years earlier—twice elation, twice regret);[4] ignorance is answered by παράλογος ('unexpectedness') for the participants (for Thucydides, Nicias, the reader, there is no παράλογος). Clearly Thucydides now complements the intellectual and emotional attitude of the initial phase by describing the mood of the Athenians facing the results of their irrational decision. But he not only complements, he nearly quotes Nicias' words of 6.20 now in 7.55: 'For these cities alone they had attacked as ones similar to themselves in character (ὁμοιοτρόποις—Nicias had, at 6.20.3, used the form ὁμοιοτρόπως), having both a democratic constitution as they had themselves, too, and possessing ships and horses and large numbers' (55.2): ἵπποι, μεγέθη (it was μεγάλαι in 6.20.2)—the whole outline of Nicias' second speech appears again, even the word μεταβολή is in both places: they had to face the fact that the cities in Sicily could not be weakened by bringing about inner changes—as Nicias had predicted.

There is no doubt at all: Thucydides now measures the Athenians' surprise about their failure by the bushel of Nicias' speech. But Alcibiades' speech, too, is recalled, and his belief in safe return through the navy: '...and when they had been defeated *even at sea* (something they would not have believed), *they were even more at a loss*' (7.55.2 end). Thucydides' kind of architecture becomes visible, reaching from speeches at the beginning of Book 6 over to near-quotation of the same speeches in the face of the events in Book 7. To repeat: the speeches are elucidated by the course of events rather than vice versa. And the reactions of those affected by the events again are an essential component of the narrative.

(ii) 7.75: The final naval battle has been lost, and the Athenians try to march away from Syracuse on foot. This chapter shows them leaving the camp, their wounded and dead, their lost hopes. Again we find verbal correspondences to another departure, namely that from Athens in 6.31–2 which then too was to be measured against Thucydides' own statements on ignorance and inadequate equipment. One short quotation may suffice: There was no relief in the thought (cf. ἐδοξάζετο) of common suffering, etc., 'especially [considering] from what sort of splendor and pride in the beginning things had descended to what sort of ending and humiliation' (75.6). Splendor versus humiliation, ignorance first versus experience later, irrational desire (ἔρως) versus inescapable suffering, beginning versus ending, dream versus awakening, speeches versus course of events: the reader is invited to compare, to follow through the history of human enterprise, to see that Thucydides' categories are apposite in describing the history of the intellectual attitudes during the war, all the way through to the participants' despondent reflections when facing the end.

One last remark: although ignorance and greed rule from the beginning, there is no word of moralizing or even triumph because the sober judgment is justified in the end, or something similar. On the contrary, Thucydides follows the Athenian soldiers through even more suffering and torture: he even offers his own voice to make their sorrows known. This is important for understanding him: his outlook is not of the simple kind that the wicked must be punished or the ignorant be taught. In spite of seeing blindness ruling from the beginning, and in spite of not agreeing with the attitude that leads to the expedition, he does not fail to pay tribute to the last terrible situation in which all men are alike. Why? Because, I propose, the Athenians' blindness is not an isolated phenomenon, but indicates (as we had reason to note before) a universal (if regrettable) fact about the human condition.

(iii) I have said already that their regret, μετάμελος, is a repetition of a former regret. Similarly, the readiness to close one's eyes is repeated when the news of the Sicilian disaster arrives in Athens. The first reaction of those at home: 'The truth is not true': they don't believe, even those who report clearly, τοῖς…σαφῶς ἀγγέλλουσι (8.1.1). But upon recognition (ἐπειδὴ δὲ ἔγνωσαν), they turn against the orators who had advocated the expedition, 'as if they had not voted for it themselves' (ὥσπερ οὐκ αὐτοὶ ψηφισάμενοι). Now they give up hope (ἀνέλπιστοι...σωθήσεσθαι, 8.1.2) as easily as they had grasped it (εὐέλπιδες...σωθήσεσθαι , 6.24.3). The reversal of moods is complete.

The third step of my argument, I said, should consist in comparing war with war, as described by Thucydides. I do believe that such a comparison is what he expects from his reader, and that when he calls the Sicilian enterprise a war not much inferior to the war in central Greece, he suggests that we look for recurrent features in both wars. The Sicilian War might even serve to indicate what the end of the Peloponnesian War would have been like had Thucydides described it. Considering the fear and suffering in Athens and Sicily in 413, we might believe that Xenophon, although with inadequate literary means, was not quite off the track when he described Athens' fall in 404 in so passionate terms and, at the same time, made the Athenians think of Athens' former evil deeds *(Hell.* 2.2.3–19). Certainly, Thucydides' presentation of Sparta's final victory and of Athens' fall would have reflected the various analyses and predictions given by the speakers in Books 1 and 2. We cannot carry out that proposed large-scale comparison *in extenso*, because we do not possess the end of the *History.* But I can indicate how it may confirm the results we gained from Books 6 and 7, thereby taking up hints I gave before.

In Book 6 the discussion at Athens is nearly duplicated at Syracuse: Nicias' counterpart is Hermocrates, who—we have to imagine the Athenian army to have left Piraeus for Corcyra at the time of his speech—vainly tries to make the truth known (περὶ τοῦ ἐπίπλου τῆς ἀληθείας λέγειν, 6.33.1: [a] that they are coming, [b] that they are coming against *all* of Sicily). He is even ridiculed by part of his audience, experiencing a Cassandra-situation similar to that of Nicias. His successful opponent argues that an Athenian expedition against Sicily would not be a sensible enterprise, and therefore one which the Athenians cannot, in all probability (εἰκός), be credited with. Thus, the truth is untrue, the real is not real—again. Of course, crediting the Athenians with common sense, means, in Thucydides' eyes, a cynical judgment on their irrational vote for the expedition. (It also shows, as before, that use of the εἰκός for an optimistic forecast is questionable.)

The other parallel: when in 432 the escalation originating from far away Epidamnus finally triggers Sparta's decision for war, the warning speech of the Athenian envoys is outweighed by the Corinthian harangue, and cautious King Archidamus, appealing—like Nicias—to the older generation and their experience of the negative aspects of war, is parodied and mocked by fiery Sthenelaidas, who asks his audience to vote by getting up and walking to two different spots: here, too, nobody likes—in Nicias' words—to 'be ashamed, fearing to appear to be cowardly, if one votes not to go to war'. The result: Sparta votes for the Peloponnesian War, and is soon in for surprise, encountering realities which King Archidamus had analysed for them before. I leave out here the parallels of Pericles and the Athenian side.

Probably these belong to the kind of recurrences Thucydides had in mind when he wrote (in 1.22) of things 'such and similar to happen again in the future according to the condition of man' (κατὰ τὸ ἀνθρώπινον).[5]

Notes

[1] The present chapter develops further my contribution, 'Speeches and Course of Events in Books 6 and 7 of Thucydides', originally published in P.A. Stadter (ed.) *The Speeches in Thucydides: A Collection of Original Essays with a Bibliography*, copyright (c) 1973 by the University of North Carolina Press. Used with permission by the publisher.

[2] See D.P. Tompkins 1972. Tompkins interprets the complexity of Nicias' speeches as a sign of his 'constant concern with himself', 'his habit of making concessions and admissions of inadequacy' (188), of his 'tendency…to use himself as his constant point of reference, and to neglect other points of view', in short, of his 'self-centered attitude' (196). On the other hand one might, by pointing to the same complexity, make a case for Nicias as the most comprehensive, intelligent and prudent speaker in the *History*.

[3] An early example of this was the Mytilene complex of Book 3 (Chapter 6).

[4] See Chapter 7.

[5] For the meaning of this phrase, see above, pp. 28 f.

LITERARY DETAIL AND
HISTORICAL CRISIS POINT:
The Sicilian Books[1]

Sir Winston Churchill reportedly answered a question about the politician's essential qualification by citing the ability to predict what will happen the next day, the next month, the next year—then, later on, convincingly to explain why it did *not* happen. The historian faces a similar dilemma. What does he expect us to learn from his work? That history on the whole is a process open to rational analysis in a way that would allow one to predict at least long-range or large-scale developments and, so, perhaps to influence or steer the future? Read along these lines, the work of Thucydides has, as we pointed out earlier, been described as a 'manual for future statesmen'.[2] On the other hand, the study of history may equally well lead to a position akin to that of Churchill (and the analysis on which it is based need not at all, if compared to its alternative, be less rational—probing, as it would, into the occurrences and influence of the unexpected in historical processes[3]).

At the ends of Chapters 7 and 9 we indicated that Athens' doomed war in Sicily of 415–413 might be viewed as a sort of paradigm or blueprint, 'writ small', so to speak, of the overall Peloponnesian War: more easily surveyed since lasting only two years, but 'not much inferior' (6.1.1) to the overall war and, so, hardly less complex. Chapter 9 has, in sweeping strokes, sketched some of the parallels which the historian's artful writing recommends to his readers. The similarities of structure, especially in the areas of planning and outcome, confirm the appropriateness of the terms and concepts chosen for our preceding analyses of Thucydidean event sequences. Confirmation will be welcome also in that grey intervening sphere of ever-changing action, where human nature and chance work singly and together (or against one another) to give the course of history its direction (or, perhaps, rather 'indirection'). If the author's interest in the 'hinges' of history, as documented in his literary detail, can be evidenced in Books 6 and 7 as it has been before (and with comparable results), the task of this monograph will be fulfilled and its thesis established.

It is good to remind ourselves at this point that the problem posed by the discrepancy between planning (usually optimistic) and outcome (often devastating) is probably as old as mankind. In Greek literature it is spelled out already in the earliest piece there is, Homer's *Iliad*. King Agamemnon, following a wishful dream purportedly sent to him by the ruler of the universe, expects to take the city of Troy on his own, without the help of his strongest warrior, Achilles; Achilles for his part, bearing a grudge against Agamemnon, is unwilling to participate in battle; on one occasion, he lends his armor to his friend Patroclus so Patroclus may go and fight in his place; Achilles confidently trusts that highest god Zeus will listen to his prayer for the safe return of Patroclus (16.233–48). But Agamemnon and Achilles both must learn that their overconfident schemes not only result in losses so painful as to exceed all expectations, but also leave them in a position much worse than their initial situation.

Similar findings are reported by Herodotus, the so-called Father of History: King Croesus of Lydia, in his insolent bid for geographical expansion, is blind to the warning contained in a prophecy issued by the god Apollo's oracle. Croesus unwittingly first destroys his own country; then, while claiming to have learned from past mistakes, he repeats his errors and causes the downfall of his advisee, King Cyrus of Persia.[4]

Unlike these earlier, myth-related approaches, Thucydides analyses the old problem in exclusively human terms. The Athenian decision of 416/15 to send out a military expedition to conquer Syracuse and Sicily is characterized as irrational, guided by greed and blind to factual obstacles. Such conduct we found described more than once in the *History of the Peloponnesian War*. During the winter of 424/3, the Spartan general Brasidas, through skillful psychology and propaganda, manages to win over a number of cities which so far have been subject to Athens. The cities deceive themselves about the true power of Athens and later will have to pay a terrible price for their defection. But at present 'they were basing their judgment more on unclear wishing than on safe forethought, accustomed as men are to entrust what they desire to thoughtless hope, but to reject with sovereign reasoning what they do not agree with' (4.108.4).

The author here comments on two points. One is the human tendency of letting irrational desires dictate our goals and actions; in this process reason is given the secondary (subordinate) role of sovereignly explaining away obstacles that may appear to be blocking the road to fulfillment of our desires. Chapter 6 has addressed this feature when analysing the speech of Diodotos. The other point concerns the usual outcome. Neglecting 'safe forethought' (together with the warning resulting from it) in favor of irrational hopes invites disaster. Chapter 8 has explicated this aspect in the behavior of the threatened Melians.

The result may be observed as in the case of the defecting subject cities, so in the failure of the Athenians' own expedition against Sicily. In either case, *safe* forethought would advise *against* undertaking the enterprise. We can draw here and expand on the preceding chapter to provide the background. The final decision at Athens to go ahead with the military campaign is taken in a popular assembly. It is characterized by a pervasive and uncontrolled irrational desire (καὶ ἔρως ἐνέπεσε τοῖς πᾶσιν ὁμοίως ἐκπλεῦσαι, 6.24.3). Those voting in favor represent the overwhelming majority, young as well as mature men: the older ones expect a successful conquest or, at least, no harm to a powerful expeditionary force; the younger ones find the spectacle offered by a far-away country alluring and foster optimistic hope for a safe return (εὐέλπιδες ὄντες σωθήσεσθαι); the great crowd (including the common soldiers) expect 'eternal wages' from the foreseen accretion to the empire. The few who are not happy with the decision keep quiet; they do not dare to vote openly against the enterprise, fearing that, in view of the excessive desire of the majority (διὰ τὴν ἄγαν τῶν πλεόνων ἐπιθυμίαν, 24.4), they might be viewed as showing ill will toward their city.

At this point already, the Athenians may appear not dissimilar to their subject allies who defected to Brasidas and who were 'basing their judgment more on unclear wishing than on safe forethought'. But the intellectual profile of this case is drawn with a much sharper stylus. Not only does Thucydides characterize the general Athenian ignorance about the far-away island (ἄπειροι οἱ πολλοὶ ὄντες, 6.1.1; cf. 6.6.1) by inserting an 'excursus' (6.1–6) on the vast geographical size and the huge as well as diverse population of the powerhouse Sicily, but his literary presentation, marked by speeches of opposing politicians, also emphasizes that the Athenians have been manifestly *warned* beforehand by rational arguments which, under normal circumstances, it would seem hard to discredit because they would meet the requirements of 'safe forethought'.

The preceding chapter has once more elucidated Thucydides' technique of confronting planning and outcome. The projections and arguments given before the Athenian assembly by the two prospective generals, Nicias and Alcibiades, are confronted, even by verbal echoes, with the bitter outcome of the Sicilian campaign. It turned out that Nicias' persona reflects the author's own views on the ill-advised enterprise. The hard facts of money, horse, hoplites, archers and grain supplies, as well as the stable constitution of major Sicilian cities, in the long run prove Nicias' analysis correct and his risk-taking, war-mongering colleague-in-office wrong.

Under many aspects, then, it looks as if the expedition was doomed from the beginning. This impression is intensified by the literary detail employed in the narrative, which likewise stresses the correspondence of unsound planning and devastating outcome. From the correspondences mentioned in the preceding chapter, I wish selectively to recall two pairs here, precisely for their literary detail. The glorious morning of the armada's departure from the Piraeus, a matter of only a few hours, is developed into a panorama painting of lasting symbolism. To Thucydides, some moments can carry a weight which may balance months of events less pregnant with historical meaning.

At sunrise, it is as if the whole population of Athens is on the move down to the harbor, citizens and foreign residents alike. A passing cloud of concern is quickly dissolved by the visual splendor and strength of the departing force. But the cloud has made its appearance: hope for conquest is briefly overshadowed by lament about the implied uncertainty of a *Wiedersehen*. 'And in the present moment, when they were already about to leave each other with an eye on the dangers, the terrifying aspect (of the enterprise) overcame them more than at the time (scil. in the assembly, 6.24) when they voted to undertake the voyage' (31.1). It is this moment of sudden awakening to the expedition's potential of personal loss on which the narrator will capitalize later. Now, the Athenians are 'escorting each their own, some their friends, others their relatives, others again their sons' (30.2). By detailing the passing premonitions as well as the multiplicity of human relations involved in the farewell scene, the author artfully provides a background for the impact which the coming disaster will have on the human level.

When, after their last naval defeat in the Syracusan harbor, the Athenian soldiers are about to abandon their camp on foot, leaving the dead and even the wounded behind, they are overcome by grief and fear 'whenever someone saw one of his close friends lying there' (7.75.3). Their 'painful' perceptions 'for eyes and mind' (7.75.2) contrast with the departure from Athens, when the sight of the proud sailing force had assuaged the Athenians' fear for their close ones (6.31.1). The wounded, 'turning to imploration and lamentation', cause those leaving the camp despair by calling on them, 'whenever someone somewhere caught sight of friends or relatives'. Some even try to attach themselves physically to their leaving tentmates (7.75.3f.). There can be no doubt that these departure and good-bye scenes are composed as a pendant to the original departure from Athens.

One more feature of correspondence between the opening and ending situations should be cited here. When the soldiers have gone aboard and the fleet is ready to leave the Piraeus, the customary prayers take place—but not separately, boat by boat. After a trumpet has commanded general silence, all the soldiers and sailors on all the ships pray together, while a herald is taking the lead. Those on the shore join in the prayer—a spine-tingling experience, considering the thousands and thousands of voices involved. The ceremony is completed by the singing of a paean and the offering of libations (from golden and silver vessels!). By another group of details Thucydides underlines the unreality of visual splendor doomed to be destroyed by disregarding objective facts. Upon proudly 'first sailing out in line', the ships then even compete against each other in a race as far as the island of Aegina: a seeming abundance of strength is displayed before the background of insufficient preparation (6.32).

As the 'greatest...reversal', μέγιστον...τὸ διάφορον (7.75.7) that 'happened to a Greek army' takes place, the historian quotes from his own report on the original departure from Athens.[5] When abandoning their camp outside Syracuse, as 'soldiers on foot rather than *shipboard warriors*', the Athenians happen to 'depart again, instead of (under) the *prayer* and *songs of victory* (paeans) with which they *sailed out* (from the Piraeus), under invocations opposite to these', (i.e. under the curses of their wounded comrades who stay behind). The verbal repetition of details (in 7.75 from 6.32) leaves no doubt that the two departures, from home and from the camp, are composed in reference to one another, thus once more confirming and validating the Thucydidean opposition of wish-dictated planning and bitter outcome.

Under these, the historian's own, terms, it is only consistent that he should from now on employ the most exacting literary detail when describing the army's death march toward the Assinaros river and to the final massacre. In a day-to-day report (7.78–84), stretching over more than a week and including fractions of days as well as night occurrences, the reader is taken along on the inevitable road of suffering to its bitter end. Those who survive to become Syracusan prisoners languish in the quarries, exposed to the most torturous physical conditions (7.87).

The course from wishful blindness to eventual blood-letting is the same we read about in the case of the Athenian subjects who defect to Brasidas. It is exemplified also by the attitude of the Melian councillors who, when their city is encircled and besieged by a vastly superior Athenian army, reject well-founded warnings (5.103, 111) and place their trust in chance (which, they say, sometimes helps the weaker side, 102), the gods (104), the Spartans (104), and in their own centuries-old heritage of liberty (112; see Chapter 8). The Melian citizens, too, in the end suffer the utmost destruction. And it would not be difficult to list other event sequences of similar import.[6]

Is, then, the Sicilian expedition perhaps just another instance of a customary development, and in it can we grasp a Thucydidean law of probability, revealing large-scale predictability in a course of events? Does the historian's use of literary detail emphasize the likely outcome of insufficiently planned enterprises? If so, we may feel that here at least we grasp a strand of predictability in the web of history.

The answer to the question just posed is both 'yes' and 'no'. Naturally, inadequate planning will tend to result in unwelcome outcome, and, as exemplified above, the literary detail will drive the point home. But outcomes do not always depend on planning alone—or, for that matter, even on the adequate or inadequate planning done by only one of the two parties involved. The defection of Mytilene on Lesbos from the Athenian empire in 427 is a classic case (3.2–50; Chapter 6). On the one hand triggered prematurely because of information leaked to Athens, and, on the other hand, confronting the Athenians with a situation they are reluctant to face at this time, the process, once started, forces either side to keep *re*-acting rather than to act. Or (to cite another notorious case which emancipated itself from the original planning categories), in the Athenian raid on tiny, uninhabited Pylos the interference of chance (τύχη), repeatedly evidenced in great detail by the historian, leads to a Spartan peace offer which could mean the end of the Peloponnesian War (were not the Athenians, made confident, to gamble away their unexpected good fortune: what chance has granted, human nature dissipates, as we said in Chapter 7). Neither of these cases displays the scope of the Sicilian Expedition of Books 6–7, the components of which amount to a war-within-a-war, according to 6.1.1. But either case can also lead us to consider that the function of the literary detail may reach beyond the simple dimension of good (or inadequate) planning and desirable (or undesirable) outcome—a dimension which would limit the ancient historian's horizon and goal to that of writing a desk manual for future statesmen. We now must approach that grey area between planning and outcome excluded from the preceding chapter, i.e. the intervening period of undecided, but frequently changing warfare, where a comparison merely of projection and outcome may appear insufficient or, occasionally, even simplistic.

A good introduction to Thucydides' complex concept of history is supplied by the surprising extent he grants the description of a non-event in the Sicilian War. Following the Athenians' departure for Corcyra, the historian describes the reaction at Syracuse to early (but multiple) messages about the approaching enemy force. Believing (and rightly so, as the attentive reader immediately recognizes) to be better informed than his fellow-citizens, Hermocrates, the Syracusan statesman, comes before the popular assembly and suggests a number of advance measures (6.34): firm up the

Sicilian alliances and form new ones, seek assistance from rich Carthage, push Corinth and Sparta to send help as well as to resume hostilities in the motherland, etc. In terms of time projection, these moves are to prepare the city for the situation which is going to evolve once the Athenian force has arrived in the area.

In addition to (and separate from) such medium range planning, Hermocrates develops an *ad hoc* plan for immediate action (34.4–35.8), which would pay off even before the bulk of the enemy fleet can think of putting out to sea from Corcyra (αὐτοὺς οὐδ᾽ ἂν ἀπᾶραι ἀπὸ Κερκύρας, 34.6) and of reaching the coast of Sicily (οὐ περὶ τῆς Σικελίας πρότερον ἔσται ὁ ἀγὼν ἢ τοῦ ἐκείνους περαιωθῆναι τὸν Ἰόνιον, 34.4). In terms of the pro's and con's offered in the preceding discussions at Athens, which dealt with predicting the success or failure of a military campaign on Sicilian soil, Thucydides here surprises his readers by confronting them with a completely new aspect which had entered neither the projections of risk-taking Alcibiades nor even those of cautious Nicias. This circumstance in itself is worth noting.

But even more surprising is the fact that an author with a reputation for succinctness should grant extensive space and literary detail to a design which will never be given a chance of entering the realm of reality. For, unlike the historian himself, the fellow-citizens of Hermocrates for the most part do not take him seriously—yes, some even ridicule the true information he gives them (35.1). His Cassandra-like situation is apt to alert us to the possibility that Thucydides is thinking in terms of greater complexity than merely those which predict success or failure of a military campaign from a set of strategic premises. However, to acknowledge such complexity, an interpreter must himself rise above the level of predominantly military rank and hierarchy, which reduces Thucydides to (as Wade-Gery characterized him in the *OCD*) 'a first-rate regimental officer' whose 'judgment of problems of high command' is considered seriously lacking.[7]

In Athenian planning terms, Hermocrates' design would constitute a first occasion where an unforeseen event might overthrow the whole enterprise—*outside* the well-established literary arch that connects the proud but closed-minded departure from the Piraeus to the open-eyed and abject final egress from the camp outside Syracuse. Here, the reader is being introduced to a new dimension.

Scholarship has encountered great difficulty in dealing with Hermocrates' plan, from declaring it not serious[8] to calamitous.[9] A lonely recent defender is Bloedow,[10] who rightly points to the high esteem which the Syracusan statesman enjoys elsewhere in Thucydides' work. But by tying the plan to, and attempting to integrate it with, the other (medium-term) measures also recommended by Hermocrates, Bloedow himself deprives the plan of its status as a separate, prophylactic enterprise, which, moreover, is designed *not* to result in military action or even confrontation. The situation is comparable to the threat intended by some modern ballistic weapons, where actual firing would mean that the intended prevention of war through deterrence has been defeated.

Though Bloedow thinks that Hermocrates 'would have attempted to avoid'[11] a pitched battle, he (like his forerunners) still discusses the possible 'chronological room for Hermocrates to have carried out his strategy, including the *amassing* of an *adequate* fleet',[12] and Bloedow also states Syracusan 'advantages' 'in either case',[13] i.e. (I understand) in case the Athenians decide to give up their campaign or to go ahead with it.

This misses Hermocrates' bluff, the point of which relies on *immediate* action *without time for preparation*. For (he says) 'most appropriate at this point in time' (μάλιστα...ἐπίκαιρον, 34.4), would be for us Sicilians 'to pull to water all the *existing (available)* fleet' (καθελκύσαντες ἅπαν τὸ ὑπάρχον ναυτικόν, cf. ἀπὸ τῶν ὑπαρχόντων, 33.3) and, with two months' supplies, to sail to Tarentum and the Iapygian promontory [at the heel of the Italian boot] to face the Athenians' (34.4; see MAP 1), so they would be scared by the idea of having to fight for crossing the sea even *before* fighting for (or: around) Sicily.

Hermocrates then goes on to develop the thought process, λογισμός (34.4 and 6), which the Athenians would be going through upon hearing the unwelcome (and probably exaggerated, 34.7) reports about a Sicilian fleet lying in wait for them. We can easily translate the λογισμός into the first person plural, i.e. into the targeted *persona* of the Athenians:

> with Tarentum as their base, the Sicilians move from friendly territory as its protectors; but for us Athenians the sea is wide to cross with our whole force (which it will be hard to keep in order because of the length of the trip), and we shall be easy targets, approaching slowly and in sections (κατ' ὀλίγον, 34.4; cf. 4.10.4 and 11.3). But if we disembarrass and concentrate our fast-sailing boats and send them all ahead on an advance attack, they will, if they have to use oars, be exhausted and easily be attacked themselves; alternatively [in case our boats encounter favorable winds], if the Sicilians choose not to attack, *they* can withdraw to Tarentum; but *our* fast-sailing boats, equipped for a naval engagement with few supplies, will be at a loss facing uninhabited areas [where they have to go ashore overnight]: either, when our boats stay, the Sicilians will besiege them, or, when trying to sail along the coast, they will leave our main force behind and, uncertain about the reception by the local cities, will be disheartened.

So far the prospective thought process, λογισμός, of the Athenians, as anticipated by Hermocrates. He is convinced that these considerations will at least induce the Athenians for now to remain at Corcyra (ὥστ᾽ ἔγωγε τούτῳ τῷ λογισμῷ ἡγοῦμαι ἀποκληομένους αὐτοὺς οὐδ᾽ ἂν ἀπᾶραι ἀπὸ Κερκύρας, 34.6) and, by first sending out spy boats, to be delayed into the winter, beyond this year's sailing season. Or, he thinks, they may, terrified by the unexpected development (τῷ ἀδοκήτῳ, 34.6 and 8), give up the expedition completely, especially so since their most experienced general is leading the expedition against his own will and would gladly seize upon the pretext. (This feature seems confirmed both by Nicias' position in the Athenian assembly and by his later suggestion to sail home, barring payments by the Segestans or other unexpected positive developments, 6.47.)

The psychological element is prevalent in Hermocrates' approach: he is counting on the intimidating effect of unexpected preventive action (as opposed to the mere show of resolve to defend oneself if attacked, 34.7);[14] and he calculates the effect rumors have on the enemy, especially so when the Sicilian defense 'force' at the Iapygian promontory will, as happens in such cases, be reported with exaggeration (34.7).

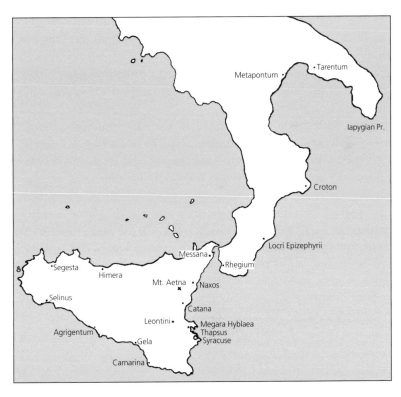

MAP 1. Southern Italy and Sicily.

The plan's reliance on rumor and exaggeration (i.e. on misinformation) renders it clear beyond doubt that Hermocrates never intended his collection of *available* ships, assembled at shortest notice, to engage the supreme Athenian fleet in actual battle. He only wanted at least to buy time for his city until next spring and, if possible, even to scare off and prevent the enemy from coming at all. It is deplorable that modern historians have blamed the Thucydidean Hermocrates for miscalculating 'strategic advantages', allegedly 'mythical'[15] in quality, which he never voiced in Thucydides' work.

The idea 'to challenge the Athenian fleet'[16] does not even occur in Hermocrates' plan. Nor does he express 'hope of deterring the Athenians with a show of *force*'.[17] This entails that it is likewise untenable to maintain that Hermocrates 'gravely underestimated Athenian numerical and tactical superiority at sea'.[18]

On the contrary, Hermocrates expressly counts more on the prospect that the Athenians will be scared by the unexpected character of such an enterprise (τῷ ἀδοκήτῳ μᾶλλον ἂν καταπλαγεῖεν, 34.8; cf. μάλιστ' ἂν αὐτοὺς ἐκπλήξαιμεν καὶ ἐς λογισμὸν καταστήσαιμεν, 34.4) 'than by the real power' (scil. of the Sicilian 'fleet'; ἢ τῇ ἀπὸ τοῦ ἀληθοῦς δυνάμει, 34.8).

This does away with two kinds of customary speculation. One of them prophesies a likely Sicilian defeat (allegedly resulting from Hermocrates' plan) and its calamitous consequences: '...the probable outcome was the annihilation of the Sikeliot fleets and the rapid imposition of Athenian rule on Sicily and South Italy'.[19]

The other speculation, connected to the first, concerns the alleged chronological impossibility of Hermocrates' plan. In Kagan's words: '...it would at least take two months to *build, gather,* and *train* a Sicilian fleet.'[20] And likewise Dover: '...if there had been time (as there was not)...';[21] as well as Westlake: 'One factor that surely rendered the plan impracticable was lack of time.'[22] It has to be said once more: Hermocrates' is *not* a long-range plan 'to *build*, gather, and *train* a fleet' or 'to *muster* a fleet' (italics mine) for an 'operation on a large scale in distant waters'.[23] The idea does, as explained above, not even enter into Hermocrates' plan. His urgent proposal *for the present moment* (μάλιστα...ἐπίκαιρον) is (to repeat it once more here) to pull *all presently available* boats (ἅπαν τὸ ὑπάρχον ναυτικόν, 34.4) into the water for (immediately) sailing to Tarentum and the Iapygian promontory. There is still something to be said in favor of a thorough and precise reading of the Greek text.[24]

Having secured the true character of Hermocrates' preventive plan, we may now determine its place within the historian's concept. This is the first time that the categories of prospective success or failure on Sicilian soil, under which the campaign had been discussed in the assemblies at Athens, are superseded by a possible and unforeseen, albeit never executed, development, viz. the delay or even termination of the expedition before it can reach its target area. The literary detail dedicated to outlining the ramifications and minute subdivisions of the anticipated Athenian reaction to the enterprise proposed by Hermocrates forces the reader to add a new category to his expectation that inadequate planning will lead to failure: what may look like a predictable train of events can be interrupted and thrown off course by unforeseen factors, here consisting of bold planning on the opposite side. The mere possibility of such a deviation, even if it never turns into reality, is to Thucydides important enough to be introduced and elaborated upon in the historical work. This observation encourages us to look for and perhaps investigate similar crisis points in Thucydides' analysis of event sequences.

Like other developments depicted in the *History*, the Sicilian War too offers a number of prominent occasions where the literary detail not only signals, as in the Athenians' death march toward the Assinaros river, the seemingly predictable final stage of failure and human suffering, but is also used to draw the reader's attention to an unforeseen situation, in which the train of events may switch tracks. A major example of this type of literary presentation is offered by the failure of the relief force which arrives from Athens under the general Demosthenes in July of 413. Having received advance information about the imminent arrival, the Syracusans attempt to win a pre-emptive victory over the Athenian fleet (and army). The naval engagement, drawn out over three days, is a success. The train of events is described with great precision and technical detail (7.36–41). But the resulting Syracusan confidence receives a severe blow by the arrival of the unexpectedly huge relief force (which, on the opposite side, boosts the morale of the already despondent Athenians).

Intent on avoiding Nicias' initial mistake of wasting the element of surprise, Demosthenes quickly embarks on a night attack against the city, launched from the high-lying plain of Epipolai (7.42–4). Extraordinarily successful in the beginning, the assault turns into an Athenian disaster when the soldiers, made confident by their apparent initial success, carelessly abandon their fighting formations. The contrast of plan (7.42.4) and bungled execution (43.7 ff.) leads to extraordinary descriptive detail,—extraordinary also because of the difficulties the author encountered in securing a reliable picture of what happened in the night battle.

Clearly, the outcome of the night attack was not predictable. Equally clear is that the outcome could have gone either way. And either swing of the pendulum, if not 'corrected' or not meeting interference from a new course of events, has the potential of determining the overall outcome of the war in Sicily. We are encountering one of the 'hinges' of history, and the historian's interest in the crisis point is marked and conveyed to his reader by the literary detail.

The possible emancipation of an event sequence from a seemingly predictable course is, then, an important feature for the historian. The result of the speeches for and against the expedition at the opening of Book 6 was sobering, and so was the outcome of the vote taken in the Athenian assembly. The reader might have expected the defeat of the ill-informed Athenians at the hands of powerful Syracuse. Meanwhile, however, we have learned that, right upon arrival, Nicias did have a chance but wasted it by spoiling the surprise effect (7.42.3; cf. 6.63.2); that Demosthenes was on the brink of re-instating the Athenian siege of Syracuse; and that the whole expedition might have been stopped in its tracks even before crossing the Ionian sea from Corcyra and reaching the coast of Sicily.

Already we may be convinced that, for Thucydides, historical developments are anything but predictable, that is, steerable. Even where the outcome appears to fulfill rational expectations as in the final Athenian disaster in Sicily, there may first have been intervening events which deviated from and then other events which again restored the original thrust, rendering the final result basically unpredictable. It is worth our while that at one point we more closely trace Thucydides' accents in presenting such a me-andering course of events. The event sequence I have in mind is remarkable because the historian dedicates to it a day-to-day account, sometimes even narrowing the focus to a time span which may rather be measured in hours or parts of hours. Under the perspective of a war that lasted twenty-seven years the brief time span under discussion must indeed be assumed to be pregnant with historical meaning.

In the summer of 414 the Syracusans, expecting the arrival of the Athenian siege army, plan to take preventive measures. They do not have to prepare too much on the eastern and southern sides of their city, where the sea protects their peninsular territory, formed by a real (though land-connected) island and the territory between the small harbor in the east and the big harbor in the south (see MAP 2).

An area of great concern, however, for the inhabitants is their exposed geographical situation on the land-side. We owe it to the groundbreaking 1969 study of H.P. Drögemüller that we are well-informed about the site and extent of the city in 415–3. I myself have, wherever possible after more than thirty years of an uninhibited building boom, checked out Drögemüller's results *in situ*, and have generally found his reasoning as well as his results superior to those of his competitors.

Syracuse is located barely outside the south-eastern corner of a plateau which rises immediately above the city. The plateau, called Epipolai, i.e. 'Upland', can roughly be described in terms of an isosceles triangle. From the short hypotenuse, which extends from the city in a northern direction for about four kilometers or 2.5 miles, the triangular Epipolai plateau slowly rises westward for about seven kilometers (four miles) to a height of 150 meters (about 500 feet), reaching, at the western end of the so-called Euryelos elevation, the point where the two long sides of the triangle meet at a very sharp angle; at this western end later a fort was built, which likewise went by the name of Euryelos.

MAP 2. Syracuse.

But there is also a rather steep rise in the terrain right from the city itself in a north-western direction before one reaches the plateau, rendering Syracuse vulnerable to attacks launched by an enemy who has climbed the northern rim of the slanting elevation and crossed it in a southward direction. For, though the rim of the plateau falls off steeply on all sides for about 10 to 15 meters to the next lower terrace (see PLATE 1: an example from the northern rim), it has five access points alone on its northern slope, and the northern rim is not visible from the city. This is one major problem the Syracusans feel they have to deal with.

> ...they believed that, if the Athenians were prevented from becoming masters of Epipolai, a steep area lying right above the city, they themselves would not easily be walled off (by a siege wall), even if they should be defeated in a battle. Therefore they intended to guard the (northern) approaches, to prevent the enemy from climbing up at these points *unnoticed*; for nowhere else (by no other route) would they be able to (scil. climb up without being noticed) (6.96.1).

The threat of an Athenian siege wall or circumvallation has been on the Syracusans' minds for a long time. Already during the preceding winter they have extended their city wall north of the city in a west-east line along the whole stretch along the south side of Epipolai (including a bulge to the west so as to enclose the Temenites with the sanctuary of Apollo) in order to make it more difficult for the Athenians to surround the city on land with a siege wall (75.1):[25] the longer the Syracusans' own defense wall, the longer the enemy will have to build their siege wall.

PLATE 1. Steep slope of Epipolai, example from the northern side.

So, with information received on the looming Athenian approach (the Athenians are sailing from the north, leaving their winter camp in Catana), the whole Syracusan army one summer morning at daybreak gathers for a review in the plain south of the city, along the left (northern) bank of the Anapus river (see MAP 2).[26] At this point Thucydides begins a day-to-day account of events, in remarkable contrast with the preceding report on the Sicilian theater, where operations of the Athenians in early summer against five different communities are summarized and compressed into the space of a single chapter (6.94).

But still before they start their general review of arms, the Syracusans pick, under their newly elected generals (Hermocrates is one of the three), six hundred select hoplites under the command of a certain Diomilos, 'in order that they might *both* be guardians of Epipolai *and* might, quickly concentrated, come to help if it should be necessary for something else' (96.3).

This arrangement does express the urgency long accorded the protection of the approaches to the northern rim of the Upland. However, by turning the six hundred heavily armed men into a *general* rapid deployment force, available also 'for something else' should the need arise, the Syracusans run the risk of weakening the primary function of their elite detachment.

Their planned availability also for other functions probably supplies an explanation of the fact that the six hundred are not sent up right away to guard Epipolai but stay down at the Anapus river together with the bulk of the army. (At least, Thucydides' report gives no indication of their immediate deployment up there, and from what follows one has to conclude that they have remained down at the river.) A conceivable strategic reason for initially keeping the force in the low-lying plain south of the city could be that the Syracusan leadership may not wholly exclude the alternative to the northern plateau, i.e. may expect the Athenians possibly again to go ashore where they landed once before last year and where they at that time set up their camp: south of the city, on the west shore of the great harbor, near the Daskon elevation and opposite the Olympieion (see MAP 2; 6.65.3, 66.2; at that time, the Athenians also destroyed the bridge across the Anapus). From that position, too, the Athenians would, by fighting their way through, be able to pose a threat to the north rim of Epipolai, as is demonstrated by the later night attack of Demosthenes, who led his troops around the western end of Epipolai and then up the same approach to the north rim which the Athenians had used the year before (7.43.3; cf. 6.97.2).

At any rate, it is clear that for the time of this morning's review of arms, Epipolai is *de facto* unprotected in spite of the fact that the rapid deployment force under Diomilos is being picked still *before* the review starts.

The Syracusan leadership does expect the Athenian assault to occur in the near future—but not this morning. And here appears to lie the historian's starting point.

For Thucydides in a flash-back now goes to a point a few hours *before* the Syracusans review their army in the plain south of the city. And his report also switches over to the Athenian side: 'But, during this [very] night on the day following which[27] they (i.e. the Syracusans) did their review [= during the night preceding the day of the Syracusan review of arms], the Athenians, [coming] from Catana, had already landed with their whole army, *unnoticed* by them (i.e. the Syracusans), at the so-called Leon, which lies six or seven stades (i.e. about 1000 meters or six tenths of a mile) distant from [the northern rim of] Epipolai. And they had [also] gone unnoticed disembarking their infantry and putting in with their ships at Thapsos' (97.1). In an aside, Thucydides then goes on briefly to inform his readers that Thapsos, only a short distance away by foot or by boat, is a peninsula, the narrow neck of which the navy crews have fenced off with a palisade; behind it, they now stay put (97.2a).

The main action continues in the second clause (97.2b), contrasted with the navy's withdrawal: '*But* the infantry *right away* moved in running mode toward Epipolai and managed to be beforehand climbing up at the Euryelos, before the Syracusans, becoming aware, could come to help from the meadow and their review.' The verbal repetition is ominous: Diomilos and his six hundred had been selected 'to be guards of the Epipolai' and elsewhere, too, to 'come to help'. Now, the Athenians climb up the northern access to Epipolai, before the Syracusans become aware of it and the presumed guards can even think of 'coming to help'. And while the Syracusans wanted to prevent them from 'climbing up unnoticed' (ὅπως μὴ...λάθωσι σφᾶς ἀναβάντες, 96.1), the Athenians are now able to land their troops without being noticed (ἔλαθον...τοὺς πεζοὺς ἀποβιβάσαντες, 97.1), and their army 'climbs up, before the Syracusans notice it' (φθάνει ἀναβάς...πρὶν τοὺς Συρακοσίους αἰσθομένους, etc. 97.2).

PLATE 2 shows a stone staircase (possibly of a more recent date) with low, wide steps, situated at the point of the Athenian ascent as determined by Drögemüller. To its right there is a likewise flat, but hardly half as wide, staircase, today almost totally overgrown.[28] For a hurried ascent the low steps are exceedingly useful. The staircase shown in PLATE 2 has in its high rim occasional holes drilled into the stone, for tying up beasts of burden. (The same kind of holes is found in the casemates of the Euryelos fort, there, however, shoulder-high, for tying horses.) PLATE 3, taken after climbing up to the plateau, not only shows in the distance (moving from left into the picture) the peninsula of Thapsos (resting place of the

Athenian naval crews), but also, in the middle ground, the sharp edge of the northern rim of Epipolai, next to which only the tops can be seen of the trees that are standing in the low plain at sea level. Only in two areas, here in the north of Epipolai and south of the city, in the vicinity of the Great Harbor (landing site of the Athenians in the preceding year, opposite the Olympieion, 6.65.4; cf. 64.1) was it possible to land a major body of troops. On the eastern rim of Epipolai the grotto coast of *Trogilos* falls off into the sea so steeply as not to allow any ascent (see PLATE 6).

PLATE 2. Ancient stone stairway, leading up to the northern rim of Epipolai.

PLATE 3. View across the north-western rim of Epipolai, towards the lower plain near the shore and towards Thapsos peninsula.

But things get even worse for the Syracusans, to whose side the narrator now returns (97.3). Diomilos and his rapid deployment force as well as the other troops move to help from the meadow as fast as everyone can (that is, without appropriate order); however, *for them* matters literally turn into an 'uphill battle'. 'But the number of stades before clashing [with the enemy] amounted *for them* from the meadow to no less than twenty-five' (97.3), i.e. 3,750 meters or two miles and a third. It is hardly necessary to say that the expression 'no less than' emphasizes that the stated number may be a minimum, or, at least, a disproportionately long distance; in order to reach their enemy, the Syracusans have to run almost four times the distance which the Athenians had to cover for reaching the top of the plateau.

Drögemüller has demonstrated that the measurements supplied here by the historian are precise. So the sheer numerical statement is apt to convey the extent of the Syracusans' disadvantage. Because of running each at his individual speed, they are in rather bad order when encountering the enemy and, so, are defeated in a battle on top of Epipolai. Diomilos and three hundred others are killed, the rest withdraw into their city, and the Athenians set up a victory monument (97.4f.).

So far, then, the disastrous outcome of what had been feared for a long time and what had been expected to be prevented by special precautions. The case is not singular in Thucydides' work. One may cite, e.g., the Thebans' attack on Plataea in the weeks before the war broke out, where likewise the relief force which was intended to prevent a negative outcome was prevented from fulfilling its task, and the enterprise led to tragic consequences.[29] The most serious consequence in the case here under discussion is that the Athenians in the course of *this very morning* are placed in a position to begin the siege of the city which, during last year's landing, they were unable to undertake. And the Syracusans now find themselves in that situation which they had most eagerly and for a long time endeavored to forestall.

If we ask what it is that causes the historian to dedicate so much literary detail to so few hours, the answer will be the same as in the two preceding cases which have been discussed so far in this chapter: it is his interest in the 'hinges of history', in those moments of crisis where things may develop either in this or in that direction. The Athenian landing and occupation of the northern area of Epipolai took hardly more than a few hours (if not less). And we must picture the Syracusans at daybreak moving out through the south gate of their city to their early morning review of arms and to the preceding selection of the Epipolai guards *at the same time* at which their enemy are taking possession of the plateau.

Thucydides does not relate in which way the Syracusans 'perceived' (αἰσθομένους, 97.2) their enemy's presence on the plateau. This could hardly have taken place through men sent out from the city to reconnoiter. For the citizens went out south with *all* their forces, πανδημεί (96.3), and the generals saw no need to send Diomilos and his six hundred guards up right away following their advance selection. So Thucydides' description leaves his reader no other than the natural way of picturing the Syracusans 'observing' or 'perceiving' the enemy's presence: there possibly appeared on Epipolai, moving along the southern rim above the steep slope, an Athenian advance detail, perhaps on horseback (the north rim stairway could accommodate horses) looking down on the Syracusans' review; whereas the Syracusans, looking up and discovering the men at a distance of about two kilometers (a mile and a quarter) as the crow flies, were startled to see them and stirred 'to come to help from the meadow and their review' (97.2). PLATE 4, taken in close vicinity to the modern race track (the ancient site of the Syracusans' review, situated a little further to the east, lies today in a barred zone) provides—especially by the two multi-story buildings on the right—a good idea of the steep southern slope of Epipolai as the Syracusans faced it.

So far, the Athenians have gained a decisive advantage. But this does not yet mean that they can use it to their fullest intent. As long as the chain of events appears open-ended, the detailed report continues, if not in terms of hours, so still for the most part in terms of days. I shall try briefly to summarize the stages Thucydides marks in the development, and then pay closer attention to those passages which are marked by even more detailed literary emphasis.

PLATE 4. View towards southern slope of Epipolai from the plain west of the area of the Syracusan review.

On the day following their occupation of and victory on Epipolai, the Athenians move down against the city itself (97.5); but when the Syracusans do not come out to meet them in battle, they go back up and build a fort on Labdalon, a place right on the north slope of Epipolai (see MAP 2), which can guard their supply lines toward Thapsos and Megara. They also receive, possibly on the same day (98.1), much-needed cavalry from Sicilian allies. And, settling their camp on Syke (an area near the Temenites, close to the north-western bulge of the new Syracusan wall), they start swiftly building the ring of their siege wall, as planned from the outset (6.44.1) and so much dreaded by the Syracusans (6.75.1; 96.1).[30] Frightened by the speed of the Athenians' construction activity, the Syracusans come out of their city to stop them, but must withdraw because of their troops' lacking order. Part of their cavalry is defeated by all the Athenian horse (98.2–4).

On the following day (the *third* one mentioned, 6.99), the Athenians work on the northern part of their siege wall, i.e. pushing from the Syke area in an eastern direction towards the Trogilos cape north of the Small Harbor; their plan is to produce the shortest connection from the Great Harbor in the south of Syracuse to the east coast north of the city.

The Syracusans, no longer risking battle with all their forces, build a cross-wall, aiming at cutting the projected line of the Athenian siege wall. Their plan works out so well that they soon feel their job is done.

> When as much of their cross-wall as had been built and palisaded seemed sufficient to the Syracusans, and the Athenians did not come to hinder them from fear of being an easier match when split up...at that point the Syracusans, leaving a single φυλή [tribe] behind as a guard of their cross-wall, withdrew into the city (100.1).

What a change within less than a day! Now it is the Athenians' turn to be afraid, and the Syracusans, when having extended their cross-work beyond the expected line of the Athenian siege wall, feel they have made 'sufficient' (ἀρκούντως, 100.1) progress for their city to be out of danger. Their newly gained sense of security even allows part of them to go home for lunch. Has then (the reader may wonder) the effect of the long-feared Athenian occupation of Epipolai finally been voided?

This is the point where the narrative delves into even greater detail. The Athenians '...observed that the rest of the Syracusans were distributed over their tents during midday; that some had *even* (καὶ) gone away into the city; ...and that those on the palisades were on guard without care' (100.1b). The reader believes he is actually following the eye movements of the Athenian soldiers who are watching what the enemy are doing (or, rather, not doing): these observations can be made in less than half an hour. And the Athenians do utilize their chance. A quickly assembled special force, attacking in running mode, takes the negligently guarded cross-wall and drives its guards into that outer work on the Temenites which the Syracusans have built last winter to make it harder for the Athenians to ring them with a siege wall. To complete the irony of the situation, the Athenians pull up the stakes of the cross-wall palisades and carry them over to the siege wall for their own use. And they set up a victory trophy (100.3). Syracusan complacency and Athenian attentiveness have in the shortest time brought about another reversal which has been unforeseeable and unpredictable because it depended on the vagaries of human nature. At the end of this day the Syracusans find themselves back from where they set out in the morning.

On the next day (the *fourth* in the series, 101) the Athenians turn to building the part of their wall which is designed to reach the Great Harbor in the south. Wishing to go the shortest possible distance, they do not mind going down the steep slope, and then through the plain and the swamp of Lysimeleia. The Syracusans respond with a second crosswork, a palisade accompanied by a parallel ditch, right through the middle of the swamp. At daybreak of the *fifth* day, the Athenians take this fortification, too, placing doors and wooden planks (what a detailed description!) on the firmer parts of the swamp area. Though victorious in the ensuing battle (101.4), the Athenians suffer some losses as well as confusion on their right wing, and they lose one of their two generals (Lamachus).

Encouraged by this unexpected turn, part of the Syracusan right wing, which had been fleeing toward the city and which now regroups, leaves the city area toward Epipolai, seeking to attack the now unprotected northern siege wall and the site of the Athenian camp. This, of course, is a severe threat to the Athenian strategic position on Epipolai. If successful, the surprise attack may result not only in the Syracusans' recovery of the plateau, but also in the Athenians' loss of their camp and of the supplies stored in it. However, *by chance* (ἔτυχε, 102.2) Nicias, the surviving general after Lamachus' death this morning, has been left behind here today because he is sick. With no soldiers to defend the place, he cannot hold the outwork, but saves the wall proper (and against all odds effects his own survival) by ordering the servants to set fire to the wooden siege equipment which lies piled up in front of the main wall.

Within the shortest time, the situation is reversed once more. The fire turns the enemy away, and Athenian troops returning to Epipolai from the low-lying battle area mean further help for Nicias and the camp. *At the same time*, the Athenian fleet, under orders to leave Thapsos this morning, sails into the Great Harbor. Seeing the ships, the Syracusans speedily withdraw into their city, no longer believing that they can prevent the siege wall from being completed down to the sea (102.4). Again, we have been witnessing a reversal within the shortest time. From the *ersatz* attack on the camp area and the fire ordered by Nicias to the return of the Athenian troops and the simultaneous arrival of their fleet there can hardly have passed more than an hour, more likely it was less time that passed between sudden hope for the city's freedom and utter hopelessness.

Here the historian ends his day-to-day report, and one can easily see why he proceeds in this way. Like the preceding days, also the fifth has shown at least the potential for a reversal: it has only been *chance* (ἔτυχε, emphasized by being positioned at the opening of the sentence, 102.2; cf. 7.2.4; 2.91.3) that has prevented the extinction of the Athenians' strategic siege position on the Epipolai plateau.

From now on, the tracks of the development appear set, at least until a new factor enters the account from outside. So Thucydides can summarize without much detail (103). The Athenians work on their double wall down the steep slope to the Great Harbor. Supplies and ships and troops keep arriving for them from everywhere, even from as far away as Etruria. Everything runs according to hope, whereas the Syracusans, with no help in sight from the Peloponnese, no longer expect to prevail. So they even, both among themselves and towards Nicias, enter (fruitless) negotiations about surrender. This is a one-way development of some duration, in which there is accented only the human factor inside Syracuse, producing distrust and despair born from misfortune (103.4). Nothing positive for the city can be expected here any longer. The crisis where things could have gone either way is over, at least for now.

A new strand of interesting details is being selected when another development gathers intensity, one which shows the potential of reversing the seemingly sealed fate of Syracuse.

Already during the preceding winter (of 415/14) Sparta, encouraged by Alcibiades' treasonable advice and pressured by Syracusan as well as Corinthian envoys, had named its general Gylippus to head the Syracusan defense effort (6.93.2f.; cf. 88.10). Gylippus ordered the Corinthians to place two ships at his disposal immediately and to send more later (6.93.3).

This strand of the story, dormant during the recent narrative, is activated now, at the point when the Syracusan situation is described as being desperate. '*But during this time*, Gylippus [...] and the ships from Corinth were *already* around *Leukas* intending to come to Sicily to help *with speed*' (104.1). 'During this time', 'already', 'with speed': the emphasis is on the time element and reflects the urgency of the situation at Syracuse, suggesting the question: can the relief effort reach the city before it is too late? Mentioning Leukas likewise carries weight in this context: not too far north of the island lies the area from where boats will usually cross over to Italy. The reader is led to understand the whole enterprise as a race against time.

But the news which Gylippus receives at Leukas (false news, that is) says that Syracuse has already been surrounded completely by the siege wall. Giving up all hope for saving *Sicily* as a whole (Syracuse is no longer mentioned), the Spartan general, accompanied by the Corinthian commander Pythen, decides in a sort of *ersatz* action to try to keep at least southern Italy from becoming Athenian. With an advance detachment of four boats, he crosses the Ionian sea 'as fast as he can' to Tarentum (see Map 1), leaving the bulk of the allied fleet (of ten Corinthian and five other boats) behind so they may cross over later (104.1).

The hopes for Syracuse are certainly dimming; and even more so since Gylippus, though being in such a hurry, encounters nothing but delays and difficulties. First (πρῶτον, 104.2) he moves from Tarentum to Thourioi (situated about halfway between Metapontum and Kroton), but is unable to turn his father's ties to the community (the details are not quite clear) into an alliance; then, when sailing on along the Italian coast, his boats are badly battered by high northern winds (characteristic of the area) and driven out to sea (again the details are debated); so he is forced to *return to Tarentum* for extensive repairs (the imperfect tense ἐπεσκεύαζεν at 104.2 is durative in meaning).

Precious time has been lost, but not only for Gylippus. Nicias, when informed of the four boats' presence in the area, disregards them (as did the Thurians before him) because of their small number, classifying them rather as pirate vessels, and accordingly at this point (πω, 104.3) fails to dispatch any Athenian guard ships. So Gylippus' weather-bound delay is compensated by the negligence of Nicias, who misses a chance of forestalling a dangerous future enemy.

After the repairs on their boats are done, Gylippus and Pythen, sailing *once more* along the coast, put in at Lokroi Epizephyrioi (a city not friendly to the Athenian expedition, 6.44.2). And here they hear 'more clearly' (σαφέστερον, 7.1.1) that Syracuse is not yet completely walled off, 'but that they can still get in via Epipolai when arriving with an army' (7.1.1). Their choice is between 'risking the danger to sail through' into Syracuse (εἴτ'...διακινδυνεύσωσιν ἐσπλεῦσαι), or first (πρῶτον) to sail through the strait of Messina to reach Himera on the northern coast of Sicily, and then to approach Syracuse later over land, after gathering an army in northern Sicily (7.1.1). Their decision in favor of the latter alternative of course means even further delay for Syracuse, and the decision has also a specific ingredient, viz. 'especially since the four Athenian ships were not yet at

Rhegium, which Nicias nevertheless had sent out when hearing that they were at Lokroi' (1.2). 'Not yet at *Rhegium*': this would mean that the Athenian guard ships would cut them off long before they could reach the narrow passageway itself (see Map 3).

So, upon hearing that the four unknown ships have left Tarentum for the second time in the direction of Sicily and now are at Lokroi, Nicias does take precautionary measures—but what he does not know is that he is actually dealing with his opposite number, a Spartan general. On the other hand, Gylippus, upon receiving, apparently while still at Lokroi, information about the four approaching Athenian vessels, prefers, rather than facing them, to anticipate their moves (and actually does manage to anticipate: φθάσαντες δὲ τὴν φυλακὴν ταύτην, 1.2) by quickly sneaking through the strait, on the way putting in at friendly Rhegium (today's Reggio di Calabria) and Messene (today's Messina).

The urgency of Gylippus' situation, once he *has* decided to take the northern route and go to Himera first, becomes clearer if we consider the

Map 3. East coast of Sicily.

local geography more closely. Apart from the use of fire or smoke signals, the northward narrowing waterway between the coasts of Italy and Sicily offers excellent observability of movements on the sea and on the opposite shore, long before a ship reaches the strait proper. The strait itself, at its narrowest point, is less than four kilometers (two miles and a quarter) wide. Today the best impression of the narrow passageway is provided by two pylons, one on either shore, which carry the power lines from Calabria to the island: the towers stand 3,650 meters or two miles apart. On a clear day, one can see Taormina (Tauromenium: twenty miles or thirty kilometers away) and even as far as Mount Etna. So there can be no doubt about the necessity for Gylippus of quickly moving northward through the strait (see PLATE 5) if he wants to escape notice of the four Athenian vessels which probably are fast sailing ships, equipped to hunt down their prey.

Making it to Himera, Gylippus is able to gather a sizable army of more than 2,800 men, consisting of his own soldiers and armed sailors, of Himeraeans and men from different tribes and cities in the area (he is aided in part by the recent death of a local king who had been friendly toward the Athenians), and he quickly leads his troops through Sicily toward Syracuse. Should then his plan, in spite of the numerous delays, be called a success, and is his decision to go north *first* (πρῶτον, 7.1.1) justified by its results? An answer obviously depends on the other question of whether the Syracusans are still upholding their defense or have meanwhile surrendered to Nicias.

It is here that the historian once more employs greater detail, and at the same time he joins the three different strands of his recent narrative: (1) Gylippus and his newly gathered troops; (2) the bulk of the relief fleet,

PLATE 5. Strait of Messina from the south.

expected to leave Greece and arrive on the Italian side later (ὕστερον, 6.104.1) than Gylippus himself and his four advance boats; and (3) the Syracusans in their city, despairing of their situation.

At this point Thucydides *first* blends in the Corinthian fleet which is coming from Greece to help as fast as possible;

> and Gongylos, one of the Corinthian commanders, putting to sea with a *single* ship *last*, is the *first* to arrive in Syracuse, *a little before* Gylippus, and, *coming upon them when they were about to hold an assembly on the deliverance from the war, he stopped them* and encouraged them (7.2.1).

He informs the Syracusans of the impending arrival of Gylippus, the Spartan general, and of the coming aid from the Peloponnese (whose non-arrival had earlier caused their despair, 6.103.3).

Again, the narrative has come down to a matter of hours rather than days or even weeks. The assembly on ending the war seems to have been prevented only briefly before it was scheduled to begin; and that a *single* ship, the last one of the relief force to leave Greece, should pass all the others and arrive first and, so, compensate for the delays in Gylippus' advance mission, can hardly be counted as a credit to the original planning. Gongylos' last-minute arrival is rather attributable to the behavior of the winds, which is unpredictable *par excellence* (or to the unforeseen personal initiative of an individual officer, gifted with special sailing and leadership skills?).

How was Gongylos able to get into the city through the Athenian blockade? I give a speculative answer: On the steep and generally inaccessible eastern shore of Epipolai (see PLATE 6), there is a tiny bay (*piccolo seno*) at the so-called Cliffs of the Two Brothers (*Coglie Due Fratelli*); here a very ancient staircase, today almost completely crumbled by the elements, leads up from the water to the tableau (see PLATE 7).[31] The location is about three-quarters of a mile as the crow flies north of the new northern city wall of 415 as reconstructed by Drögemüller. Since the eastern rim of the plateau is situated slightly lower than the western territory next to it, Gongylos could here remain undetected by the Athenians.[32]

One thing is clear: *without Gongylos' unscheduled early arrival, Gylippus himself, at his own arrival, might well have found the city in Athenian hands.* With regard to the aspect of timing, which has dominated the historian's narrative ever since the reader left the Syracusans in their predicament (6.103.4; cf. 104.1), Gylippus' earlier decision to avoid the Athenian guard ships by going to Himera first turns out to have been too risky: his own planning would not have allowed him to be back before the decision on surrendering the city had been made. If Gongylos could get through into the city on a *single* ship, one out of Gylippus' *four* advance ships would have had an even better chance to escape the four Athenian guard ships. It

PLATE 6. Steep, unscalable east coast of Epipolai (Trogilos).

PLATE 7. Weathered ancient staircase on the steep east coast of Epipolai, about three-quarters of a mile north of the Syracusan wall of 415, affording ascent directly from the sea.

possibly further adds to the delay that, when the Syracusans, in response to Gongylos' arrival, march out with all their force to meet Gylippus and his army, he in passing again is spending precious time then (τότε) on taking Ietai, a small Sicel fortification (7.2.3).

215

The final irony of the situation may well be indicated by the remark that, before attacking the Athenian siege wall on Epipolai, Gylippus and his troops have 'climbed up at the Euryelos, *precisely where* also the Athenians [climbed up] the first time' (ᾗπερ καὶ οἱ Ἀθηναῖοι τὸ πρῶτον, 7.2.3; cf. 6.97.2). The Athenians might have known better, recalling their own original surprise occupation of the Epipolai plateau, at that time likewise unguarded.

The historian's concluding statement is preceded by yet another emphatic consideration of the chance-dependent timing: Gylippus '*happened to come at this critical point of time*' (ἔτυχε δὲ κατὰ τοῦτο τοῦ καιροῦ ἐλθών, 7.2.4), when (I summarize the rest) the Athenians had almost finished their double wall down to the Great Harbor, and for the rest of the wall north of the city (toward Trogilos) the stones had been put in place and some parts even been worked upon already.

The concluding statement itself recalls and secures the essence of the narrative: 'To such a degree of danger came Syracuse', παρὰ τοσοῦτον μὲν αἱ Συράκουσαι ἦλθον κινδύνου (2.4). The emphasis, distributed upon opening and ending of the sentence, παρὰ τοσοῦτον...κινδύνου, lies on the degree of danger the city was exposed to. The phrasing gains in historical weight because Thucydides has used the same formula once before for a comparable situation regarding the city of Mytilene on Lesbos (3.49.4; see Chapter 4).

The climax of the narrative is the relief of the city from danger, at least for the time being. The next *detailed* report (7.3–8) will be given under a very different aspect, viz. that of the deteriorating situation of the *Athenians*, which will first culminate in the letter Nicias sends home, asking the Athenian assembly for a relief army.

So it is clear that the sentence about the degree of danger Syracuse was exposed to forms the conclusion to a long train of events; it started with the prophylactic Syracusan endeavor to prevent the Athenians from taking possession of the Epipolai plateau. In view of the ups and downs, the delays and 'almost' situations, especially the unforeseen reversals emphasized by the narrative detail, the meaning of the climax itself becomes clear: *for Syracuse, things could, more than once and up to the last link in the chain, have gone either way* during this stretch of the war. This leads to an important insight into Thucydides' concept of history and of the historian's task.

Our original question, asked at the opening of this chapter, has been whether Thucydides' findings, as expressed in the literary detail of his narrative, advocate a degree of probability, predictability and even 'steerability' of historical and political processes. The overall picture of the Athenian expedition (which he calls 'a war not much inferior to the one against the Peloponnesians', 6.1.1) may initially suggest to the reader that inadequate planning has led to predictable disaster, and that this, to a degree, applies also to the Syracusan side, where the true information presented by Hermocrates to the assembly is not taken seriously by his audience—an attitude which leads to bitter consequences.

But the historian himself also shows the change in direction which unforeseeable chance and unpredictable human nature may give to a train of events beyond the original planning categories. *Rational analysis may uncover the irrationality of history.*

If then in the beginning we observed that insufficient planning and false splendor at the departure of the Athenian force are, by verbal referencing, compared to and contrasted with suffering and disaster at the end, so the overall picture may have looked like the predictable outcome of insufficient preparing. But this picture now turns out to have been preliminary and in need of modification insofar as the negative result of insufficient preparation proves not to have been *a priori* determined.

The view which holds that the course of historical development is on principle predictable would be simplistic in the eyes of Thucydides. That is the 'lesson' which his narrative conveys by the use of literary detail whenever critical points are reached in the overall development—points where the course of history may be switched from one track to another: one may use the metaphor 'hinges of history'. A railway engineer might prefer actually to speak of 'points'.[33]

In the stretch of events considered last, which describes the repeatedly changing danger for Syracuse, the eventual outcome does not allow one to claim any predictability. The same is true in the case of the Athenian night attack, led by Demosthenes, on Epipolai. Both instances have the solid weight of researched facts on their side to give them the status of evidenced history. But our third example (actually it was the first one presented in the series of this chapter), the proposal of Hermocrates to dupe the threatening Athenian force before it arrives, is even more informative. It shows that the historian is interested in a possibility even if those involved in the situation do not avail themselves of it. For him it is enough to have demonstrated, in a thought experiment with a detailed dichotomy, that at this point already, before even reaching Sicily, the train of the Athenian campaign could have been derailed.

The present chapter has been able, perhaps even more systematically and conclusively than some earlier ones, to establish how the literary detail helps the historian to define crisis points[34] and further, how at such points the chain of events tends to develop independently from the direction it so far has seemed to observe, and independently also from the factors originally considered by the planners on either side.

It is always desirable to check how an author's literary practice relates to his theoretical position. When citing from the historian's chapter on the method and purpose of his work (1.22), especially from that section (4) which deals with its purpose, I should first point out how Thucydides expresses disdain both for the ephemeral fame of a rhetorical show-piece (ἀγώνισμα ἐς τὸ παραχρῆμα ἀκούειν) and for the pleasing story-telling that usually goes with it (καὶ ἐς μὲν ἀκρόασιν ἴσως τὸ μὴ μυθῶδες αὐτῶν ἀτερπέστερον φανεῖται).

Such an attitude does not exclude a strong self-confidence. However, in view of the work's cautionary character, one will expect to find such confidence reflected hardly in the area of practice, but rather in the realm of insight and comprehension. Such a contemplative tendency and remoteness from the *vita activa* go well both with the precise wording of the core sentence and with its modesty (a modesty emphasized in the original by being stated at the final position in the sentence: ...ἀρκούντως ἕξει): '... it will be *sufficient* if all those judge it (i.e. my work) to be useful who will wish to *see clarity* both of what happened and of what at some time again will be—according to the human condition[35]—such and similar'.

For the reader, then, present and future will be as unsteerable and unpredictable as was the historical past.

In this context, it is worth recalling from the preceding chapters that arguments of probability, if used by warners (Archidamus in Book 1; Nicias in Book 6), are verified by the later course of events—and are used by the historian himself for the purpose of securing knowledge of the *past*;[36] but, when they are used to sketch a rosy picture of the future (the final pro-war speech of the Corinthians and even Pericles in Book 1; Alcibiades and Athenagoras in Book 6), the outcome is due to be disappointment and even disaster. On the whole, one may say that warning predictions in Thucydides tend to be justified (and, besides, hardly ever listened to), but optimistic calls for action, if accepted, lead to failure.

Our overall study of the *History*, then, has confirmed the interpretation that was given in Chapter 2 of the programmatic sentence on the work's purpose.[37] The literary detail, as examined especially in the present chapter, likewise advises against recasting the clear wording of the program sentence so as possibly to mean that the author intends to provide a practical handbook for future statesmen. For the investigation of historical details has led the historian to discovering the unceasing recurrence of the incalculable and unforeseeable, even in cases such as the Sicilian Expedition, where on the surface the result appears to flow smoothly from and to be wholly consistent with the originally identified premises. In this, the more deeply searching view, then, the process of gaining *clarity* about lasting and similarly recurring components of the human condition aims hardly at successful manipulation but rather at insight.

At this point, there enters Thucydides' hope for his work's everlasting value: 'And it has been written as a possession for ever rather than a declamation piece to listen to for the moment' (1.22.4). Accordingly, the work would fulfill the author's intention if today's readers, when being acquainted with the events and vicissitudes of Greek history as detailed by him, could likewise, in an act of recognition, gain clarity about constitutive elements of the history of their own time—elements which, though recurring with inescapable constancy, nevertheless, since being variables, cannot be concretely calculated beforehand.

Notes

[1] An earlier version of this Chapter was given as a lecture before the 1999 convention of the *Mommsen-Gesellschaft* in Jena, Germany, as well as at the Universities in Augsburg, Lisbon, Munich and Pittsburgh. An enlarged German version appeared in *Rheinisches Museum für Philologie* 144 (2002).

[2] 'Now to Thucydides the supreme requisite for a politician is his πρόγνωσις—his ability to foresee—and the *History* itself is, in essence, *a manual for future statesmen*' (Finley 1947[2], 50; italics mine). On the work's alleged usefulness, see also Chapter 2, pp. 15 ff.

[3] De Romilly (1990, 381) seems to think that conclusions about (discoveries of) irrational event sequences in Thucydides' work are a matter of the individual scholar's inclination. With regard to weighing the rational and the irrational she states: 'Selon leur tempérament, certains savants sont sensibles à un aspect ou à un autre' ('According to their temperament certain scholars are sensitive to one aspect or the other.'). De Romilly herself is clearly inclined to discover in Thucydides a technician set on rationally steering historical processes. Precise analysis of the text (as submitted in this and preceding chapters), however, establishes that the ancient historian leaves his reader no latitude for personal inclinations.

[4] For this aspect see Stahl 1975, esp. 23–30.

[5] The fact of the quotation causes me (and in this I differ from Kern 1989, 78) to see the contrasting correspondence intended by the historian in this passage and not in the vivid scene when the army from the harbor shore watches the final naval battle.

[6] In the catastrophe in Sicily, Nicias' well-reasoned warnings prove to be correct (and Alcibiades' irresponsible projections have turned out to be untenable). In comparable fashion, the destruction of Melos confirms the warning predictions of the Athenian generals (and the irresponsible, irrational hopes of the Melians have not been confirmed).

Before we turn to cases of higher complexity in the literary detail, let us here already, from the angle of the dimension observed so far, point to the—at best—limited applicability of de Romilly's position mentioned earlier: 'et les mauvaises [scil. prévisions] elles-mêmes sont une leçon de prévision. Grâce aux prévisions non verifiées, on découvre où résidait l'erreur; et l'on apprend' ('And the wrong [scil. previsions] themselves are a lesson of prevision. Thanks to previsions not verified, one discovers where the mistake lay; and one learns accordingly.') (1990, 382).

What have the Athenians learned from their Sicilian catastrophe? What (applicable) lesson to draw from their mistakes ('tirer une leçon de ses erreurs' ['draw a lesson from one's mistakes']) remained for the Melians before being executed? ('Le principe qui consiste à tirer une leçon de ses erreurs est à la base de la *technè* qu' élabore Thucydide' ['The principle which consists of drawing a lesson from one's mistakes is fundamental to the *techne* which Thucydides builds up.'], l.c.).

In Thucydides' eyes, one deals not only with the easily underrated role of chance (played down in vain even by Pericles, when he calls the plague the '*only* matter of all which has developed beyond expectation': πρᾶγμα μόνον δὴ τῶν πάντων ἐλπίδος κρεῖσσον γεγενημένον, 2.64.1; cf. 65.3) but precisely also with the dimension of irrational human conduct, which further complicates the problem of correct prevision.

[7] Cf. *OCD* (1996, 1517), where Wade-Gery also ascribes to the ancient historian 'pride in the soldier's profession'.

[8] Westlake 1969, 181 f.: Hermocrates' plan is called by Westlake a mere 'debating manoeuvre' not intended to be carried out but presented to the assembly in order to win acceptance of his preceding, less bold proposals.

[9] Gomme *ad* 6.34.4: 'If Hermocrates' proposal had been adopted and if there had been time (as there was not) to put it into effect, the probable outcome was the annihilation of the Sikeliot fleets and the rapid imposition of Athenian rule on South Italy.'

[10] Bloedow 1993, 115–24.

[11] Bloedow 1993, 122: 'Dover and Kagan appear to envisage a major "pitched" battle. But it would seem clear that this is something that Hermocrates would have attempted to avoid.'

[12] Bloedow 1993, 122 (my italics).

[13] Bloedow 1993, 124.

[14] Bloedow (1993, 123 f.) appears to misread this sentence.

[15] Kagan 1981, 221.

[16] Westlake 1969, 182.

[17] Kagan 1981, 221 (my italics).

[18] Kagan 1981, 221. Cf. Westlake 1969, 181: '...there were palpable dangers to the Siceliots in trying to intercept so far from their own bases [? Hermocrates speaks of Tarentum as the basis of the Syracusans!, 34.4] an enemy whose seamanship they could not hope to match.'

[19] Dover in *HCT* IV, 299 (*ad* 6.34.4).

[20] Kagan 1981, 221 (italics mine).

[21] Dover in *HCT* IV, 299 (*ad* 6.34.4).

[22] Westlake 1969, 181.

[23] Westlake 1969, 181 f.

[24] One will hardly follow Westlake (1969, 182) in assuming that Hermocrates himself deems his plan impracticable (he 'can hardly have been blind to the diffi-culties of putting his plan into operation') and introduces it only as a 'debating manoeuvre'; and adduce for this view that Hermocrates in the end says that the Athenians 'are already almost here' (6.34.9). If anything, then, this last statement by the Syracusan politician is a 'debating manoeuvre', put forward with the intent of raising awareness of the threatening danger in the minds of his audience. (Cf. τὰς μετὰ φόβου παρασκευὰς and ὡς ἐπὶ κινδύνου in the immediately preceding sentence, as well as the subjective ὡς οὖν ἐν τάχει παρεσομένων, 33.3.)

[25] Details on 'die neue Nordmauer' are provided by Drögemüller (1969, 71–3, with Abbildung 14 on p. 72). Drögemüller is certainly right in assuming that the ἄκρα Τεμενῖτις (= via Agnello and viale G.E. Rizzo [Rizzo was the excavator of the Temenites]), with the altar(s) of Apollo and the Greek theater, was situated inside the extension of the wall built in the winter of 415/14.

[26] This must be the area south of the swamps. Drögemüller (1969, 118) locates it around today's C. Cutreri, C. Bucceri, Mass. S. Nicola and Mass. Santannera. The area is now not open to the public.

[27] 'Which'—ἧ—here is an insertion by Classen (and Poppo), certainly correct. After the relative pronoun was lost, the verb 'they held a review' could no longer be referring to the Syracusans. So 'both' (καὶ) was understood as 'and', as if connecting 'landed' and 'held a review', the subject to both now being the Athenians. (Understood correctly, the three participles dependent on ἔλαθον ought to be viewed as connected by καὶ…καὶ…τε. Alternatively, one might follow Steup (and Madvig) in declaring the first καὶ a later addition, made after ἧ had dropped out. For more details, see Steup's *Anhang ad loc.*) But for the context it is utterly irrelevant whether or not the Athenians, after successfully landing without being noticed by the Syracusans, for their part, too, held a review. What counts is their swift progress up the approach to Epipolai, emphasized by 'right away' (97.2b).

[28] Drögemüller 1969, 76 f. with *Tafel X*.

[29] See Chapter 3.

[30] There is nothing out of the ordinary about the use of the article with 'siege wall' in the Greek text (99.1): it means 'the planned' (or 'feared') wall, which Thucydides has alluded to several times before. Drögemüller (1969, 79 with n. 23) has thoroughly disproved Didot's (1833) invention of a 'ring fort' (still found in Dover's commentaries: vol. IV, 473; 1971, 96 f. *ad* 6.98.2), allegedly built by the Athenians on Epipolai: why would a (defensive) 'ring fort' scare the daylights out of the Syracusans? Though I do admit that some passages may appear ambiguous, a wording like 'for *the rest of the ring* stones had already for the major part been placed along toward the Trogilos in direction of the other sea and…' (7.2.4) can refer only to the siege wall, not to a 'ring fort'. See also Drögemüller's discussion of 6.98–101 (1969, 123–7).

[31] A picture of the complete staircase may also be found in Drögemüller (1969), *Tafel* X.

[32] Similarly, the Syracusans could later move undetected when they joined Gylippus and his relief army (7.2.2); Drögemüller (1969) 90, 93.

[33] Accordingly, occasional instances of correct prediction (whose success, however, may itself be subject to unforeseen limitations, as for instance through the death of Pericles, 2.65.5–7) can be generalized and raised to the level of a principle only if the interpreter diminishes the emphasis placed by the historian on the influence of vicissitudes in a course of events.

[34] Present-day scholarship likes to describe narrative technique in the nomenclature of narratology. S. Hornblower, in a chapter entitled 'Narratology and Narrative Techniques in Thucydides', has called the first edition of this (along with de Romilly's) book 'particularly notable, as straight forward, *jargon-free* analysis' (1996, 136; italics mine). Accordingly, I have refrained in this chapter, too, from conducting the investigation in terms of, e.g., 'focalization' or of a 'Thucydides narrator'. See C. Dewald 1999, 242.

[35] For the translation of τὸ ἀνθρώπινον see above, pp. 28 ff.; 97 f.

[36] See pp. 4 f., *ad* 6.55.1–3.

[37] See especially pp. 14–17 on 'useful' lessons allegedly intended by Thucydides.

BIBLIOGRAPHY

A. EDITIONS, COMMENTARIES, ETC.

Thucydidis Historiae, iterum rec. brevique adn. crit. instr. H.S. Jones; app. crit. corr. et aux. J.E. Powell, Oxford 1951/53 (reprint of the 1942 edition).

Thucydides, La Guerre du Péloponnèse. Texte établi et traduit par J. de Romilly, R. Weil, L. Bodin. Bk I 2nd edn., II, III, VI/VII. Paris 1955—.

Thucydides. Ed. O. Luschnat. Bk I/II. Leipzig 1960, 2nd edn.

A Historical Commentary on Thucydides, A.W. Gomme, A. Andrewes, and K.J. Dover, 5 vols., Oxford, 1945–81.

Θουκυδίδου συγγραφή mit erklärenden Anm. herausgegeben von K.W. Krüger. 1st–3rd edn, Berlin 1858–68.

Thucydidis de Bello Peloponnesiaco Libri Octo. Ad optimorum librorum fidem editos expl. E.F. Poppo; editio altera (or tertia) quam aux. et em. I.M. Stahl, Leipzig 1875 ff.

Thukydides erklärt von J. Classen, bearbeitet von J. Steup. 3rd–5th edn, Berlin 1900–22. (Repr. Berlin 1963, mit Nachwort und bibliographischen Nachträgen von R. Stark.)

Thucydides. Book VI, Book VII. With an Introduction and Commentary by K.J. Dover, Oxford 1971 (repr. with corrections of the 1965 edn).

A Commentary on Thucydides. Vol. II: Books IV–V.24. Ed. S. Hornblower, Oxford 1996.

A Commentary on Thucydides. Vol I: Books I–III, Ed. S. Hornblower, Oxford 1997.

Scholia in Thucydidem ad optimos codices collata edidit C. Hude. Leipzig 1927.

Lexicon Thucydideum confecit E.-A. Bétant, Hildesheim 1961 (repr.).

Index Thucydideus ex Bekkeri editione stereotypa confectus a M.H.N. von Essen, Berlin 1887.

B. SECONDARY LITERATURE

Abbott, G.F.
    1925   *Thucydides, A Study in Historical Reality,* London.

Adcock, F.E.
    1951   'Thucydides in Book I', *JHS* 71, 2.
    1963   *Thucydides and his History,* Cambridge.

Alberti, G.B.
    1959   'L'uso delle particelle nella formula di correlazione πρῶτον...ἔπειτα', *Maia* 11, 44.

223

Aly, W.
 1928 'Form und Stoff bei Thukydides', *RhM* 77, 361.
Andrewes, A.
 1959 'Thucydides on the causes of the war', *CQ* 9, 223.
 1960 'The Melian dialogue and Pericles' last speech', *PCPhS* 186, 1.
 1961 'Thucydides and the Persians', *Historia* 10, 1.
 1962 'The Mytilene debate', *Phoenix* 16, 64.
Bayer, E.
 1948 'Thukydides und Perikles', *WJA* 3, 1.
Bender, G.F.
 1938 *Der Begriff des Staatsmannes bei Thukydides*, Würzburg. Diss. Erlangen, 1937.
Berve, H.
 1938 *Thukydides. Auf d. Wege z. nationalpolit. Gymnasium* 5, Frankfurt.
Bill, C.P.
 1937 'τὰ καινὰ τοῦ πολέμου', *CPh* 32, 160.
Bizer, F.
 1937 *Untersuchungen zur Archäologie des Thukydides*. Diss., Tübingen.
Bloedow, E.F.
 1993 'Hermocrates' strategy against the Athenians in 415 BC', *Ancient History Bulletin* 7, 115–24.
Bodin, L.
 1914 'Thucydide et la Bataille de Naupacte', cf. *REG* 27, 49.
 1932 'Isocrate et Thucydide', *Mélanges Glotz* 1, 93, Paris.
 1935 'Thucydide et la Campagne de Brasidas en Thrace', *Mélanges Navarre*, Toulouse, 47.
 1940 'Diodote contre Cléon. Quelques aperçus sur la dialectique de Thucydide', *REA* 42 (Mél. Radet) 36.
Bogner, H.
 1937 *Thukydides und das Wesen der altgriechischen Geschichtsschreibung*, Hamburg.
Bradeen, D.W.
 1960 'The popularity of the Athenian empire', *Historia* 9, 257.
Braun, E.
 1953 'Nachlese zum Melier-Dialog', *Jahresh. d. Österr. Arch. Inst.* 40, Beibl. Sp. 231.
Brunt, P.A.
 1952 'Thucydides and Alcibiades', *REG* 65, 59.
Büchner, K.
 1953 'Thukydides I 40, 2', *Hermes* 81, 119.
Burrows, R.M.
 1908 'Pylos and Sphacteria', *JHS* 28, 148 (*JHS* 18 (1898) 147).
Bury, J.B.
 1958² *The Ancient Greek Historians*, New York. 1st edn. 1909.
Calder, W.M.
 1955 'The Corcyrean–Corinthian Speeches in Thucydides I', *CJ* 50, 179.

Cassiman, R.
1937/8 *Thucydides*, Thèse de lic. Louvain.

Chambers, M.H.
1957a 'Thucydides and Pericles', *HSPh* 62, 79.
1957b 'Studies in the Veracity of Thucydides', cf. *HSPh* 62, 141.

Cochrane, Ch.N.
1929 *Thucydides and the Science of History*, London.

Compton, W.C. and H. Awdry
1907 'Two notes on Pylos and Sphacteria', *JHS* 27, 274.

Cornford, F.M.
1907 *Thucydides Mythistoricus*, London.

Corsen, P.
1915 'Der Charakter der perikleischen Politik im Lichte der Darstellung des Thukydides', *ZG* (Sokrates) 69, 321.

Couch, H.N.
1943/4 'Emphasis in Thucydides', *CW* 37, 125.

Danninger, O.
1931/2 'Über das εἰκός in den Reden des Thukydides', *WS* 49/50, 12.

Deffner, A.
1933 *Die Rede bei Herodot und ihre Weiterbildung bei Thukydides*. Diss., Munich.

Deininger, G.
1939 *Der Melier-Dialog*. Diss., Erlangen.

Dewald, C.
1999 'The figured stage: focalizing the initial narratives of Herodotus and Thucydides,' 212–52 in Thomas M. Falkner, Nancy Felson, and David Konstan (eds.) *Contextualizing Classics—Ideology, Performance, Dialogue*, Lanham and Oxford.

Didot, A. Firmin
1833 (2nd edn 1868–79) *Thucydide: Histoire de la guerre du Péloponnèse (Traduction française)*, t. III (= Livr. 6–8), Paris.

Diesner, H.J.
1956 *Wirtschaft und Gesellschaft bei Thukydides*, Halle.
1959 'Peisistratidenexkurs und Peisistratidenbild bei Thukydides', *Historia* 8, 12.

Dietzfelbinger, E.
1934 *Thukydides als politischer Denker*. Diss., Erlangen.

Diller, H.
1962 'Freiheit bei Thukydides als Schlagwort und als Wirklichkeit', *Gymn.* 69, 189.

Dow, St.
1961 'Thucydides and the number of the Acharnian "hoplitai"', *TAPhA* 92, 66.

Drobig, B.
1958 *Psychologie und Begrifflichkeit bei Thukydides, dargestellt an den Problemen seiner Furchtsynonyma*. Diss. (typescript), Bonn.

Drögemüller, H.-P.
  1969 'Syrakus. Zur Topographie und Geschichte einer griechischen Stadt',
        Gymnasium, Beiheft 6, Heidelberg.
Ebener, D.
  1955/6 'Kleon und Diodotos. Zum Aufbau und zur Gedankenführung eines
        Redenpaares bei Thukydides', *Wiss. Ztschr. d. M. Luther-Univ. Halle-
        Wittenberg* 5, 1085.
Eberhardt, W.
  1954 'Die Geschichtsdeutung des Thukydides', *Gymn.* 61, 306.
  1959 'Der Melier-Dialog und die Inschriften *ATL* A9 (*IG* I² 63+) und *IG* I²
        97+', *Historia* 8, 284.
Egermann, F.
  1942 'Die Geschichtsbetrachtung des Thukydides.', *Das Neue Bild der Antike*
        1, 272.
  1961 'Zum historiographischen Ziel des Thukydides', *Historia* 10, 435.
Ehrenberg, V.
  1947 'Polypragmosyne: a study in Greek politics', *JHS* 67, 46.
Erbse, H.
  1953 'Über eine Eigenheit der thukydideischen Geschichtsbetrachtung', *RhM*
        96, 38.
  1961 'Zur Geschichtsbetrachtung des Thukydides', *Antike und Abendland* 10,
        19.
Ferrara, G.
  1956 'La politica dei Meli in Tucidide', *PP* 11, 335.
Finley, J.H.
  1938 'Euripides and Thucydides', *HSPh* 49, 23.
  1939 'The origins of Thucydides' style', *HSPh* 50, 35.
  1940 'The unity of Thucydides' history', *HSPh* Suppl. vol. 1, 255.
  1947² *Thucydides*, Cambridge, Mass.
Fitton Brown, A.D.
  1958 'Notes on Herodotus and Thucydides', *Hermes* 86, 379.
Fliess, P.J.
  1960 'War guilt in the History of Thucydides', *Traditio* 16, 1.
v. Fritz, K.
  1954 'ὅπερ σαφεστάτη πίστις. Thukydides I 35, 5,' *Festschrift* I. Kapp.
        Munich, 25.
  1956 'Die Bedeutung des Aristoteles für die Geschichtsschreibung', *Entretiens*
        (Fondation Hardt) 4, 85.
Gomme, A.W.
  1923 'Thucydides and Sphacteria', *CQ* 17, 36.
  1937 *Essays in Greek History and Literature*, Oxford.
  1948 'Thucydides notes', *CQ* 42, 10.
  1951 'Four passages in Thucydides', *JHS* 71, 70.
  1953 '*IG* I² 60 and Thucydides III 50, 2', in *Studies Presented to D.M. Robinson
        on his 70th Birthday*, vol. 2, 334, St. Louis.

1954   *The Greek Attitude to Poetry and History*, Sather Class. Lectures, 27, Berkeley.

1962   'Thucydides and Kleon,' in *More Essays in Greek History and Literature*, 112, Oxford.

Gomperz, T.

1896   *Griechische Denker I. Eine Geschichte der antiken Philosophie*, Leipzig.

Gregor, D.B.

1953   'Athenian imperialism', *G&R* 22, 27.

Grene, D.

1950   *Man in his Pride. A study in the political philosophy of Thucydides and Plato*, Chicago.

Großkinsky, A.

1936   'Das Programm des Thukydides', *NDF* 68 *Abt. Klass. Phil.* 3, Berlin.

Grossmann G.

1950   *Politische Schlagwörter aus der Zeit des Peloponnesischen Krieges*. Diss., Basel.

Grundy, G.B.

1948   *Thucydides and the History of his Age*, I 2nd edn., II, Oxford.

Gundert, H.

1940   'Athen und Sparta in den Reden des Thukydides', *Antike* 16, 98.

Hammond, N.G.L.

1936/7 'The campaigns in Amphilochia during the Archidamian War', *ABSA* 37, 128.

1939   'The structure of Thucydides' thought in the *Archaeologia*', *PCPhS* 172–4, 10.

1940   'The composition of Thucydides' History', *CQ* 34, 146.

1947   'Thucydides I 142, 2–4', *CR* 61, 39.

1952   'The arrangement of the thought in the proem and in other parts of Thucydides I', *CQ* 46 (n.s. 2), 127.

Harrison, E.L.

1959   'The escape from Plataea: Thuc. III 23', *CQ* 9, 30.

Heinimann, F.

1945   *Nomos und Physis*, Schweiz. Beitr. z. Altertumswiss. H 1. Basel.

Henderson, B.W.

1927   *The Great War between Athens and Sparta. A companion to the military history of Thucydides*, London.

Herter, H.

1950a   'Freiheit und Gebundenheit des Staatsmannes bei Thukydides', *RhM* 93, 133.

1950b   'Macht und Idee', cf. *Gymn.* 57, 315.

1953   'Zur ersten Perikles-Rede des Thukydides', in *Studies Presented to D.M. Robinson on his 70th Birthday*, vol. 2, 613, St. Louis.

1954   'Pylos und Melos. Ein Beitrag zur Thukydides-Interpretation', *RhM* 97, 316.

1955   'Comprensione ed azione politica. A proposito del capitolo 40 dell' Epitafio tucidideo', *Studi Funaioli*, 133, Rome.

Hornblower, S.
    1987   *Thucydides*, Baltimore.
    1996a *Greek Historiography*, Oxford.
    1996b 'Narratology and Narrative Techniques in Thucydides', 131–66 in
             S. Hornblower (ed.) *Greek Historiography*, Oxford.
Hornblower, S. and A. Spawforth, eds.
    1996   *Oxford Classical Dictionary*, 3rd edn, Oxford.
Howald, E.
    1944   'Thukydides', in *Vom Geist antiker Geschichtsschreibung*, 46, Munich.
Hudson-Williams, H.Ll.
    1950   'Conventional Forms of Debate and the Melian Dialogue', *AJPh* 71,
             156.
Immerwahr, H.R.
    1960   'Ergon. History as a monument in Herodotus and Thucydides', *AJPh*
             81, 261.
Jacoby, F.
    1929   'Thukydides und die Vorgeschichte des Peloponnesischen Krieges',
             NGG, Philologisch-historische Klasse 1.
Jaeger, W.
    1934   *Paideia I*, Berlin.
Jebb, R.
    1907   'The speeches of Thucydides', in *Essays and Addresses*, 359, Cambridge.
Kagan, D.
    1981   *The Peace of Nicias and the Sicilian Expedition*, Ithaca and London.
Kakridis, J.Th.
    1961   *Der Thukydideische Epitaphios. Ein stilistischer Kommentar*, Zetemata
             26.
Kapp, E.
    1930   Review of W. Schadewaldt, *Die Geschichtsschreibung des Thukydides*,
             Gnomon 6, 77.
Katicic, R.
    1957   'Die Ringkomposition im ersten Buche des Thukydideischen Geschich-
             tswerkes', *WS* (Festschr. Mras) 70, 179.
Kern, P.B.
    1989   'The turning point in the Sicilian Expedition', *Classical Bulletin* 65,
             77–82.
Kierdorf, W.
    1962   'Zum Melier-Dialog des Thukydides', *RhM* 105, 253.
Kirkwood, G.M.
    1952   'Thucydides' words for "cause"', *AJPh* 73, 37.
Kolbe, W.
    1930   *Thukydides im Lichte der Urkunden*, Stuttgart.
Lang, M.
    1954/5 'The murder of Hipparchus', *Historia* 3, 395.
Landmann, G.P.
    1932   *Interpretation einer Rede des Thukydides: Die Friedensmahnung des*
             Hermokrates, Kiel. Diss., Basel, 1930.

Laqueur, R.
1937 'Forschungen zu Thukydides', *RhM* 86, 316.

Lendle, O.
1964 'Die Auseinandersetzung des Thukydides mit Hellanikos', *Hermes* 92, 129.

Lesky, A.
1963[2] 'Thukydides', *Geschichte der griechischen Literatur*, 496, Bern and Munich.

Levi, M.A.
1953 'Il dialogo dei Meli', *PP* 8, 5.

Littré, E.
1839–61 *Oeuvres Complètes d'Hippocrate*, Paris.

Lohmann, J.
1953 'Das Verhältnis des abendländischen Menschen zur Sprache', *Lexis* 3, 5.

Lord, L.E.
1945 *Thucydides and the World War. Martin Class. Lectures 12*, Cambridge, Mass.

Ludwig, G.
1952 *Thukydides als sophistischer Denker*. Diss. (typescript), Frankfurt.

Luschnat, O.
1942 'Die Feldherrenreden im Geschichtswerk des Thukydides', *Ph. Suppl. Bd. 34*, H. 2. Leipzig.
1954 'Eine Interpretation von Thuk. I 142,3', *Festschr. f. Lammert*, 37, Stuttgart.
1970 'Thukydides', *RE* Suppl. 12, 1147.

MacKay, LA.
1953 'Latent irony in the Melian Dialogue', *Studies Presented to D.M. Robinson on his 70th Birthday*, vol. 2, 570, St. Louis.

Macon, R.W.
1927 'Herodotus and Thucydides', *CAH* 5, 398.

Martin, C.B.
1930 'Thucydides', *The Martin Class. Lectures I*, 30, Cambridge, Mass.

Mathieu, G.
1940 'Quelques notes sur Thucydide', *REA* 42, 242.

Méautis, G.
1935 'Le Dialogue des Athéniens et des Méliens', *REG* 48, 250.

Meister, C.
1955 *Die Gnomik im Geschichtswerk des Thukydides*, Winterthur. Diss., Basel.

Meyer, C.
1955 *Die Urkunden im Geschichtswerk des Thukydides*, Zetemata 10.

Meyer, Ed.
1899 *Forschungen zur Alten Geschichte II*, Halle.
1913 'Thukydides und die Entstehung der wissenschaftl. Geschichtsschreibung', *Mitteil. d. Wiener Vereins d. Freunde d. hum. Gymn.* Heft 14.

Meyer, E.
   1939   *Erkennen und Wollen bei Thukydides*. Diss. Göttingen.
Michaelis, S.
   1951   *Das Ideal der attischen Demokratie in den Hiketiden des Euripides und im Epitaphios des Thukydides*. Diss. (typescript), Marburg.
Momigliano, A.
   1930   'La composizione della storia di Tucidide', *Memoria d. r. Accad. d. scienze di Torino* 68.1, 1.
Moraux. P.
   1954   'Thucydide et la rhétorique', *LEC* 22, 3.
Müller, Fr.
   1958   'Die blonde Bestie und Thukydides', *HSPh* 68 (Stud. Jaeger), 171.
Müller-Strübing, H.
   1881   *Thukydideische Forschungen*, Vienna.
Münch, H.
   1935   *Studien zu den Exkursen des Thukydides*, Qu. u. St. z. Gesch. u. Kultur d. Altertums u. des M.-A., Reihe D, Heft 3, Heidelberg.
Müri, W.
   1947   'Beitrag zum Verständnis des Thukydides', *MH* 4, 251.
Nesselhauf, H.
   1934   'Die diplomatischen Verhandlungen vor dem Peloponnesischen Kriege', *Hermes* 69, 286.
Nestle, W.
   1934   'Thukydides als politischer Erzieher', *U&F* 6, 157.
   1938   'Hippocratica', *Hermes* 73, 1.
   1940   'Thukydides', in *Vom Mythos zum Logos*, 514, Stuttgart.
   1948a   *Griechische Studien*, Stuttgart.
   1948b   'Thukydides und die Sophistik', in *Griechische Studien*, 321, Stuttgart.
   1948c   'Apragmosyne. Zu Thuk. II 63', in *Griechische Studien*, 374, Stuttgart.
   1948d   'Zum Rätsel der Ἀθηναίων πολιτεία', in *Griechische Studien*, 387, Stuttgart.
Neu, K.R.
   1948   *Die allgemeinen Antriebe der Geschichte bei Thukydides und bei modernen Geschichtsschreibern des Peloponnesischen Krieges*. Diss. (typescript), Marburg.
Notopoulos, J.A.
   1945/6   'Thucydides' πρόγνωσις and the oracles', *CW* 39, 29.
Oehler, K.
   1963   'Der Entwicklungsgedanke als heuristisches Prinzip der Philosophiehistorie', *ZPE* 17, 604–13.
Oliver, J.H.
   1951   'On the Funeral Oration of Pericles', *RhM* 94, 327.
   1955   'Praise of Periclean Athens as a mixed Constitution', *RhM* 98, 37.
Oppenheimer, K.
   1933   *Zwei attische Epitaphien*. Diss., Berlin.

Otto, W.F.
1949   'Herodot und Thukydides', in *Große Geschichtsdenker. Ein Zyklus Tübinger Vorlesungen*, 11, Tübingen.

(Milman-)Parry, A.
1981   *Logos and Ergon in Thucydides*, New York. Diss. Cambridge, Mass., 1957.

Pavan, M.
1961   'Postilla a Tucidide', *Historia* 10, 19.

Pasquali, G.
1927   'L' "ultimatum" spartano ad Atene nell' inverno 431–30', *St. It.* n.s. 5, 299.

Patzer, H.
1937   *Das Problem der Geschichtsschreibung des Thukydides und die Thukydideische Frage*. NDF Abt. Klass. Phil. VI, Berlin.
1955   Review of J.H. Finley, *Thucydides*, *Gnomon* 27, 153.

Pearson, L.
1943   '3 notes on the Funeral Oration of Pericles', *AJPh* 64, 399.
1947   'Thucydides as reporter and critic', *TAPhA* 78, 37.
1952   'Prophasis and Aitia', *TAPhA* 83, 205.
1957   'Popular ethics in the world of Thucydides', *CPh* 52, 228.

Peremans, W.
1956   'Thucydide, Alcibiade et l'expédition de Sicile en 415 av. J. C.', *AC* 25, 331.

Plenio, W.
1954   *Die letzte Rede des Perikles (II 60–64)*. Diss. (typescript), Kiel.

Pohlenz, M.
1919   'Thukydides-Studien I, II (u. III)', *NGG, Philologisch-historische Klasse* 95 (1920, 56).
1920   'Thukydides und wir', *NJA* 45/46, 57.
1936   'Die Thukydideische Frage im Lichte der neueren Forschung', *GGA* 198, 281.
1953   'Nomos und Physis', *Hermes* 81, 418.

Raubitschek, A.E.
1963   'War Melos tributpflichtig?', *Historia* 12, 78.

Regenbogen, O.
1930   *Drei Thukydides-Interpretationen. 250 Jahre Weidmannsche Buchhandlung*. Beil. zu H. 4 d. Monatszeitschr. f. Höh. Schulen, 21.
1933   'Thukydides als politischer Denker', *HG* 44, 2.
1935   'Politik und Geschichte im Werk des Thukydides', cf. *HG* 46,100.

Rehm, A.
1934   'Über die sizilischen Bücher des Thukydides', *Ph* 89, 133.

Reich, L.
1956   *Die Rede der Athener in Sparta (I 73–78)*. Diss. (typescript), Hamburg.

Reinhardt, K.
1960   'Thukydides und Machiavelli', in *Vermächtnis der Antike*, 184.

Rittelmeyer, F.
1915   *Thukydides und die Sophistik*, Leipzig. Diss. Erlangen, 1914.
Rohrer, K.
1959   'Über die Authentizität der Reden bei Thukydides', *WS* 72, 36.
de Romilly, J.
1951²   *Thucydide et l'impérialisme athénien*, Paris.
1956a   *Histoire et raison chez Thucydide*, Paris.
1956b   'La crainte dans l'œuvre de Thucydide', *C&M* 17 (Mélanges Hoeg),
        119.
1956c   'L'utilité de l'histoire selon Thucydide', *Entretiens* (Fondation Hardt) 4,
        39.
1962   'Le Pseudo-Xénophon et Thucydide', *RPh* 36, 225.
1990   'Les prévisions non vérifiées dans l'œuvre de Thucydide', *REG* 103,
        370–82.
Roscher, W.
1842   *Leben, Werk und Zeitalter des Thukydides*, Göttingen.
Saar, H.G.
1954   *Die Reden des Kleon und Diodotos und ihre Stellung im Gesamtwerk des
        Thukydides*. Diss. (typescript), Heidelberg.
de Ste. Croix, G.E.M.
1954   'The character of the Athenian Empire', *Historia* 3, 1.
Schadewaldt, W.
1929   *Die Geschichtsschreibung des Thukydides*, Berlin.
Scharf, J.
1954   'Zum Melier-Dialog des Thukydides', *Gymn.* 61, 504.
Schmid, Walter
1947   *Zur Enstehungsgeschichte und Tektonik des I. Buches des Thukydides*. Diss.
        (typescript), Tübingen.
1955   'Zu Thukydides I 22,1 u. 2', *Ph* 99, 220.
Schmid, W. (-Stählin, O.)
1948   'Die Klassische Periode der griech. Literatur', in I. v. Müllers *Handbuch
        d. Altertumswiss.* Abt. VII, Teil I, Bd. V, 2. Hälfte, 2, Abschn, p. 3,
        Munich.
Schröder, O.
1931   'Zwei Interpretationen. I. Über einen Abschn. aus der Leichenrede des
        Perikles', *Hermes* 66, 355.
Schuller, S.
1956   'About Thucydides' use of αἰτία and πρόφασις', *RBPh* 34, 971.
Schwartz, E.
1929²   *Das Geschichtswerk des Thukydides*, Bonn.
Sealey, R.
1957   'Thucydides, Herodotus, and the causes of war', *CQ* 51 (n.s. 7), 1.
Smith, R.E.
1941/2 ''Αληθεστάτη πρόφασις', *G&R* 11, 23.
Smith, S.B.
1941   'The economic motive in Thucydides', *HSPh* 51, 267.

Solmsen, F.
1931 'Antiphonstudien', *NPhU* 8, 1.
Stahl, H.-P.
1966 *Thukydides. Die Stellung des Menschen im geschichtlichen Prozess, Zetemata* Heft 40, Munich.
1973 'Speeches and course of events in Books Six and Seven of Thucydides', in P.A. Stadter (ed.) *The Speeches in Thucydides: A Collection of Original Essays with a Bibliography*, Chapel Hill.
1975 'Learning through suffering? Croesus' conversations in the *History* of Herodotus', *YClSt* 24, 1–36.
Stenzel, J.
1926 Review of F. Taeger, *Thukydides, Göttingische gelehrte Anzeigen* 7–8, 193–206.
Strasburger, H.
1936 'Zu Thukydides VI 15', *Ph* 91, 137.
1954 'Die Entdeckung der politischen Geschichte durch Thukydides', *Saeculum* 5, 395.
1957 *Introduction to Horneffer's translation of Thucydides*, Bremen.
1958 'Thukydides und die politische Selbstdarstellung der Athener', *Hermes* 86, 17.
Strassler, R.B.
1988 'The harbor at Pylos, 425 BC', *JHS* 108, 198.
Taeger, F.
1925 *Thukydides*, Stuttgart.
Täubler, E.
1927 *Die Archäologie des Thukydides*, Leipzig.
Thibaudet, A.
1922 *La campagne avec Thucydide*, Paris.
Tompkins, D.P.
1972 'Stylistic characterization in Thucydides: Nicias and Alcibiades', *Yale Classical Studies* 22, 181–214.
Topitsch, E.
1942 'Die Psychologie der Revolution bei Thukydides', *WS* 60, 9.
1943/7 "Ανθρωπεία φύσις und Ethik bei Thukydides', *WS* 61/2, 50.
1946 *Mensch und Geschichte bei Thukydides*. Diss. (typescript), Vienna.
Toubeau, A.
1947 *La crainte et l'ardeur chez Thucydides I-V 24*. Thèse de Lic., Louvain.
Treu, M.
1953/4 'Athen und Melos und der Melier-Dialog des Thukydides', *Historia* 2, 253.
1954/5a 'Athen und Karthago und die thukydideische Darstellung', *Historia* 3, 41.
1954/5b 'Nachtrag', *Historia* 3, 58.
1956 'Der Stratege Demosthenes', *Historia* 5, 420.
Ullrich, F.W.
1845/6 *Beiträge zur Erklärung des Thukydides I/II*, Hamburg.

Umfahrer, H.
1946 Δύναμις *bei Thukydides*. Diss. (typescript), Vienna.

Vogt, J.
1950 'Dämonie der Macht und Weisheit der Antike', *WG* 10, 1.
1956 'Das Bild des Perikles bei Thukydides', *HZ* 182, 249.

Wade-Gery, H.T.
1996 'Thucydides', in S. Hornblower and A. Spawforth (eds.) *Oxford Classical Dictionary*, 3rd edn., 1516, Oxford.

Walbank, F.W.
1960 'History and tragedy', *Historia* 9, 216.

Walker, P.K.
1957 'The purpose and method of the "Pentekontaetia" in Thucydides, Bk. Γ', *CQ* 51, 27.

Wassermann, F.(M.)
1930 'Thukydides', *V&G* 20, 1.
1931 'Das neue Thukydidesbild', *NJW* 7, 248.
1947 'The Melian Dialogue', *TAPhA* 78, 18.
1952/3 'The speeches of King Archidamus in Thucydides', *CJ* 48, 193.
1954 'Thucydides and the disintegration of the polis', *TAPhA* 85, 46.
1956 'Post-Periclean democracy in action: the Mytilenean debate (Thuc. III 37–48)', *TAPhA* 87, 27.

Weidauer, K.
1954 *Thukydides und die Hippokratischen Schriften. Der Einfluß der Medizin auf Zielsetzung und Darstellungsweise des Geschichtswerkes.* Diss., Heidelberg.

Westlake, H.D.
1941 'Nicias in Thucydides', *CQ* 35, 58.
1955 'Thucydides and the Pentekontaetia', *CQ* 49 (n.s. 5), 53.
1958a 'Thucydides II 65,11', *CQ* 52 (n.s. 8), 102.
1958b 'ὡς εἰκός in Thucydides', *Hermes* 86, 447.
1960 'Athenian aims in Sicily, 427–424 BC. A study in Thucydidean motivation', *Historia* 9, 385.
1962 'Thucydides and the fall of Amphipolis', *Hermes* 90, 276.
1969 'Hermocrates the Syracusan', in his *Essays on the Greek Historians and Greek History*, Manchester and New York, 174–202.
1989 *Studies in Thucydides and Greek History*, Bristol.
1989 'Personal motives, aims and feelings in Thucydides' = Chapter 14 in his *Studies in Thucydides and Greek History*, Bristol, 201–23.

v. Wilamowitz-Moellendorff, U.
1913³ 'Von des attischen Reiches Herrlichkeit', *Reden und Vorträge*, 30.
1915 'Der Waffenstillstandsvertrag von 423 v. Chr.', *SPA* 39.2, 607.
1919 'Das Bündnis zwischen Sparta und Athen', *SPA* 49, 934.
1921 'Sphakteria', *SPA* 17, 306.
1929 'Lesefrüchte', (CCLIX) *Hermes* 64, 476.

Wille, G.
  1965 'Zu Stil und Methode des Thukydides', in *Synusia* (Festschr. Schade-
       waldt), 53, Pfullingen.
Woodhead, A.G.
  1960 'Thucydides' portrait of Cleon', *Mnem* S IV vol. 13, 289.
Zahn, R.
  1934 *Die erste Periklesrede* (Thuk. I 140–44), Leipzig. Diss., Kiel, 1932.
Ziegler, K.
  1928 'Thukydides und die Weltgeschichte', *Greifswalder Univ.-Reden* 19, 3,
       Greifswald.
  1929 'Der Ursprung der Exkurse in Thukydides', *RhM* 78, 58.
Zimmern, A.E.
  1928 'Thucydides the imperialist', in *Solon and Croesus and Other Greek Essays,*
       81–104, Oxford.

INDEX RERUM

INDEX NOMINUM

Customary usage of modern and Latinized forms (Aegina, Thucydides) is observed. Otherwise, Greek forms (Aristogeiton, Salaithos) are preserved.

INDEX VERBORUM GRAECORUM

INDEX LOCORUM

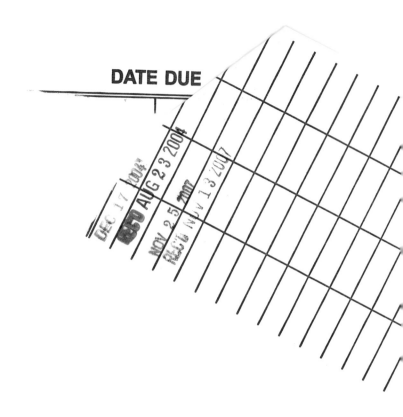